S0-AIU-895

The Shaping of an American Islamic Discourse

South Florida-Rochester-Saint Louis
Studies on Religion and the Social Order

ISLAM AND THE WORLD SUBSERIES
Edited by Tamara Sonn

THE SHAPING OF AN AMERICAN ISLAMIC DISCOURSE

edited by
Earle H. Waugh
and
Frederick M. Denny

The Shaping of an American Islamic Discourse

A Memorial to Fazlur Rahman

edited by
Earle H. Waugh
and
Frederick M. Denny

Scholars Press
Atlanta, Georgia

The Shaping of an American Islamic Discourse

A Memorial to Fazlur Rahman

edited by
Earle H. Waugh
and
Frederick M. Denny

Published by Scholars Press for the University of South Florida, University of Rochester, and Saint Louis University

Funds for the publication of this volume were provided by
The Tyson and Naomi Midkiff Fund for Exellence
of the Department of Religious Studies at the University of South Florida
The Max Richter Foundation of Rhode Island
and
The Tisch Family Foundation of New York City

Library of Congress Cataloging in Publication Data

The Shaping of an American Islamic discourse : a memorial to Fazlur Rahman / edited by Earle H. Waugh and Frederick M. Denny.
p. cm. — (South Florida-Rochester-Saint Louis studies on religion and the social order ; 17)
ISBN 0-7885-0436-3 (cloth : ;alk. paper)
1. Rahman, Fazlur, 1919- . 2. Islam—20th century. I. Waugh, Earle H., 1936- . II. Denny, Frederick Mathewson. III. Rahman, Fazlur, 1919- . IV. Series.
BP161.2.S524 1998
297'.092—dc21 98-9469
CIP

Printed in the United States of America
on acid-free paper

DEDICATION

To Fazlur Rahman,

Philosopher, savant, alim, friend and guide

Thou are the painter; thy design
Inspires and moves this brush of mine;
Thy hands the living world adorn,
And shape the ages yet unborn.

M. Iqbal, *Zabur-i Ajam*, #29.

TABLE OF CONTENTS

Note on Transliteration

Although their styles differ, in general, authors have adhered to the system established in the *International Journal of Middle East Studies*. Arabic words that can be normally found in dictionaries do not carry diacriticals, e.g., hadith. Words that appear repeatedly in an article are italicized with diacriticals marking long vowels the first time only; however, in those chapters that focus on issues of translation, diacriticals and italics are used throughout.

INTRODUCTION

Earle H. Waugh

This book has been written to encourage the North American reading public to look beyond the headlines to understanding some of the forces at work in an important world religion: Islam. There are many reasons for this but three will suffice here. The first is that at the turn of this century North America is experiencing the transplanting of a major world religion into its very fibre: Islam is now becoming a North American religion. The significance of this fact should not be lost on anyone. We have available to us the fashioning of a new religious environment at the same time as we have the technology and analytic skills to study its ramifications. What form will it take? Who will be its leaders? What kind of social and cultural impact will it make? These and a host of other questions stand ready for pursuing.

The second is a corollary of the first but its focus is different: American Muslims will begin in the next century to play a role in the shape of international Islam. This will have a dramatic and perhaps disturbing impact upon the traditional centers of Islamic power. How will many third world countries, rich in Islamic history but poor in terms of intellectual and economic resources, respond to an admittedly youthful, yet dynamic American Islam? Is it possible now to sketch some of the directions that this North American religious movement might take? Even if these questions seem to generate more questions than answers, it seems obvious that this movement is intimately connected to the world of Islam and will play a prominent part in intellectual and cultural developments. Attempting to determine the discourses that have taken place and will continue to take place will open up another perspective on this fascinating story. Our concern here will be to indicate how one leading individual has already had important influences. This will suggest discussions underway and directions the discourses might take.

The third is that we have now had more than a quarter century of professional schools and universities with specialists in Religious Studies who have developed their own institutional and professional skills in understanding Islam. We have had first-hand experience with talented and sensitive Muslim scholars who have begun the process of establishing an intellectual tradition of studying Islam on this continent. What you will read in this book is the first generation result of this interaction. True, it deals with only one distinctive slice of that interaction. Nevertheless, it does indicate important trends. We can now see that the main parameters of North American intellectual response to Islam are becoming evident, and the intensity of scholarship here demonstrates the depth of the encounter.

"How can non-specialists possibly come to grips with Islam today when it is clear that the specialists themselves can't?" This plaint came from a student, but newspaper reporters, television commentators and even the next-door neighbor have all voiced much the same concern. Usually enshrouded by the popular press with exotic or terrifying images, and nurtured by the Arabic language that is beyond the reach of only the most dogged and talented researchers, Islam remains a conundrum to ordinary North Americans. This, after Zen Buddhism or Hindu Yoga have found an acceptable place in their mental universe. Hence, the solution to understanding Islam will not be found by wishing away how the public feels about the tradition. Clearly, the problems remain, despite the work of intellectuals. We shall turn now to address some of the more contentious aspects of this cultural situation.

SCHOLARLY DISCOURSES AND THE NEW ISLAMIC PHENOMENON

It is not that specialists cannot deal with Islam—they often write copiously on the subject—but when they do, they are often accused of distortion. Sometimes they are told bluntly that they do not have the religious capacity to be fair to the tradition. In Islamic studies, this issue has solidified around the issue of "orientalism" but it is really larger than that, for the claim is made by fundamentalist groups and Aboriginal peoples too. The ordinary observer concludes it is beyond his/her capability to venture into this minefield.

The basic distortion of a religion by outside observers has taken one very contentious direction in recent days. Students of others' religions are challenged by the claim from a whole range of fields that there can only be "insider" knowledge, never true "objective" knowledge.[1]

Believers most often make this claim. Even within the academy, a vocal minority emphasizes the ultimate authority of the distinctive group's experience as the fundamental yardstick for all understanding. While the perspective is being propelled onward by the immense success of women's viewpoints within Religious Studies in North America, the liberation movement around the world has also had a profound impact on our perception of biased knowledge.[2] Ethnic groups as well as North American Muslims often espouse the viewpoint as a means to protect identity and to further distinctive traditions.

It is the mark of our common confusion that at precisely this moment the world is becoming a village through the miracles of communications, trade and travel. While there is not much evidence for its reality, the phrase "the new world order"[3] does signify profound adjustments in the way peoples relate to each other and hence come to know each other. Whatever that might mean in terms of politics, the reality is present among us: quite simply, there is now no more room to hide. Wars halfway around the world are now in our living rooms every night, and issues occupying our fellow human beings anywhere are now our issues. Thus, when Muslims raise concerns in Cairo or Karachi, even the most remote of our North American communities are drawn into the discussion.

The basic proposition is that we must find ways of dealing with the diverse kinds of peoples who call themselves Muslim because they now number more than one billion, and even more importantly, they now are our neighbors just next door. Islam is now part of our continental landscape. How we do that in some important part will depend upon how we take up and discuss the various conceptions we have of Islam in our history and in our present scholarship.

DISCUSSIONS ARISING FROM PAST IMAGES

We should first note that there are both public and scholarly conceptions of Islam, that they often are interrelated but that they do not often converge. What scholars want from Islam differs decisively from what the public needs. Twentieth century North American treatments of Islam, whether in academic circles or in the intellectual community within Islam itself, have been marked by several contrasting emphases. While each of these emphases has contributed an important element to the general understanding of the tradition, the mix has not been consistent nor the picture easily deciphered. The following are important public images.

IMAGE ONE: ISLAM THE EXOTIC

Toward the end of the nineteenth century, the exotic and fascinating aspects of Islam attracted attention, especially among the cultured elites who revelled in the rich colors and distinctive art forms associated with Islam. Who could remain untouched by the beauty of the Taj Mahal? It is hard to conceive now, but at one time every sophisticated private library had at least one multi-volumed set of *A Thousand and One Nights*. Associating Islam with this perspective allowed thinkers and literati to find a place in the hierarchy of religions for the tradition, equal to the other "world" religions, but clearly only one of several similar claimants to the earth's soul. The *Parliament of Religions* in Chicago enshrined this attitude.[4]

A positive result of this emphasis was that, at least on one level, Islam became part of the current imaginative world of North Americans, with equivalent claims and acceptances as Hinduism or Buddhism. This was not just a trend operative solely in a distant and nebulous past. The Disney film "Aladdin" is a good example of a continuing involvement in a symbolic world that arises out of an Islamic milieu. Thus, it is surely correct to say that "Islam the exotic" has helped to sustain a certain romanticism about Islamic culture and has vitiated some of the antipathy toward the tradition among the public at large.

Such an emphasis is now very diversified. The most fascinating aspects live on in stories and novels of intrigue in the Middle East,[5] in popularizing Sufi writers[6] and in the steady sale of regional Muslim folk literature.[7] Importers of such cultural artifacts as carpets continue to trade on this conception. All this would seem to promote a more engaging attitude toward things Islamic. Unfortunately, one consequence of the exotic vision has been that serious issues like Muslim marriage and family life are plagued by images of harems and secluded women; belly-dancing dies hard in the popular North American mind.

It would be unjust to relegate this popular fascination about Islam to commercial manipulation by Western entrepreneurs. Some elites from Islamic countries who have become popular interpreters in North America have tended to present the Islam of this exotica as the real Islam to a devoted clientele.[8] Even in more serious environments, such as colleges and universities, courses trade on the exotic. A scholarly residue of this perspective is still perceived in the discipline of Religious Studies and its various cognate areas. Certain aspects of Islamic experience, notably its mystical traditions, excite and attract many different kinds of scholars. Sometimes the result is an almost evangelistic pursuit of the "spiritual core" of Islam,[9] suggesting that political and legalistic forms are either incompatible with Religious Studies or are somehow less significant in Islam's rich life.

IMAGE TWO: ISLAM THE "PROBLEM" RELIGION

Another perspective, arguably more powerful, was articulated by major Christian missions to the Middle East and India early in the century. It could be roughly summarized as "Islam, the religious and cultural problem." For some Christians, this perspective may well have begun when Islam first moved out of its Meccan environment,[10] but it is evident in several forms today. Academic attitudes to it range along a spectrum from antipathy towards Islamic doctrine to an acknowledgement that Islam needs special kinds of interpretive methodologies.[11] While it is clear that rivalry between Islam and other religions was a key ingredient in its initial growth, in the West generally, and in North America in particular, the rivalry has been perceived as exclusively with Christianity since the time of the Crusades.[12]

In conjunction with that, to much of the North American popular mind, the rivalry has almost always been cast in terms of military dominance. For much of the American public, traditional Islam equals jihad. The military conquests of Islam's early days are amplified into a fundamental warlike character that is interwoven with personal piety throughout the length and breadth of Muslim consciousness. The history of two traditions is solidified into opposite sides of a fence: two great religious cultures pitted against each other, with the winner providing the truth for the world's salvation. If history is not clear in proving the scenario, then the bloodshed of today's fundamentalist certainly does. Islam becomes a difficult and militant "other." It is a troubling image, emotionally and psychologically powerful.

Lost or forgotten are the claims of peace at the heart of Islam, and the stellar examples of Jews, Christians and Muslims working for the common good as they did in Muslim Spain. Lost are scores of shared inheritances, of similar values, notions, beliefs, hopes and outcomes. Hundreds of books every year in major languages of the world articulate the troubled vision of Islam as a "problem," and North Americans collect a good many of them. Well-meaning scholars sometimes get involved in this. While it might be regarded as beneficial to have such a barrage of analysis aimed at "understanding" Islam, often the explication is done, not to comprehend the tradition itself but to "read" and "weigh" it on the scoreboard of the preconceived rivalry. The tide of rivalry tends to sweep all before it.

IMAGE THREE: ISLAM OFF OUR THEORETICAL MAP

While it is manifestly unfortunate, we have not as yet developed structures by which to address the general view that Islam is a "foreign" tradition. How can this be when so many of the basic elements of Islam are similar to that of Judaism and Christianity? Scholars make claims to be able to probe universal categories of religious experience. Yet as much as the urge for universality might be at the heart of scholarship, often Muslims believe that the subtext is an implied critique of current Islamic practice. Somehow the theory cannot bring the Islamic tradition into focus.

This debate is also part of a larger discourse concerning the biases of Western understanding of all non-Western cultural traditions, biases that can be conveniently summed up in the literature as "orientalism." Since Edward Said's famous book of the same name,[13] there has been a general acknowledgement that many and perhaps all Western Islamic scholars have been seriously infected with this malady; in truth, however, some scholars were aware of the problem long before Said's work. For example, the Euro- and ethno-centricity of much historical writing motivated Marshall Hodgson not only to try to write a history of Islam within its own context, but to try and understand it within a larger world history, a history in which the now-dominant West plays only a minor and relatively recent role.[14] Even if we acknowledge that differences between the two traditions are not nearly as black and white as assumed, the problematic is still at the centre of an ongoing discourse.

SHAPING INTELLECTUAL DISCOURSES

As a discipline, Religious Studies adheres to the need to be both objective and empathetic to all religions, both as the guarantor of its continuation as a "science of religion" and of the legitimacy of all religious forms. But where the line should be drawn on empathy before one has lost one's objectivity is not clearly demarked in the discipline. It is difficult to see how someone could devote a lifetime of study to Islam without being attracted to it at an emotional as well as a theoretical level. Still the line remains and serious political repercussions can result from someone who is said to have "gone over" to Islam.[15] At the same time the objectivity of scholars born within the tradition can be readily questioned if they hew too closely to traditional doctrinal lines.

The problematic cuts two ways, for Islam may be a problem for the current way of studying other religions, or Islam itself may reject the assumptions by which it is being studied. The genre can involve issues as complicated as theological evaluation, such as those found in the work of Cragg or Anawati,[16] to the adequacy of contemporary Religious Studies methodology, as in Adams or Martin.[17]

Certainly, some of the problem lies in the way in which our major intellectual traditions developed. Surely, it is true that the now universally-accepted bifurcation of scholarly tradition in the West between the humanities and social sciences has significance for how Islam is treated.

First, humanist concerns: These developed out of the Renaissance when the ancient Greek thinkers began impacting on Europe, and Western explorers encountered diverse cultures abroad. The challenge to a hegemonic Christian doctrine posed by these influences continues today in the academy, for both conceptions aided in the development of a critical and "objective" science of humanity, unfettered by the demands of faith.

Apart from the search for objectivity within the academic community is the very different life-experience of the two religions. Christianity was dependent upon the Greek tools of rational discourse for its creedal formulation. Islam was also subject to those norms, but in a much different and less critical manner. Very early Islam rejected the bifurcation between science and religion implicit in Greek sources because it saw all human activity under the beneficent hand of God. Religion framed all of life, even the intellectual's life. Islamic scholarship confronts the humanist dimension of Western study because there are basic disagreements over the limits of human knowledge. A wide-ranging discussion is taking place around these issues today, and some of the essays in this volume broach the topic.

Moreover, the subterranean humanist assumption that human knowledge has a singular nature has been challenged in the latter half of the twentieth century by postmodernism and poststructuralism. These approaches critically denigrate the objectivitist agenda, arguing for a more limited and relativist stance on what humans may say about knowledge at any one time. It is too early to determine what impact this might have on Islamic studies, but it is certain that it will have an impact. More than likely, these notions will affect everything from Qur'anic studies to the definition of Islam itself.

Second, the growth of scientifically-modelled studies of other cultures and peoples: It is probably safe to say that North American views of Islam have felt these kinds of studies in greater proportion than has Europe. Such studies eventually brought the disciplines of anthropology, sociology and psychology into birth. These envisaged the amassing of details about places and people, and their analysis on the basis of structural or organizational principles. The European move to North America presented the opportunity to study the peoples already here and this fostered local scholarship ranging from studies of folk literature to Amerindian religious traditions. The result has been a bewildering array of approaches, all purporting to present a picture of the religio-cultural terrain.

Despite its universalist assumptions, studying other people is not a neutral enterprise. Social scientists treat religion, if at all, as if it were one element on an equal par with many others. It is not seen to be foundational and generative of the others. Muslim and other scholars have insisted such forms of scholarship have either modified the way Muslims see themselves (that is, they often feel after reading them that they themselves are less purely "Muslim")[18] or are driven by incipient colonialism,[19] in which case even the most innocuous student is exercising some kind of political power over the subject. In the academy, studies of religion have had to deal with this problem on a number of levels and from a number of critics.[20] Several of the essays here implicitly deal with this issue.

Students of Islamic tradition have found much of value in the studies of social scientists, especially those who were interested in the phenomenon of Islam itself wherever it might be found. For example, Geertz's "religion as a cultural system"[21] has been approvingly utilized by many Islamicists to account for the various types of Muslims that seem to exist around the world. This allows the academy to acknowledge the diversity of form that Islam can take without broaching the fundamental Muslim claim of unity (*tawhīd*).[22] Still, Muslim tradition cannot accept any theory that explicitly or implicitly holds that religious meaning is dependent upon other kinds of meanings, even if they are as significant as politics or economics. Some of the essays here deal with the conflict between the different demands intellectual life places on the faith.

Our writers do not belong to one disciplinary approach, and have not collaborated to present a thematic development of these issues. Rather, we want the variety of approaches to indicate how diverse is the intellectual tradition so you will see how broad the spectrum can be. The discussions underway here reflect concerns that will surface again in other contexts and with other participants, but they will provide an outline of several very key elements as Islam in America moves to take its place in the larger context of religious growth and change.

NOTES

1. The most radical views of this are found in fundamentalist groups; they would even condemn those within the tradition who do not follow their viewpoints. Thus, Shukri Mustafa, founder of al-Takfir wa'l-Hijra in Egypt could say: "Every Muslim who is reached by the call of the Society of the Muslims and does not join is an infidel." He follows this with, "Infidels deserve death." Quoted in Abdel Azim Ramadan, "Fundamentalist Influence in Egypt: The Strategies of the Muslim Brotherhood and the Takfir Groups," in Martin E. Marty and R. Scott Appleby, eds., *Fundamentalisms and the State: Remaking Politics, Economics,*

and Militance (Chicago: University of Chicago Press, 1993), p. 158. Less radical, but still disturbing, is the statment by the liberal philsopher Sayyid Jamāl al-Dīn al-Afghānī: "All religions are intolerant, each in its own way." See *An Islamic Response to Imperialism: Political and Religious Writings of Sayyid Jamāl al-Dīn al-Afghānī*, trans. and ed. Nikki R. Keddie (Berkeley: University of California Press, 1968), p. 87.

2. Readers will find a primer on liberation theology in South America in Leonardo Boff, *Church: Charism and Power* (New York: Crossroads, 1985).

3. The term is usually associated with former president George Bush. Most observers think it means only that the basis of world order will be American power and influence. A brief description is found in Graham Evans and Jeffrey Newnham, *The Dictionary of World Politics*, Revised Edition (New York and London: Harvester/Wheatsheaf, 1993), pp. 219–220. It must have struck a responsive chord around the world, for many books and articles were spawned by it, as for example, Hazrat Mirza Tahir Ahmad, *The Gulf Crisis and the New World Order* (Maple, Ontario, Canada: Islam International Publicatons, 1992).

4. See *The World's Congress of Religions*, J.W. Hanson, ed. (Chicago: International Publishing Co., 1894), where Islam is represented as "Mohammedanism." The Muslim "representative" was a convert Russell Webb, who spoke about the relationship between Islam and Christianity. Yet a number of photos in the volume are of Islamic mosques in several countries.

5. See, for example, Manucher Farmanfarmaian and Roxanne Farmanfarmaian, *Blood and Oil: Memoirs of a Persian Prince* (New York: Random House, 1996); Soheir Khashoggi, *Mirage* (New York: Forge Books, 1996).

6. Fazal Inayat-Khan, *Old Thinking, New Thinking: The Sufi Prism* (San Francisco: Harper & Row, 1979); Mojdeh Bayat and Mohammad Ali Jamnia, *Tales from the Land of the Sufis* (Boston: Shambala, 1994).

7. Ahmed and Zane Zagloul, *The Black Prince and Other Egyptian Folktales* (Garden City, New York: Doubleday & Company, Inc., 1971); Barbara Cohen and Bahija Lovejoy, *Seven Daughters and Seven Sons* (Toronto: McClelland and Stewart, Ltd., 1982); Dorothy Gilman, *Mrs. Pollifay and the Whirling Dervish* (New York: Fawcett Gold Medal, 1990).

8. Thus, Javad Nurbakhash, *A Brief History of Sufism* (New York: Khaniqahi-Nimatullahi Publications, 1982) and the idolization of Idris Shah by the New Agers, etc.

9. A sophisticated interpreter with this idea in mind is Roger Arnaldez, *Three Messengers for One God*, trans. Gerald W. Schlabach, et. al. (Notre Dame, Indiana: University of Notre Dame Press, 1994).

10. Muslim sources claim that Muhammad was recognized as a prophet by a Monophysite monk on one of his trips north; see Ibn Ishaq, *Sīrat Rasūl Allah*, A. Guillaume (trans.), *The Life of the Prophet* (Oxford: Oxford University Press, 1955), pp. 79–81; but the relationship between Christians and Arabs had been established long before that. Some of the pre-Islamic controversies are explored in Irfan Shahid, *Byzantium and the Arabs in the Fourth Century* (Washington, D.C.: Dumbarton Oaks Research Library and Collection, 1984).

11. One very influential writer among evangelical Christians was Samuel M. Zwemer. His *The Influence of Animism on Islam: An Account of Popular Superstition* (New York: Macmillan, 1920) was an element in encouraging an American Christian attitude that Islam was inferior.

12. For a particularly obsessed novel of this rivalry, see the recent best-seller Roger Elwood, *Wise One* (Chicago: Moody Bible Institute, 1991).

13. Edward Said, *Orientalism* (New York: Pantheon Books, 1978).

14. See Marshall G.S. Hodgson, *The Venture of Islam: Conscience and History in a World Civilization*, 3 vols. (Chicago: The University of Chicago Press, 1974).

15. The accusation that many lower-level Arabists in the State Department who had "gone over" was made by those who favored an Israeli stance. Inspired by Robert D. Kaplan's *The Arabists* (New York: The Free Press, 1993); another view can be read in Peter Grose, *Israel in the Mind of America* (New York: Alfred A. Knopf, 1983), and Donald Neff, *Fallen Pillars: U.S. Policy Towards Palestine and Israel since 1945* (Washington, D.C.: Institute for Palestine Studies, 1995).

16. Canon Cragg has published some 26 books on Islam; perhaps his most representative is *The Event of the Qur'an* (London: Allen & Unwin, 1971). A brief example of Georges C. Anawati's stance can be found in "An Assessment of the Christian-Islamic Dialogue," in Kail C. Ellis, ed., *The Vatican, Islam, and the Middle East* (Syracuse, New York: Syracuse University Press, 1987), pp. 51–68.

17. Charles J. Adams, "The History of Religions and the Study of Islam," Joseph M. Kitagawa, Mircea Eliade and Charles H. Long, eds., *The History of Religions: Essays on the Problem of Understanding* (Chicago & London: The

University of Chicago Press, 1967), pp. 177–193; Richard C. Martin, ed. *Approaches to Islam in Religious Studies* (Tucson: University of Arizona Press, 1985).

18. "I don't know where I am in his book...I don't recognize anything about myself." The plaint of one of my Muslim students after reading V.S. Naipaul, *Among the Believers: An Islamic Journey* (New York: Vintage, 1982), but also heard from quite moderate Muslim scholars about Western-oriented books on Islam.

19. The most aggressive view of this is found in the Iranian Jalal Al-e Ahmad's (d. 1969) critique of Iranian society, summed up in the phrase Westoxification (*gharbzadagi*), but is also to be found in Rashid Rida's notion that contemporary believers were really only "geographical Muslims" (*muslimūn jughrfiyyun*), Muslim only for having been born in a Muslim country, as expressed in his exegesis on Qur'an 5:44–48 in *Tafsīr al-Manār* (Cairo: al-Manār, 1906–34).

20. The current emphasis on deconstruction is surely one of the most important. Readers who wish to explore this critique at its root could explore the work of Gadamer through an effective interpreter: Joel C. Weinsheimer, *Gadamer's Hermeneutics: A Reading of Truth and Method* (New Haven and London: Yale University Press, 1985). Past structuralist analyses by anthropologists are critiqued by S.J. Tambiah in *Buddhism and the Spirit Cults in North-East Thailand* (Cambridge: Cambridge University Press, 1970).

21. Clifford Geertz, "Religion as a Cultural System," in Michael Banton, ed., *Anthropological Approaches to the Study of Religion*, Association of Social Anthroplogists of the Commonwealth, Monograph No. 3, (New York: Praeger, 1966), pp. 1–46.

22. For the concept of tawhīd, see Tamara Sonn, "Tawhīd" in *The Oxford Encyclopedia of the Modern Islamic World* (Oxford: Oxford University Press, 1995) Vol. 4., pp. 190–198.

PART I.
ISLAMIC PRIORITIES AND THE CONTEXTUALITY OF DISCOURSE

Chapter 1

BEYOND SCYLLA AND KHARYBDIS: FAZLUR RAHMAN AND ISLAMIC IDENTITY

Earle H. Waugh

Islamic identity is a key element in the debate that constitutes the current study of Islam.[1] As it has developed, the issue of identity for Muslims is not just a matter of affirming certain abiding traditional values; it has involved relationships with and critiques of and from the West. The recriminations by orientalists, the strictures of colonialism, and religious exclusivity have all exacerbated the matter, adding a conspicuous "foreign" dimension to Islamic self-awareness. One result of this situation is that the chasm between Islam and the West becomes almost mythic, reminiscent of Scylla and Kharybdis.[2] Navigating beyond the clamor requires virtually the same kind of epic voyage.

It is generally acknowledged that Muslims who live in the West must face additional problems of self-definition, including the suspicion of being less than true "Muslims" by their confreres in Muslim lands. Moreover, large numbers of Muslims in the West undermine the mentality of "them against us" so explicit in ideological debates. These factors make the cultural divide between the West and Islam even more complicated than in the early part of this century.[3] Even if there are areas where the problematic seems less significant, as, for example, among the Hui of China, factoring in the West means that no doctrinal or traditional definition of being Muslim will encompass the experience that contemporary Muslims have of themselves.

The Muslim intelligentsia is particularly open to these issues. Nevertheless, arguing for a more balanced view of relations between Islam and the West, as the Muslim intellectual might do on academic grounds, is regarded suspiciously by many believers. To some the stance towards the West becomes a loyalty test set by fellow Muslims. This is particularly so regarding Western scholarship on Islam; not a few Muslim academic colleagues would demand uniform condemnation of Western scholarship on Islam.[4] Rather than being of minor importance, then, the West has become a critical ingredient in the present-day debate over the nature of Islam. For the non-specialist, such twists and turns make Islamic identity even more difficult to comprehend.

I wish to take another perspective on this problem. I do not want to argue for any one definition of being Muslim. Rather, my working thesis is that the meaning of Islam is a series of debates, affirmations and counter-claims, made from within the community itself and enshrined in the life and work of leading practitioners. It is, in short, a cluster of community discourses.

Naturally, this short essay cannot analyze all these clusters; what I hope to do is to provide one model for treating such an issue, by examining how Fazlur Rahman encountered and expressed his Islam. At the end, we should have some idea of how the parameters of Islam can be mediated for us by this methodological technique.

CONTEXT FOR DISCOURSE: MUSLIMS AND "WESTERN MENTALITY"

During my research in Cairo during the late 1970s, it became a commonplace to hear President Sadat described as an "American Muslim." Both the tone and the implication were that he had betrayed some deeply-significant Muslim characteristic in his politics. Whatever was initially intended by this phrase, for purposes of this essay it also implied something critical about the way people in "the West" thought. There was an insidious element in this thinking.

Muslims have always been sensitive to "external" detractors, beginning from the time of Islam's first engagement with Semitic pagans and then Christians and Jews, but what scholarship from abroad says about Islam has been of even greater Muslim concern in this century. Western students have not always been motivated by an innocuous will to learn about Islam's rich tradition. Often they have applied Western-conceived tactics to the understanding of Islamic religious life and history regardless of the resulting distortion. Essential to such an "orientalist" enterprise is the belief that these tactics are "objective." A corollary is that Islam-specific methodologies are not.

Muslim responses to these methodological rejections have been varied, indicating, among other things, that they have had serious repercussions on Islamic self-definition. Typically, Islam's reaction follows one of four paths: (1) to categorically and even radically reject any interpretation that does not assume a monolithic and integrationist position about Muslim identity; (2) to use arguments against what is said by those both without and within the tradition who deviate from a perceived normative interpretation of Muslim identity; (3) to proclaim an Islam that is in keeping with a "traditional" view of Islam regardless of what critics say; (4) to engage in an intellectual reconstruction of Islam, taking modern trends both within and without the tradition into consideration.[5] Clearly, each of these responses has different emphases within as well as connections to others. And just as clearly, each has different ramifications for understanding Islamic identity.

Most Muslim scholars of international stature are cognizant of Western studies. They and the Muslim intelligentsia have responded by attacking their methodological assumptions. To state the matter simplistically, these attacks normally consist in reducing the offending Western approach to some kind of ideology (Westernism, modernism, colonialism, orientalism), and then demonstrating the inherent weaknesses of those positions. A good example of this approach is in an influential Arabic four-volume study on Arabic and Islamic philosophy published in 1973.[6] In it, Anwar al-Jundī devotes one whole volume to *al-da'wa al-haddāma* or "Destructive Ideologies" in which he addresses those influences deemed to have arisen outside the tradition but which have had a detrimental effect on it. Concerning Westernization, he writes:

> Westernization, in its simplest conception, is the conditioning of Muslims and Arabs to willingly accept the Western mentality and reject the fundamentals (of Islam) which impose (on Muslim society) a particular identity and a specific Islamic character. In addition, it seeks to raise doubts concerning Islam's educational, social, intellectual and legislative principles.[7]

That so much time and effort in this important study should be expended on these Western "destructive ideologies" is testimony to their perceived importance. The equivalent would be a text on European philosophy with a large prolegomena on influences from India—it might be done, but it would not be regarded as mainstream.

Almost all such studies rest on the assumption of the ontological fixedness of this "Western mentality." Surely, the question has to be raised as to what this Western mentality may be and how it operates, for anything that is so much part of the very structure of Muslim knowledge as this should receive widespread critical evaluation. Books like al-Jundī's are responding to this requirement, but what is not done is to examine the assumed fixedness of this way of thinking.

The issue cannot remain solely an academic one, for Muslims have for many years travelled to the West and drunk deeply from its intellectual resources. Their impact on the West's understanding may have been minimal, but when they returned "home" they left lasting legacies in their dissertations, studies and students they trained. Just how much significance should be attributed to returning academics?

Even more critically, Islam has now become a religion of the West.[8] Once Islam itself has taken root in the heart of this "Western mentality," it becomes less convincing to condemn the West with blanket statements. That fact alone has made the issue of knowledge larger than the simplistic dichotomy so prevalent in studies such as al-Jundī's. If Islam now becomes part of the religious landscape of the West, then Muslims themselves must contend with this mentality directly. Worse still, they themselves may express it. Thus, being an American Muslim adds another level to the problematic by which Islam is understood, not only by Western scholars, but by Muslims themselves.

One scholar who thought the Western mentality argument was fundamentally wrong-headed was Fazlur Rahman. Both in his life and work, he attempted to build bridges. He is also interesting because he was a vigorous conservative scholar within Sunnī Islam who nevertheless both developed and ended his career in the West. Like many of his Muslims colleagues teaching at universities in the West, Fazlur Rahman had to face the difficulties encountered when trying to communicate to non-Muslim graduate students. He had to find ways of relating to and opening young minds to the intellectual traditions of Islam while being aware of his students' background and intellectual environment.

Fazlur Rahman's first response was to lead his students into an appreciation of the depths of Islamic intellectual tradition, because he believed that tradition had fostered a strong Islam in its early flowering. Moreover, he held that that tradition had secure linkages with the Western intellectual tradition. He also believed it could stand the rigors of Western critique, just as Christianity had thrived despite the most withering assault by its own Western critics.

The second response was more subtle. Whether by design or through dint of character, Fazlur Rahman practiced mediating Islam to these students through the personal power of his own engagement with Islam. In effect, these students encountered Islam as embodied in the cultured, intellectually tolerant character of a respected teacher, an encounter that undercut the validation accorded the reified "Western mentality." The image of a committed mind wrestling with the great philosophical issues of his tradition in an open manner overrode the mythic nature of the Islam/West split. His students willingly joined him in that intellectual odyssey.

There are four principle areas of discourse to which Fazlur Rahman made significant contributions: the problematic of traditional sources, recovering Islamic philosophy, the nature of Islamic statehood, and modernizing Muslim law. In what follows we will examine each of these discourses.

FAZLUR RAHMAN AND THE PROBLEMATIC OF TRADITIONAL SOURCES

Fazlur Rahman's graduate work at Oxford brought him in touch with both British and Continental philosophy, especially those analyses that dealt with culture. Thinkers like Julian Huxley and René Dubois were arguing vigorously for a natural interpretation of human life, a position with direct connections to the European humanist tradition; religious philosophers were dealing with the assault on theology from existentialism and Kantianism; religious methodology was engaging the hermeneutics of Schleiermacher in Hans-George Gadamer and Bernard Lonergan. At the same time, Islamic Studies in the West was firmly in the hands of the Orientalists.

Fazlur Rahman moved to develop a contextual understanding of history and truth in Islam out of an environment that militated fully against one of the basic presuppositions of Islam: humans cannot be understood in their totality without presupposing their relationship with God. Indeed, the obsession with finding a knowledge separate from and sometimes in contradiction to the existence of God is the cornerstone of modern Western philosophy, and has been since the time of the Enlightenment. Moreover, Christian concern for propositional statements of belief and the need to provide evidence for their truth-value has shifted the concern away from community definitions of what is true to that of accumulation of data, of evidence and specialist analyses of an "objective" sort. The interpretation of history and the manner it amasses evidence and renders it into "causal" theses was highly refined and sophisticated. When these norms were applied to Islamic evidence, inevitably Western humanists came up with interpretations that differed or conflicted with the view long held in Islamic scholarly circles.

Fazlur Rahman did not reject the evidence slowly mounting about Islam in the West with regard to Islam's distinctive historiography. Nor did he reject the general contention of Western humanism that religious understanding is subject to change. Rather, he turned to European interpreters of Christian realities like Hans-George Gadamer to provide a hermeneutical articulation to apply to the Qur'ān and Sunna; his interpretation of Gadamer's first principle of that articulation is: "All experience of understanding presupposes a preconditioning of the experiencing subject."[9]

Gadamer had insisted that classical texts were not just used by the early humanists to pass on information about the past, but as a standard by which to judge their own achievements. Hence, he says:

> As "humanists," they take pride in recognizing the absolute exemplary nature of classical texts. For the true humanist his author is certainly not such that the interpreter would claim to understand the work better than did the author himself. We must not forget that the highest aim of the humanist was not originally to "understand" his models, but to imitate or even surpass them.[10]

It is this possibility of bringing expectations to the text that frees the interpreter from any absolute rendering of the text. Put another way, all attempts to uncover an objective meaning in history must fail because human consciousness has already built in assumptions, both about what should be known and what can be said to be and these are "read" into what is found in the text. *Vorurteil*, or pre-judgment, means that we already have a structure in place that allows us to project an initial meaning on the text:

> A person who is trying to understand a text is always performing an act of projecting. He projects before himself a meaning for the text as a whole as soon as some initial meaning emerges in the text. Again, the latter emerges only because he is reading the text with particular expectations in regard to a certain meaning. The working out of this fore-project, which is constantly revised in terms of what emerges as he penetrates into the meaning, is understanding what is there.... This constant of new projection is the movement of understanding and interpretation.[11]

In comprehending what is there, one uses all the interpretive material at hand, grammar, rules of expression, history of notions, ideas in the text. Once this methodology has finished its task, it is really up to the interpreter to encounter what all this means. The process then becomes one of the interpreter relating that to "the movement of understanding and interpretation." That is why, for example, no original meaning can be uncovered, since the original meaning presupposes a constituting individual from that moment in history and that moment is now dead. Therefore, one must interpret as the text speaks at the present moment.[12]

Fazlur Rahman applied this modern humanist methodology to his project of understanding the Qur'ān and the Sunna and, indeed, the whole problematic of Muslim identity. He accepted the Western contention that revelation had a historical context. He believed that Islam, uniquely among the monotheistic traditions, is aware of its historic contextualization. This was symbolized in the very institutionalization of the Islamic calendar. The significance of the hijra (the emigration from Mecca to Medina in 622 C.E.) for him is that the long process of revelation of the covenant, beginning with Prophet Abraham, was completed with Prophet Muhammad. Thus, history was essential for the meaning of the revelation, and the revelation could not escape it. Indeed, Tamara Sonn, who has analyzed his methodology in a recent article, sees Rahman affirming a historicist awareness at Islam's core.[13]

Insofar as modernists are to be defined by accepting history as an ultimate constraint on intellectual understanding, he accepted the designation modernist.[14] However, Fazlur Rahman actually belongs in a distinctive group of Islamic modernists, that is, those who call for a new hermeneutical stance to be taken to the whole Islamic corpus. This group includes such noteworthy scholars as Hasan Hanafī, Muhammad Arkun, Muhammad al-Jābrī, 'Abd Allah al-'Arwī (Abdallah Laroui) and Abdullahi al-Na'īm, all of whom consciously address the interpretive methodology by which the Islamic legacy has been produced.[15]

Once one accepted that God had delivered His Word at specific times and places, then one had also to accept that interpretations of revelation were also subject to the specificity of those times and places. The Muslim scholar has the task of re-examining each piece of revelation within its precise historical context, determining what motivated it and then reformulating it in ways appropriate to present circumstances. This entire undertaking must be based on a clear understanding of the overall spirit of the Qur'ān as well as the dynamics of today's complex society.[16] Put in Gadamer's terminology, understanding the Qur'ān is a process that involves a distinctive fore-project. The scholar unearths how, why and when a specific revelation was given and then determines what its message is to the scholar encountering it today. As he said in an interview in 1979:

> All the passages in the Qur'ān came out of a concrete situation. Whenever a special problem arose Muhammad made a reply. The background for his reply is contained in the "occasions of revelation." It is my firm belief that modern Muslims must study the "occasions" because it is there that the dynamics of faith are found. The rationales, the reasons behind the laws, are the essence of the revelations.[17]

Once one had determined the "essence of the revelations," one could extrapolate as to how God wanted the revelation to be understood today.

It is essential that the ultimate meanings of the Qur'ān depend on contemporary understanding and cannot be fixed for all time; its meaning must be constantly renewed and reaffirmed for each generation of Muslims. At the same time, the application of the Qur'ān to contemporary life is always a dialogue between the contemporary scholar's highly nuanced sense of existence and what the Qur'ān has to say to such a person for guidance. In effect, Muslims are in a dialogue with the Qur'ān on its meanings for today.

Many Muslim scholars currently interested in Islamic hermeneutics are influenced by the European post-structuralist concern with principles of interpretation. Muhammad Arkun, for example, and 'Abd Allah al-'Arwī, mentioned above, build upon the work of French post-structuralists Jacques Derrida and Michel Foucault. Fazlur Rahman, however, formulated his methodological stance purely in terms of Islamic descriptors, founded principally on Islamic hermeneutic principles, even if his basic orientation towards the text of the Qur'ān and the hadith belongs to the same family as the post-structuralists. Thus, apart from the initial stance towards the texts, the hermeneutical process is one of a living faith encountering the truths that shaped it. The activity of concretizing the faith, then, is the task God has left to humans, and the humans must labor to bring into being the ideal community envisaged in God's revelation.

For this reason, he saw no need to fret about situations in the Qur'ān that seem to conflict or were beyond interpretation. Humanity had all the revelation it needed: it was enjoined with the task of creating in society the same equality all humans share in the eyes of God. That is at once the challenge and the purpose of human existence, the *amāna* or trust accepted by humanity at creation. It is the measure according to which Muslims will be judged in eternity.

Yet there is no eternal formula in the sense of specific social, economic or political institutions that can guarantee social justice. There is, rather, the example, established by Prophet Muhammad himself, of how the principle of human equality in fact was made the *raison d'être* of a society. To find out the principles of God's understanding of that equality, humans must continually return to the record of how that example was articulated in the concrete environment of Mecca and Medina, as expressed in the Qur'ān. Although that example does not give the specific details for how all just societies will operate, it does provide a perfect example, and to the open heart—the motivation to implement the same principles in changed and changing historical circumstances.

Fazlur Rahman saw this historicism within the Qur'ān itself. For example, the Qur'ān states,

> He it is Who sent down to thee the Book. In it are verses that are *muhkamāt*, and those are the source [or essence] of the Book, and others are *mutashābihāt*. As for those in whose hearts is perversity, they follow the latter seeking discord, and seeking its inner meaning; and none knows its interpretation except God. (Surah 3:5–7)

The question is, of course, what do the terms *muhkamāt* and *mutashābihāt* mean? Who was to decide? The traditional answer, at least among Sunnis, was that the scholars and interpreters of Muslim belief were the ultimate authority. Fazlur Rahman disagreed with this view. Yet, as classical commentators described the differences between the verses that had a plain and unequivocal meaning *muhkamāt* and those destined for more metaphorical understanding *mutashābihāt*, and in the way in which they formulated the interpretive task, the range of options was significantly limited, even to those verses that were regarded as open to interpretation.[18] For those texts that were to have only one meaning, it was the 'ulamā' that were held to give the authentic reading. Everything else had to be left to God. The input of believers, even of the most sophisticated and educated kind, in any field related to these fundamental Muslim understandings was very little.

Fazlur Rahman thought otherwise. Interpreting Islam's meaning was the believer's responsibility, not the specialist's. Moreover, he insisted there were very few verses of the Qur'ān which were not open to the ongoing efforts of interpretation and application. The Qur'ān, he asserted, was a revelation, not a legal code, a distinction that seems simple enough in the stating, but which has huge ramifications when scholarship begins its work. It "exhibits an obvious direction towards the progressive embodiment of the fundamental values of freedom and responsibility in fresh legislation,"[19] and understanding it requires one to look behind the historic details contextualizing the verses in order to come to a full realization of the principles involved.

Here then is another way in which the community of Islam and its meanings are expressed through the work of Fazlur Rahman. He assented to the notion that Islam could not escape its historicity, and hence historicity must live with Islam in its interpretation. The discourse around these topics continues in the work of Fazlur Rahman's students as will be evident below.

FAZLUR RAHMAN: RECOVERING THE IMPORT OF ISLAMIC PHILOSOPHY

As is characteristic of many Muslims who study in the West, Fazlur Rahman underwent a crisis of his faith, a crisis that forced him into a personal search of Muhammad's role as Prophet and the meaning of prophecy in Islam. In his book *Prophecy in Islam*,[20] he vigorously explored traditional conceptual formulations. Unlike al-Jundī and those who dichotomize Islam and the West, and who then end up blaming the West as a way of overcoming the conflicts, Fazlur Rahman more profoundly saw the dilemma to be rooted in Islam itself, where the problem is best encountered in the tensions between traditional Muslim theologians and those Islamic philosophers whose inspiration arose from Aristotle, Neo-Platonism and Stoicism.[21] In his view, what had to be negotiated was a compromise between the intellectual rigor of Islamic philosophers and the powerful activism of a living God within Islamic history. Even though the philosophic tradition in Islam is generally held to have been destroyed by 'Asharism and the Sufi al-Ghazālī, Fazlur Rahman asserted that it had been redirected into the mystical tradition, where it transformed that movement.[22] Thus, there was no need for Muslims to go outside the resources of the Islamic tradition to discover a legitimate philosophic tradition; it was enshrined in the literature and theodicy of Sufism. Philosophic inquiry was not then "foreign" to Islam, but endemic to it.

Fazlur Rahman's response to the challenge of the West was to follow the deeper veins of that Islamic philosophic culture, and thus enriched, to turn to the explication of central Islamic doctrines. With this orientation, he explored the Qur'ān and the life of Muhammad to develop a renewed means of constituting Islam for his day. Most of his subsequent writings dealt in one way or the other with issues encountered while promoting this philosophical re-stating of Islamic identity.

It should be noted that Fazlur Rahman did not conceive of Islam's renewal via philosophical discourse because of his personal propensity. Rather, he was looking for a normative Islamic moment in Muslim history that had the broadest and most creative impact. He saw such a procedure as a return to a particularly dynamic time in Muslim history when the standards of international intellectual achievement were being laid down in Islamic society. He searched for a time when Islam confidently engaged all manner of intellectual sources in its drive to build God's true society. Moreover, he saw that moment as a validated expression of true Islam because people from all walks of life and from all areas of the empire contributed to its growth. It represented the most congruent moment when the Qur'anic ideology of equality was in tune with the intellectual expectations of Islamic society. The result was a society shaping itself according to divine precept. It was an enterprise of the whole Muslim society, not just an elite.

By founding a contemporary Islam on the discovery and elucidation of these first principles, Fazlur Rahman vaulted Islam into the universal discourse of what human society should be. He realized that cross-cultural, cross-religious debate had been under way in the West since the time of the Renaissance, and that criticisms of Islam were but one form it took. Hence, the ground rules would have to rest on accepted non-sectarian conceptualization which the West itself had not yet sorted out. Fazlur Rahman wanted the universal dimensions of Islam to be part of that debate. Anything less than that left Muslims talking to themselves, and ultimately abandoning their identity to a privileged religious caste, with little to say to the coming global culture.

At the same time, he also held that Islamic reform could not proceed until it came to terms with the intellectual principles that had been essential for its formation. To reform itself without doing so was to deny its own history. Thus, he insisted that a critical assessment of this legacy was the *sine qua non* of any further reconstruction of Islamic society.

FAZLUR RAHMAN IN PAKISTAN: MUSLIM IDENTITY IN THE MODERN STATE

As news reports from the world's Muslim capitals underscore, Muslims are today in a crucial debate about the role of government in mediating true Islam. Fazlur Rahman's career is an important gauge of the topic, since an essential element of his life was his contribution to establishing an "Islamic" state. In the years leading up to the 1960s, Pakistan had been founded, and the government had to deal with implementing an Islamic vision of a modern state. The Sharī`a (Islamic law) obviously had to play a leading role in the resulting debate.

As Berry indicates in the next chapter, General Ayyub Khan established Pakistan's Central Institute for Islamic Research to promote modernist interpretations of Islam compatible with his regime's interests. Fazlur Rahman returned home from Canada to be the director of that Institute in 1961. Immediately he was plunged into the clash between Ghulam Ahmad Parwez and the conservative 'ulamā'. Parwez particularly rejected the traditional scholars' use of the Sunna (customary practices) of the Prophet to adjudicate contemporary political/moral issues, not because the Sunna did not contain legitimate points of piety, but because there was no ground for an objective historical validation of their contents. Parwez held that without confirmed historical truth, neither the Sunna nor the sayings of the Prophet (*hadīth*) was of much present significance. He also interpreted Muslim history in a particularistic manner, for he held that the Islamic state was the true heir of Prophetic authority, a view that Shī'a believers had always rejected.

Since Fazlur Rahman was regarded as a prime consultant for Ayyub Khan, the 'ulamā' saw in this a veiled attempt by the Ayyub government to bypass their authority, a view that government actions on a number of fronts seemed to bear out. As head of the Institute, Fazlur Rahman was in a direct line of fire between the contestants. He responded with a series of articles on the Sunna and hadīth that eventually were collected into a book entitled *Islamic Methodology in History*.[23] There his views on the application of the Qur'ān and Sunna were directly spelled out.

It is well known that the Qur'ān and Sunna are the foundations of Muslim law. That law was held to be of divine provenance, because it was established on the infallible word of God in scripture and on the exemplary life of the Prophet. If the reports about the life and norms of the Prophet contained in a hadīth could be shown to be inauthentic, or if they were even shown to be manufactured at a later date, the whole structure of Sharī'a law would be on very shaky ground, perhaps even collapse. Fazlur Rahman agreed that much of the Sunna of the Prophet was likely a construct of later times, but he did not then draw the conclusions that Ghulam Ahmad and others did; rather, he argued that the Sunna represented the normative collective viewpoint of the developing Muslim community, fed as it was by the example of the Prophet, and inspired by the awareness of Muslim values as they became explicit. Hence, an analogue of the legal principle of *ijmā'* or consensus was operative in the formation of the Sunna. He maintained that "although *Hadīth* verbally speaking does not go back to the

Prophet, its spirit certainly does, and *Hadīth* is largely the situational interpretation and formulation of the Prophetic model or spirit."[24]

When Ayyub Khan appointed Fazlur Rahman to his newly-formed advisory body, the Council of Islamic Ideology, in 1964, the Council became the target for conservative and 'ulamā' opposition. Fazlur Rahman was at the center of the ensuing storm. His philosophical views of Islamic history were openly contested by the opposition, and his understanding of Islam was widely criticized. He left Pakistan under a cloud in 1968, when he moved to U.C.L.A. as a visiting professor; he then shifted to the University of Chicago in 1969, where he remained the rest of his life.

Fazlur Rahman's experience in modern nation-state planning portrays the key role that government plays in defining the contemporary meaning of Islam. Islamicist arguments that believers must return to the normativity of the Prophet's time are, in effect, spoiled. Whatever Islam was in Muhammad's time, it cannot be again, because the shape of the tradition must deal with the issue of statism that has defined Islam as it moved beyond Mecca and Medina. The reality is that Islam is now embodied in Muslim nation-states. Hence, the meaning that has for Islam is one of the essential discourses in which all Muslims are engaged today.

Yet Fazlur Rahman did not cease to form a nation just by moving to the United States. He then became a voice for the fledgling movement of Islam within America. The role Islam should play in molding Muslims in a supposedly secular environment is of heightened significance in the American context. The central issue is still governance.[25] The basic problem in founding an American congregation within a general mosque organization (where the congregation is the local mosque, and the general mosque the national structure) is not the foreignness of the structure, but the lack of direct access to state political power deemed necessary as the "container" for those institutions inherent in the Muslim system. Instead of forming exclusively religious organizations based firmly on principles of Islamic provenance, other characteristics prevail: sectarian, ethnic, national and regional. Traditional sectarianism continues in America. Mosques tend to fragment along ethnic lines, or congregational leadership remains tied to customs deriving from home states, to the detriment of an American Islamic agenda.[26] Political activism arises out of national consciousness, imposing regional and even local agenda in a setting far removed from its relevance. Notions that Islam as religion requires Islam as state continue to plague Muslim thinkers. Current fundamentalist agitation only underlines this essentially statist mentality. Rahman held that the essence of Islam resides rather in the ethical norms of Islamic law.

DISCOURSE ON MODERNIZING THE LAW: THE PRIMACY OF AN ETHICAL ORDER

Almost all modern interpreters of the Qur'ān have argued for a reinstatement of *ijtihād*, that process once a key ingredient of applying the generality of the law to the minutiae of human life but slowly eliminated in the medieval period. It is fundamental to Fazlur Rahman, as well. He liked to call it intellectual jihad. Ijtihad was absolutely essential to Islamic hermeneutics, because none of the conceptions we have explored is possible without the interpretation of the Qur'ān's message in the light of current circumstances.

Fazlur Rahman held that the absolutely basic premise of Islam was the construction of an egalitarian, ethical social order.[27] Any attempt to build such a social order is an interpretive activity, since the meanings of "ethical" and "egalitarian" are historically defined. It is "the effort to understand the meaning of a relevant text or precedent in the past, containing a rule, and to alter that rule by extending or restricting or otherwise modifying it in such a manner that a new situation can be subsumed under it by a new solution."[28] He blames the stagnation that has characterized the Islamic world since the Middle Ages, in fact, on the limitation and eventual cessation of ijtihād:

> Most modern Muslim thinkers have laid the blame...on the destruction of the caliphate in the mid-thirteenth century and the political disintegration of the Muslim world. But...the spirit of Islam had become essentially static long before that; indeed, this stagnation was inherent in the bases on which Islamic law was founded. The development of theology displays the same characteristics even more dramatically than does legal thought.[29]

For although the early Muslim leaders clearly exercised independent judgement regarding how best to implement Islamic principles and achieve the Islamic goal of social justice, they failed to stress the need for continued ijtihād, much less to institutionalize it:

> There is no doubt that early scholars of Islam and leaders of the community exercised a good deal of freedom and ingenuity in interpreting the Qur'ān, including the principles of ijtihād (personal reasoning) and qiyās (analogical reasoning) from a certain text of the Qur'ān and arguing on its basis to solve a new case or problem that has certain essential resemblances to the former. There was, however, no well-argued-out system of rules for these procedures, and early legal schools sometimes went too far in using this freedom. For this reason in the late eighth century c.e., al-Shāfi'ī successfully fought for the general acceptance of "traditions from the Prophet" as a basis of interpretation instead of ijtihād or qiyās. Yet the real solution lay only in understanding the Qur'ānic injunctions strictly in their context and background and trying to extrapolate the principles or values that lay behind the injunctions of the Qur'ān and the Prophet's Sunna. But this line was never developed systematically, at least by Sunnī Muslims.[30]

Like many modern Muslims, Fazlur Rahman believed the ideals of society laid down by the Qur'ān exemplified the greatest gift God had given human society. The sense of order and equality provided humans with a stable and uplifting worldview within which to work out their ordinary lives. The self-consciously ethical ethos implicit in the religion of Islam provided Muslims with the blueprint for a genuinely religious environment. Yet, as fundamentalism grew, liberal notions about the priority of this ethical vision withdrew.

Fazlur Rahman faced the integrationist agenda of the so-called fundamentalists head-on. In an article entitled "Roots of Islamic Neo-Fundamentalism" published in 1981,[31] he saw Islam currently fragmented into four ideological camps, one of which, the neo-fundamentalists, he pointedly attacked.[32]

He regarded the traditional-conservative camp quite differently from the fundamentalist; the former held Islamic history and tradition as their construct, and were willing to defend and affirm it. At the same time, they were stuck within their construct. The latter, whom he designated as the original fundamentalists, shifted away from the message to obey God because of eternal rewards and punishments, to a narrower obedience to God rendered in terms of behaving properly in this world. This obedience had no flexibility because it was entirely literalist. Empirical data was eschewed by these interpreters because obedience to God was entirely transcendental.

The neo-fundamentalists, among whom he classified Ayatollah Khomeini, were likewise out of touch with the world. However, they went beyond the conservatives' simple disengagement with the real world, as well as the literalist rigidities of the original fundamentalists. The neo-fundamentalists were far more sophisticated because they were postmodernist in thrust, and had been influenced by it. Moreover, the positing of foreign influences was absolutely required by the neo-fundamentalists. He thus defined neo-fundamentalism as:

> an Islamic bid to discover the original meaning of the Islamic message without historic deviations and distortions and without being encumbered by the intervening tradition, this bid being meant not only for the benefit of the Islamic community but as a challenge to the world and to the West in particular.[33]

Fazlur Rahman felt the neo-fundamentalists actually propagated positions that were dangerous. He believed it was more than an error to hope that Muslims could straighten out the problems of the world without solid intellectual effort and with only catchy slogans. It had the potential for dangerous mistakes. He pointed out that while they talked vigorously about ijtihad, they had not moved significantly to reinterpret any of the stale atmosphere of traditionalism. They could not, he held, because they were reacting both to the modernists' agenda of imposing Western solutions to Islamic problems and because they were not schooled enough in Islam itself to produce a genuine Islamic response. By reacting against both the West and modernists within, their primary motivating power came from negativity. By insisting on a form of Islam completely divorced from the real world of Muslims, the neo-fundamentalist thus cut himself off from his own Islamic traditions. Fazlur Rahman points out:

> There is no one among the fundamentalists that I know of—with the exception of Ayatollah Khomeini—who is a well-trained *'alim* in the traditional sense. So far as Islamic learning is concerned, they are dilettantes: indeed, neo fundamentalism is basically a function of laymen, many of whom are professionals—lawyers, doctors, engineers.[34]

Fazlur Rahman was willing to concede that the neo-fundamentalists had an emotional power unrivalled in the contemporary world and that, properly channelled, they could be a dynamic force for change in the Muslim world, but he believed their approach was poorly thought-out, defensive, and ultimately doomed to failure. "This fundamentalism will not last long. It's a phase in the internal dynamics of Islamic society. The modernist trends in Islam are irreversible," he concluded.[35] If the ferocity of the movement is any indication, the discourse over modernism will be acrimonious and prolonged. As is evident, it is already deadly.

The community today is somewhat deflected away from a wide-ranging debate as to whether Fazlur Rahman's ethical interpretation of Islam is the most basic. His views are eclipsed in the welter of charges and counter-charges encountered in the discourse on Islamic identity. But there can be no doubt that the sense of ethics it applies to worldly structures will force the debate back into the forefront. Determining what is essential and what is specifically particularistic, and therefore dispensable in the new world of Islam, will ultimately result in that occurring.

CONCLUSIONS

Extrapolating from these principles, then, became his hermeneutic for contemporary Islam. It was a process that brought the condemnation of many of his countrymen and contention among Muslims all over the globe. Nevertheless, in his view, that is the intellectual project that Muslims were called to shoulder in today's world. It is also the intellectual legacy which he bequeathed to students.

Fazlur Rahman's interpretive methodologies provide avenues of movement beyond the Scylla and Kharybdis of West/Islam. Thoroughly modern in his concern for hermeneutics, he nevertheless applied those interpretive principles in a manner that kept them within the orbit of Islamic tradition. He agreed with the perspective taken by all Muslim reformers that Islam had seriously deviated from "the straight path," but he rejected the view that the West was entirely responsible for that deviation. Rather, he believed that some of the deviation came from a misunderstanding of what the straight path was from the outset; in effect, the deviation began in the Islamic community itself when it failed adequately to understand the nature and role of God's revelation.

Fazlur Rahman's arguments demonstrate how key Islamic issues have been expressed through the ongoing debate between an impressive intellect and his own tradition. His solution to the vexing problems of Islamic identity in the latter part of the twentieth century are thus larger than himself and really reveal a religion debating with itself over its role in the rapidly shrinking world.

In many ways his principles militate against restricting him to a definite place in the modernist-conservative spectrum. Some American scholars might try to affix him within the moderate wing of Muslim conservative scholars, since it is doubtful his views will attract the allegiance of any student with orientalist tendencies. At the same time, his views obviously conflict with both traditional 'ulamā' and radical Islamists of today. As is well-known, Muslim critics often regarded him as a thoroughgoing modernist.

Despite the lack of success in fixing him in the spectrum, the tenor of his scholarship is progressive, for the impasse looks neither as formidable nor as insurmountable as the trenchant dichotomy between Islam and the West had suggested. Fazlur Rahman's engagement with Islam reflects a genial scholarly tolerance for other perspectives coupled with firmly held commitments to Muslim tradition; his personal legacy provides genuine insights into a kind of Islamic intellectual universalism of much importance for the future of religious understanding and scholarly endeavor. The potential of that approach can be seen in the essays from his students that follow.

NOTES

1. See G.E. von Grunebaum, *Modern Islam—The Search for Cultural Identity* (Berkeley: University of California Press, 1962), pp. 128ff for a statement of the identity crisis; also Tilman Nagel, "Identitatskrise und Selfstverstandis: Eine Berachtung zum zeitgenossischen muslimischen Geschichtsverstandnis," *Welt des Islam*, XIX (1979), pp. 76ff. On methodology in Islamic studies see, Richard C. Martin, ed., *Approaches to Islam in Religious Studies* (Tucson: University of Arizona Press, 1985).

2. Scylla and Kharybdis are legendary Greek rocks that clash together whenever approached by a ship.

3. For a flavor of this see Earle H. Waugh, "Reducing the Distance: A Muslin Congregation in the Canadian North" in *American Congregations*, J. Wind & J. Lewis, eds. (Chicago: University of Chicago, 1994), vol. 1, pp. 572–611.

4. The term "American Muslim" has become pejorative in Egypt since the death of Sadat. It implies an Islam that is nothing more than a veneer. Sadat, of course,

was labelled such after his peace treaty with Israel.

5. Three of these approaches undergird Haddad's analysis of Islam and history. See Yvonne Yazbek Haddad, *Contemporary Islam and the Challenge of History* (Albany, NY: State University of New York, 1982). She adduces the apologetic, the traditional and the intellectual, pp. 81–113. I have added a rejectionist category because of the hermetically sealed mindset implied by the radical integrationist. Absolutely nothing that is not read as Islamic will be tolerated in the ingredients of such an Islam; even arguing with others gives more credence than they deserve, and should be fought against and destroyed. See Muhammad 'Abd al-Salām Faraj, *al-Farīda al-Ghaiba* [The Missing Religious Obligation] (Cairo: NP: 1980). Faraj was a member of the radical organization *Tanzīm al-Jihād* responsible for Sadat's assassination. For a review of the radical Islamic group's involvement in the assassination, see A. Chris Eccel, "'Alim and Mujahid in Egypt: Orthodoxy Versus Subculture, or Division of Labour?" *The Muslim World*, 78(3–4), pp. 189-208.

6. Anwar al-Jundī, *al-Mausū'a al-'Arabiyya,* 1st ed. Beirut, 1973.

7. This selection is quoted from Mahmoud Ayoub, "Roots of Muslim-Christian Conflict," *The Muslim World*, 79(1), p. 38.

8. See, for example, *The Muslim Community in North America,* Earle H. Waugh, Baha Abu-Laban and Regula B. Qureshi, eds. (Edmonton: The University of Alberta Press, 1983); outside of North America, see, for example, Philip Lewis, *Islamic Britain* (London: J.B. Tauris, 1994). Popular magazines like *Washington Report on Middle East Affairs* regularly have a section reporting on American Muslims, and a fine periodical which analyzes Muslim publications, *Islam in America*, edited by Mohamed Alibhai, appears regularly.

9. Fazlur Rahman, *Islam and Modernity* (Chicago: University of Chicago Press, 19), p. 9.

10. H.-G. Gadamer, *Wahrheit und Methode* (Tubingen: J.C.B. Mohr, 1965), trans. *Truth and Method* (New York: Crossroad, 1985), p. 171.

11. *Truth and Method*, p. 236.

12. *Truth and Method*, p. 149.

13. See Tamara Sonn, "Fazlur Rahman's Islamic Methodology," *Muslim World*, 81 (3–4) (1991), pp. 212–230.

14. Scholars such as Jamāl al-Dīn al-Afghānī (d. 1897 c.e.), Muhammad 'Abduh (d. 1905), and Muhammad Iqbal (d. 1938) have the term modernists applied to

them because they call for the application of Islamic principles to new or changed circumstances. They arrive at these principles on other grounds, however, than Rahman's source analysis.

15. 'Abd Allah al-'Arwī, *The Crisis of the Arab Intellectual: Traditionalism or Historicism?* (Berkeley: University of California Press, 1976), translated from the French by Diarmid Cammell (Paris: Librairie François Maspero, 1974). For additional bibliography, see below, Chapter 6, note 7.

16. See Fazlur Rahman, *Islamic Methodology in History* (Karachi: Central Institute of Islamic Research, 1965).

17. See the *Chicago Sun-Times*, "Collapse of Islamic Fundamentalism Seen," 3/31/79.

18. See Jane Dammen McAuliffe, "Quranic Hermeneutics: The Views of al-Tabarī (d. 923 c.e.) and Ibn Kathīr (d. 1373 c.e.)" in *Approaches to the History of the Interpretation of the Qur'an*, Andrew Rippin, ed. (Oxford: Clarendon Press, 1988), pp. 46–62.

19. Fazlur Rahman, *Islam*, p. 38.

20. Fazlur Rahman, *Prophecy in Islam* (Chicago: University of Chicago, 1979).

21. *Prophecy in Islam: Philosophy and Orthodoxy*, 2nd ed.

22. *Islam*, 2nd ed. (Chicago: University of Chicago Press, 1979), p. 126.

23. The articles were: "Concepts Sunnah, Ijtihād and Ijmā in the Early Period," *Islamic Studies*, 1 (1) (1962), pp. 5–21; "Sunnah and Hadīth," *Islamic Studies* 1 (1) (1962), pp. 1–36; "Post-Formative Developments in Islam," *Islamic Studies* 1 (4) (1962), pp. 1–23. The collection was published as *Islamic Methodology in History* (Islamabad, 1965). They were also published in Urdu and Arabic.

24. *Islamic Methodology*, p. 80.

25. It must be acknowledged that Fazlur Rahman had little impact within the burgeoning Muslim community on his doorstep, that is, the rapidly expanding Black Muslims whose center of influence was no more than a few blocks south of the University of Chicago. Elijah Muhammad's group instituted one of the most dramatic religious conversion processes in modern history, when inner-city neighborhoods turned towards Islam as the means to affirm distinguished ancestry denied to it by American culture. Until that time, Islam had made negligible inroads into American society.

Yet the Black Muslims, when they did look to the outside for assistance, called in Isma'il al-Faruqi, doyen of Religious Studies at Temple University, who argued for the development of the "Islamization of knowledge", a process of creating distinctive areas of intellectual endeavor formulated around categories of Western disciplines, but based entirely on traditional Islamic notions like "tawhid". Fazlur Rahman rejected this approach as another kind of fundamentalism, resting on the hope that something in place now could be replaced with a true "Islamic" element, presumably because it had been eliminated from Islam at some point in the past. He saw no evidence that such a patchwork approach would promote Islamic revival because the Islamization of knowledge had not developed organically within the Islamic tradition itself, but arose in response to Western structures of understanding. A critique of al-Faruqi's program and an affirmation of Fazlur Rahman's is found in Yasien Mohamed, "Islamization of Knowledge: A Critique," *The American Journal of Islamic Social Science*, 11 (2) (Summer 1994), pp. 282ff.

26. See Waugh, "Distance," *American Congregations*.

27. See *Major Themes*, p. 38.

28. *Islam and Modernity*, pp. 7–8.

29. Ibid., p. 26.

30. Ibid., p. 18.

31. Fazlur Rahman, "Roots of Islamic Neo-Fundamentalism" in *Change and the Muslim World*, Philip H. Stoddard, David C. Cuthell, Margaret W. Sullivan, eds. (Syracuse: Syracuse University Press, 1981), pp. 23–35.

32. The *Sun-Times* article, "Collapse of Islamic Fundamentalism Seen," has slightly different categories, namely the secularist, the modernist, the traditionalist and the neo-fundamentalist. His shift to neo-fundamentalism appears to rest upon his belief that the reformist tradition, what he calls "Islamic positivism," was an eighteenth and nineteenth-century phenomenon. See "Roots," p. 25. See Tamara Sonn "Fazlur Rahman's Islamic Methodology," where his categories are spelled out.

33. Fazlur Rahman "Roots," p. 33.

34. Ibid., p. 34.

35. See his "Collapse of Islamic Fundamentalism Seen."

Chapter 2

DR. FAZLUR RAHMAN (1919–1988): A LIFE IN REVIEW

Donald L. Berry

> I passionately believe that we Muslims owe it to ourselves and to the world to resurrect the Qur'ānic vision from the debris of history, for in the Qur'ān the real and the ideal coalesce....Islam at present stands radically polarized and is in unmistakable ferment and transition. Medieval conservatism cannot...supply genuine and effective answers to today's problems. It appears largely to be a reaction against Western colonialism. I am therefore confident of the eventual success of the pure Islam of the Qur'ān, which is fresh, promising, and progressive. It will take a few years and considerable effort, however, for the current obscurantism to be laid to rest in its grave. During the ensuing years of my life the bulk of my activity will be directed toward the realization of this end.[1]

The refreshing candor and vitality of Fazlur Rahman has thoroughly permeated the field of Islamic Studies in North America. His unmistakable passion for the Qur'ān and his courage to challenge the weaknesses of Islamic traditionalism and Western scholarship provided his students with a well-rounded view of the Qur'ān. His diverse background and his unquenchable thirst to discover the Qur'ānic hermeneutic challenged his students and his readers to use all available resources to unearth the élan of the Qur'ān. The legacy he left has and will continue to impact the study of Islam in North America and throughout the world.[2]

BACKGROUND

Fazlur Rahman was born on September 21, 1919, in pre-partition India. He was raised in a traditional home where his father provided religious instruction.

> My mother and father had a decisive influence in the shaping of my character and earliest beliefs. From my mother I was taught the virtues of truthfulness, mercy, steadfastness, and above all, love. My father was a religious scholar educated in the traditional Islamic thought. Unlike most traditional religious Islamic scholars of that time, who regarded modern education as a poison both for faith and morality, my father was convinced that Islam had to face modernity both as a challenge and an opportunity. I have shared this belief with my father to this very day.[3]

Fazlur Rahman completed his M.A. from the Punjab University in 1942 and completed his Doctor of Philosophy degree from Oxford in 1949. While at Oxford he experienced an intense personal conflict between his modern and traditional educations. *Prophecy in Islam* represented his dilemma in written form as he discussed the head-on collision between the views of the traditional Islamic theologians and the Islamic philosophers who were heavily influenced by Aristotelian, Neoplatonic and Stoic thought. The philosophers were intellectually clever, excelling in subtlety of argument, but their god remained a bloodless principle—a mere intellectual construct, lacking both power and compassion. Although intellectually less skillful, the theologians were nevertheless instinctively aware that the God of religion was a full-blooded, living reality who responded to prayers, guided people individually and collectively, and intervened in history: "He speaks and acts," as Ibn Taymiyya so poignantly put it.[4] Fazlur Rahman sought to discover the Islam which incorporated the intellectual prowess of the Islamic philosophers and the dynamic nature of the living God as described by the Islamic theologians. Although many scholars assert that the Hellenistic perspective of the Islamic philosophers succumbed to the power of the Islamic theologians, Fazlur Rahman held that the impact of the Islamic Philosophers "did not die with the orthodox attack of al-Ghazali as is commonly supposed by modern scholarship," but that its spirit transmigrated into the Sufi movement.[5] This discovery forced him to take a fresh look at the Qur'ān and the life of Muhammad in an effort to re-evaluate traditional Islam.[6] He sought to rediscover the vitality of the Qur'ān by means of a contextual, exegetical study of the Qur'ān.[7] Fazlur Rahman spent the rest of his life trying to accomplish this task.

In August of 1962, Fazlur Rahman became the director of the Central Institute of Research in Pakistan. This position enabled him to actualize a Pakistani rediscovery of the Qur'ān and its subsequent societal reconstruction as Pakistan faced the challenge of modernity. He was responsible for interpreting "Islam in rational and scientific terms to meet the requirements of a modern progressive society."[8] Following the 1964 elections, President Muhammad Ayyub Khan appointed him to the newly formed Advisory Council of Islamic Ideology. The council's task lay in "making specific recommendations in the field of Islamic policy and law."[9] *Islam*, the first of three influential books which has shaped North American Islamic Studies, was born during this period. Although he received more than his share of grief for his attempts to wed Qur'ānic idealism and sociopolitical realism, he never lost sight of what Islam could become in the context of modernity.[10]

Fazlur Rahman's teaching career in North America began in 1958 at McGill University in the Institute of Islamic Studies. He left McGill to begin his career as a religio-political advisor in 1961 and returned to North America in 1968. After serving as a visiting professor at U.C.L.A., he joined the faculty of the University of Chicago in 1969. In Chicago, he found a haven where he could continue to develop his understanding of the role of Islam in the context of modernity and bring Islamic Studies into the larger arena of Religious Studies. During his tenure at the University of Chicago, he found time to serve as an advisor to the Indonesian government in the establishment Higher Education in Islamic Studies and as a consultant to the United States State Department and the White House. Two important writings emerged during his teaching career in Chicago, *Major Themes of the Qur'ān* and *Islam and Modernity*. His last published manuscript, *Health and Medicine in the Islamic Tradition*, has added much to the study of Islamic ethics and his last unpublished manuscript dealt with Islamic Neo-Fundamentalism. Although one can never fully estimate the impact of Fazlur Rahman's contributions to North American Islamic Studies during his Chicago tenure, one can see the overwhelming presence of Fazlur Rahman in his former students. Fazlur Rahman's students have captured a major place in the field of Islamic Studies and have worked diligently to link Islamic Studies with the larger discipline of Religious Studies.

CONTRIBUTIONS

Fazlur Rahman contributed many things to the field of Islamic Studies and these contributions will be exposed in the remaining chapters of this volume; however, five important contributions must be acknowledged to reflect Fazlur Rahman's influence on Islamic Studies in North America. First, Fazlur Rahman brought a unique multicultural blend of Sunni Islamic traditionalism, progressive Islamic modernism and Western scholasticism. His background in the traditional Islamic sciences enabled him to be well-versed in Islamic jurisprudence and the hadith. His foundation in Islamic modernism enabled him to see that one could recapture the vibrancy of Islam and face the challenges of modernity with enthusiasm. His training in Western philosophy exposed the Hellenistic influence on the Islamic philosophers and on traditional Islam as a whole. His encounters with figures like Abul A'la Mawdudi enabled him to capture a keen insight to the pulse of influential neo-fundamentalist groups like the Jamaat-i Islam.[11] Although he shared their passion for reform, but he could not condone their solutions because he recognized a glaring absence of serious scholarship in movements like these. His education at Oxford provided an opportunity to become well-read in a variety of significant writings that have shaped Western culture. The experience at Oxford, coupled with his teaching experience in North America, exposed Fazlur Rahman to material in Islamic Studies written by Western, non-Muslim authors and to the larger field of Religious Studies. His appointment by President Ayyub Khan enabled Fazlur Rahman to use his diverse background to face the sociopolitical realities of Islam in the context of modernity. He had the fortune to advocate a move from Qur'ānic orthodoxy to Qur'ānic orthopraxy in Pakistan.

Second, Fazlur Rahman's search for truth led him to challenge attitudes in traditional Islam and in Western writings on Islam. He had the courage to be innovative amidst rigid Islamic and Western attitudes. His stands on particular social, political, religious issues in Pakistan produced much controversy. For example, his stand on the Muslim Family Laws Ordinance, the appropriateness of family planning devices, the advocacy of modern banking methods and the appropriateness of the mechanical slaughter of animals for food all led to private and public denouncements of Fazlur Rahman. However, the stand that caused the greatest furor was Fazlur Rahman's dynamic view of the Qur'ānic revelation, advocated in his book *Islam*. Fazlur Rahman felt this view of the Qur'ānic revelation could be found in the writings of al-Ghazali, Shah Wali Allah of Delhi and Muhammad Iqbal, but when the first two chapters of his book were published in the *Fikr-o-Nazar* the response was intense.[12] Fazlur Rahman painfully reflected on this encounter.

> I defended the idea of the verbal revelation of the Qur'ān, which is the universal belief. However, it seemed to me that the standard orthodox accounts of revelation give a mechanical and externalistic picture of the relationship between Muhammad and the Qur'ān— Gabriel coming and delivering God's messages to him almost like a postman delivering letters. The Qur'ān itself says that the Angel "comes down to the heart" of Muhammad. I stated that the Qur'ān is *entirely* the Word of God insofar as it is infallible and absolutely free from falsehood, but, insofar as it comes to the Prophet's heart and then his tongue, it was entirely his word.[13]

Immediately following this event, conservative journals such as the *Al-Bayyinat*, declared that Fazlur Rahman was a *munkir-i Qur'ān* (disbeliever in the Qur'ān). In spite of price the paid for challenging Islamic traditionalism, he continued to advocate the necessary ingredients for a true Islamic reformation. Fazlur Rahman not only challenged Islamic traditionalism, but he also disputed many of the Western attempts to understand Islam. Many of the early Western attempts to understand Islam portrayed it as a fatalistic, archaic, and static creature with very little to contribute to Western scholarship. Fazlur Rahman represented a refreshing voice which exposed the West to an Islam that it had never seen before.[14]

Third, Fazlur Rahman's methodology was interdisciplinary to the core. The holistic, multi-disciplinary study of Islam challenged the students of North America to view Islam in its contextual expressions throughout the world. His approach demanded that the student of Islam be well-versed in the political, social, economic and religious backgrounds of the Qur'ān and in today's Muslim countries. He often team-taught courses with faculty from other departments to broaden the perspective of his students. His methodology insisted that historical research be linked with reality of contemporary settings. This methodology allowed the students of Islam to discover the dynamism of the Muslim experience. Fazlur Rahman's commitment to an interdisciplinary approach can be seen in the comments of Richard Martin.

> What the present volume highlights is the need for an interdisciplinary approach, not just in terms of the "orientalist" and "social scientist"...but in terms of several disciplines with defined methods of research. For the former without the latter remains myopic, resulting in dangerous generalizations, while the latter without the former becomes abstract, in fact, chimerical.[15]

Fazlur Rahman's approach opened the door for Islamic Studies to dialogue with the broader field of Religious Studies.[16]

Fourth, Fazlur Rahman's demeanor has done much for the receptivity of his work. His gentle, kind spirit combined with his keen intellect have done much for Islamic Studies in North America. Many preconceived ideas of Muslim behavior were dispelled by his hospitable, gracious manner. The writer of this article observed his warm, gracious nature the first time he met Fazlur Rahman at the University of Chicago. The author has also spoken with numerous Muslims from North America and all have spoken kind words about character of Fazlur Rahman. His timely presence in North America and his genuine demeanor won him a hearing by many students and colleagues throughout the world.

Lastly, Fazlur Rahman left a legacy in the form of his students. He will continue to impact the study of Islam in North America through their influence. The contributors of this volume represent the heartbeat of Islamic Studies in North America. Fazlur Rahman's students can be found teaching in many of the major colleges and universities throughout the United States and Canada. His constant striving for a better understanding of Islam in the context of modernity has been transmitted to his students. Many of his students have contributed important works to the field of Islamic Studies and continue to seek a place for Islamic Studies in the larger field of Religious Studies. Fazlur Rahman's students and admirers represent a legacy of Islamic scholarship which can never be content with simplistic assertions, but always strives for depth, accuracy, and viability.

Frederick Denny, a former student of Fazlur Rahman, wrote the following in a memorial to his professor:

> As a Muslim intellectual, Fazlur Rahman could never stand still. His mind changed and his positions evolved, but his central coordinate was always the Qur'ān. A measure of this leading thinker's impact is that wherever I have traveled in the world—whether here in North America, or to Egypt, Jordan, the West Bank, the Peninsula, Bangladesh, Pakistan, Malaysia, Indonesia, or Europe—I have never met a Muslim scholar or other specialist on Islam who has not heard of Fazlur Rahman or who is neutral about his contributions to the making sense of life in Islamic ways. There was a phrase in one of the early attempts at doctrinal formulation of early Islam that goes, "Difference of opinion in the community is a token of the divine mercy." Fazlur Rahman has shown us how "that ancient insight continues to bear fruit fulfilling the task while enjoying the fit of God's command."[17]

CONCLUSION

The full impact of Fazlur Rahman's thought, methodology, and writings cannot be fully measured. The fact that his works have been translated into several languages reveals that his work appeals to the hearts of Muslims from a variety of socio-cultural contexts. The fact that one can find his name referenced in large portion of works in Islamic Studies reflects that his thoughtful reflections and daring articulations are indeed noticed by those working in Islamic Studies. The fact that he was often asked to contribute to volumes that focused on religious dialogue reveals that his thoughtful reflection was seen by those outside of the field of Islamic Studies.

Whether one agrees with Fazlur Rahman or not, his works and influence must be acknowledged. Probably the one summation of Fazlur Rahman's attempt to discover the lively, fresh, dynamic élan of the Qur'ān is that he was one who was not afraid to search for truth in a variety of places. The Qur'ān states, "Truth stands out clear from error."[18] Fazlur Rahman was so confident in the truth revealed in the Qur'ān that he could read Muslim and non-Muslim writings to enhance his personal and professional life. He was convinced that one could be both a scholar and a devoted Muslim without compromising either commitment. His legacy has encouraged those in the field of Islamic Studies to enter into a dialogical relationship with those in the broader field of Religious Studies. The author is convinced that both fields of study have received enrichment from his relationship and that Fazlur Rahman played, and his writings still play, a major role in bringing these two fields together.

NOTES

1. Fazlur Rahman, "My Belief-in-Action" in *The Courage of Conviction*, Phillip L. Berman, ed. (Santa Barbara: Dodd Mead and Co., 1958), pp. 198, 200.

2. Fazlur Rahman's *Islam* (1966), *Major Themes of the Qur'ān* (1980), and *Islam and Modernity* (1982) have been translated into Urdu, Indonesian, Serbo-Croatian, Turkish and Italian.

3. Fazlur Rahman, "My Belief-in-Action," p. 154. Fazlur Rahman's father graduated from the Deoband Seminary in northern India and tutored him in the traditional Islamic sciences while Fazlur Rahman was attending a modern college.

4. "My Belief-in-Action," p. 155. See Fazlur Rahman, *Prophecy in Islam: Philosophy and Orthodoxy*, 2nd ed., and Chapter Seven of Fazlur Rahman's *Islam*, 2nd ed., for his critique of Muslim theologians.

5. Fazlur Rahman, *Islam*, p. 126.

6. Fazlur Rahman, "My Belief-in-Action," p. 196.

7. Fazlur Rahman, *Islam and Modernity: Transformation of an Intellectual Tradition*, pp. 1–11.

8. Fazlur Rahman, "Some Islamic Issues in the Ayyub Khan Era" in *Essays on Islamic Civilization, Presented to Niyazi Berkes*, Donald P. Little, ed. (Leiden: E.J. Brill, 1976), p. 285. This statement was originally written in the *Pakistan Gazette* in July of 1961.

9. Fazlur Rahman, "Some Islamic Issues," p. 285.

10. For a discussion of some specific issues and stands that led to strong opposition, see Donald L. Berry, "The Thought of Fazlur Rahman as an Islamic Response to Modernity," Ph.D. dissertation, The Southern Baptist Theological Seminary, 1990, pp. 50–61.

11. The best source for Fazlur Rahman's use of "neo-fundamentalism" is his "Roots of Islamic Neo-Fundamentalism," in *Change in the Muslim World*, Philip H. Stoddard, et al., eds. (Syracuse: Syracuse University Press, 1981), pp. 23–35.

12. *Fikr-o-Nazar*, September 1967, pp. 249–68.

13. Fazlur Rahman, "Some Islamic Issues in the Ayyub Khan Era," p. 299. See also *Islam*, p. 31: "But orthodoxy...lacked the intellectual capacity to say both that the Qur'ān is entirely the Word of God and, in an ordinary sense, also entirely the word of Muhammad."

14. See Fazlur Rahman, "Approaches to Islam in Religious Studies: A Review," *Approaches to Islam in Religious Studies*, Richard C. Martin, ed. (Tucson: University of Arizona Press, 1985), pp. 189-202; Fazlur Rahman's article "Some Recent Books on the Qur'ān by Western Authors," *Journal of Religion*, 64, no. 1 (1984), pp. 157–162; and the Introduction to his *Major Themes of the Qur'ān*, pp. xi–xvi.

15. Richard Martin's, "Approaches to Islam in Religious Studies," p. 202.

16. To review Fazlur Rahman's dialogical encounters with Judaism and Christianity, see "Islam's Attitude Toward Judaism," *The Muslim World*, 72 (1982), pp. 1-13; "A Muslim Response to Christian Particularity and the Faith of Islam," *Christian Faith in a Religiously Plural World*, Donald G. Dawe and John B. Carman, eds. (Maryknoll, NY: Orbis Books, 1978) pp. 69–79; and "The People of the Book and the Diversity of Religions," (a reprint of Appendix II of *Major Themes of the Qur'ān*), in *Christianity Through Non-Christian Eyes*, Paul J. Griffiths, ed. (Maryknoll, NY: Orbis Books, 1990).

17. Frederick. M. Denny, "Fazlur Rahman: Muslim Intellectual," *The Muslim World*, 79, 2 (April 1989), pp. 100–101.

18. Qur'ān, 11:256

PART II.
ISLAM AND PHILOSOPHY

Chapter 3

THE TRIUMPH OF SCRIPTURALISM: THE DOCTRINE OF NASKH AND ITS MODERN CRITICS

Daniel Brown

As modern Muslims have faced the challenge of rebuilding or reshaping social, political and legal structures on a foundation that is in some sense "Islamic," they have often been sharply divided over the foundations of religious authority—that is, over what texts, authorities or methods of interpretation can provide an authentic basis for Islamic norms. The result has been an ongoing crisis of religious authority that has frequently erupted in public controversies over both particular questions of Islamic law or practice and general questions surrounding the application and interpretation of the sources of Islamic law.

Throughout his career Fazlur Rahman was both an acute observer of and energetic participant in such controversies. During his tenure as director of Pakistan's Central Institute for Islamic Research he took center stage in several controversies—over the legality of bank interest, inheritance law, and marriage and divorce regulations. Perhaps more importantly, with a series of articles published in the journal *Islamic Studies* and later collected in *Islamic Methodology in History*, he became a major participant in debates over the theoretical foundations of religious authority.[1] In the Subcontinent, and indeed throughout the Islamic world, these debates have focussed primarily on the second source of Islamic law, the Sunna of the Prophet. Since the mid-nineteenth century the authority of Sunna and the authenticity of the tradition literature (hadīth) which is its material source have been intensely scrutinized and the source of fierce debate. Fazlur Rahman's approach to Sunna was at once critical and cognizant of the centrality of Sunna to the integrity of the Islamic tradition. His great contribution was an effort to salvage the authority of Sunna from the ravages of modern hadīth criticism by attempting to redefine Sunna as the community's collective interpretation of the Prophetic example—what the Prophet would have done in a given circumstance.

But while the Sunna has been subjected to such intense criticism and scrutiny by Muslim scholars—a process of which Fazlur Rahman's work represents a culmination of sorts—the Qur'ān has enjoyed a different fate. By analogy with the modern experience of other religious traditions we might expect the Qur'ān, like the Sunna, to have also attracted the critical scrutiny of modern Muslims and to have suffered the same sort of de-sacralizing methods that biblical critics have unleashed on Jewish and Christian scriptures. Yet this has most emphatically not been the experience of modern Muslims with the Qur'ān; in fact, Western scholars have frequently commented on the reluctance of modern, even modernist Muslims, to subject the Qur'ān to the methods of historical and literary criticism. The Qur'ān has seemed strangely above the fray—immune to the sort of criticism and controversy that has been part and parcel of modern debates over Sunna. Fazlur Rahman himself perhaps came as close as any modern Muslim scholar to the application of a historical-critical method to the Qur'ān but his approach seems cautious in the extreme when compared to the work of non-Muslim scholars in the tradition of Bell or Wansbrough, or to trends in biblical studies. Certainly in his later work, especially in *Major Themes of the Qur'ān* and *Islam and Modernity*, Fazlur Rahman was centrally concerned with the development of a viable modernist hermeneutic of the Qur'ān, but he continued to maintain a cautious attitude toward the text itself, built on an unwavering conviction of its divine origins.

Why have Muslims—even scholars of the sophistication of Fazlur Rahman—been so cautious in their approach to the Qur'ān? Is this caution simply the perpetuation of medieval Muslim doctrinal scruples, as Welch seems to suggest?[2] Have Muslim attitudes toward Qur'ān somehow escaped unchanged from the maelstrom of modernity? To the contrary, I will argue here that Muslim attitudes toward the Qur'ān have changed markedly and on a wide scale during the modern period. The directions of that change, however, turn out to be quite surprising. The main focus of my inquiry will be one aspect of Muslim attitudes toward the Qur'ān, and a topic of intrinsic interest, that is, the doctrine of abrogation, or *naskh*. Modern Muslim attitudes toward abrogation reflect, I suggest, a wider tendency in modern Muslim treatments of the Qur'ān—a tendency which I will label scripturalism. Scripturalism provides a convenient label for a complex of mutually reinforcing tendencies in modern Muslim religious thought which have resulted from an elevation of the Qur'ān and its isolation from other parts of the tradition. As other sources of authority within the tradition, particularly the Sunna, have been undermined, the Qur'ān has borne an increasingly heavy burden as the primary source of religious authority. Hence scripturalist tendencies have included the drawing of sharp boundaries around the Qur'ān; an emphasis on interpreting the Qur'ān by the Qur'ān, in isolation from other sources; heavy stress on the universality and perfection of the Qur'ān and its independence from specific historical or cultural context; and deep sensitivity to any apparent challenge to the integrity or universality of the Qur'ān.

In his own work Fazlur Rahman was both a critic and a product of these scripturalist tendencies. On the one hand, a work like *Major Themes of the Qur'ān* is unavoidably scripturalist in its assumptions: that the Qur'ān can and must speak directly, and as a coherent whole, to contemporary Muslims; that scriptural interpretation need not be bound by the weight of tradition; that the Qur'ān's best interpreter is the Qur'ān itself; and that its essential message is universal, uncircumscribed by historical circumstance. On the other hand, Fazlur Rahman was a sharp opponent of those Qur'ānic fundamentalists like Ghulām Ahmad Parwēz who seem to rip the Qur'ān entirely out of its original context. His own approach was one which elevated the Qur'ān, yet applied a sophisticated hermeneutic involving, as he put it, a double movement from present situation to the original Qur'ānic context and back, in order to formulate a principle, a *ratio legis*, applicable to the contemporary Muslim situation.[3] Fazlur Rahman's scripturalism, then, was neither rigid nor simplistic in approach. But among those with less acute historical sense, the consequence of scripturalism often has been a rigidity which was foreign to the classical exegetical tradition.

• • •

The contrast between classical approaches to the Qur'ān and modern tendencies is well illustrated by the contrast in attitudes toward the theory of abrogation.[4] The notion of *naskh* is, on the surface of it, quite simple. Put in the most general of terms, the doctrine of abrogation tells us that some of God's commands replace others. The abrogating command, *al-nāsikh,* supersedes the abrogated command, *al-mansūkh*, which then no longer carries force. The idea suggested by the notion of *naskh*—that revelation is by nature progressive—is unsurprising in a Muslim context. From very early on Muslims accepted as fundamental to their construction of Islam that later revelations replace earlier ones. Islam superseded Christianity just as Christianity superseded Judaism. Naskh at this level is not controversial, and might be superficially compared to the Christian notion of the New Covenant. In fact naskh at this level—the macro level—is central to Muslim self-definition, for Muslims see Islam not simply as building on the foundation of earlier dispensations, but as replacing them *in toto*. Unlike Christians, Muslims have no temptation to appropriate and reinterpret earlier scriptures—such scriptures have been replaced by something better and hence are irrelevant except as artifacts which from time to time might be useful to provide background for Qur'ānic exegesis.

The Qur'ān clearly supports some idea of a progression in revelation. Two verses in particular suggest later revelations replace earlier ones:

> 2:106: And for whatever verse we abrogate or cast into oblivion We bring a better verse or one which is equal to it. Knowest thou not that God is powerful over everything?
>
> 16:101: When we exchange one verse for another—and God knows best what he sends down—The say, "You are but a forger." But most of them do not know.

Seen in context these verses give support for a general idea of abrogation, and they might be understood as a defense of the replacement of rules from earlier dispensations with new commands in the Qur'ān. Moreover, there are numerous other verses which support a general notion of progression and revision of revelation.[5] If left at this general level, the Muslim doctrine of naskh would have remained a rather minor curiosity. But in the mid-eighth century—the early

Abbasid period—we begin to see large-scale interest in the notion of naskh in early legal texts and Qur'ān commentaries. Yet, surprisingly, Muslim scholars show little or no interest in the abrogation of prior revelatory dispensations. The understanding of naskh as primarily an inter-textual phenomenon—the replacement of one scripture by another—is almost completely suppressed in favor of an intra-textual theory of abrogation.[6] Hence all of the attention in these first Muslim treatments of naskh is on the application of the doctrine of naskh within the Islamic sources themselves—that is, the abrogation of one Qur'ānic command by another, or the abrogation of one Sunna by another, or the abrogation of Qur'ān by Sunna or Sunna by Qur'ān.[7]

This theory of naskh, labelled by Burton the "special theory," and understood as the abrogation of revealed commands within the Islamic sources, came to be well-developed among scholars by the early ninth and almost universally accepted by the tenth and eleventh centuries.[8] The application of naskh was, in theory, quite simple: In its most common form all that was required to apply the doctrine was to (1) establish conflict between two revealed texts, and (2) establish a chronology of texts in order to determine which is later. This rather straight-forward application of naskh is nicely illustrated by the treatment of wine in the Qur'ān: verses reflecting praise and ambivalence toward wine are ultimately abrogated by its condemnation.[9] A more dramatic case of abrogation is the famous "sword verse" (2:190) which commands Muslims to kill unbelievers ("Slay the idolaters wherever you find them, and take them, and confine them, and lie in wait for them at every place of ambush"), and which is believed by some to abrogate 124 other verses of the Qur'ān including all verses which describe the Prophet as merely a warner, and all verses in which Muhammad is instructed to be patient.[10] Qur'ān commentators disagreed, of course, over specific cases of abrogation, and the precise number of verses that were abrogated—totals varied from a high of 238 to a low of 5—but the occurrence of this form of abrogation was almost universally accepted.

The theory of naskh also had more complex and controversial applications, however. Some parts of revelation, for example, were thought to be lost completely—"cast into oblivion"—without replacement. Such an application of naskh could make sense of early traditions, indicating that there were parts of revelation left out of the final version of the Qur'ān.[11] One companion of the

Prophet, for example, held that Sura 9 had originally been 3 or 4 times longer than in its final collected form. Another recalled the existence of two long suras which never made it into the final collection. Most dramatically, the Prophet's wife Aisha reported that there were some passages of the Qur'ān under her bedding at the time of the Prophet's death which ended up becoming food for a domestic animal.[12]

A final form of abrogation involves cases in which a part of revelation is alleged to have been omitted from the Qur'ān, while the command still remains in effect. The Prophet's companion Umar, for example, claimed that there had been a verse in the Qur'ān which established the penalty of stoning for adulterers, that he remembered this verse, but that since no one else did he could not put it in the Qur'ān. Nevertheless, stoning remained the penalty for adultery, even though the Qur'ān seems to call for 100 lashes.[13]

These examples give some indication of both the functions and the importance of abrogation. Jurists and Qur'ān commentators thought that understanding abrogation was among the essential branches of knowledge—crucial for understanding the Qur'ān, for understanding Islamic law, and for piety. According to a statement attributed to Ahmad ibn Hanbal, "He who does not know the sound from the unsound in hadith or cannot tell the nāsikh from the mansūkh is no scholar." Similarly, "Anyone who makes public pronouncements on the law without expert knowledge of naskh runs the risk of endangering not merely his own immortal soul, but those of his followers."[14] We may be tempted to see this as merely the hubris of the naskh specialist, desperate for someone to read his book. But in fact there is good reason to suggest that the doctrine of naskh is every bit as important as these scholars claim. If one believes that obedience to the particular law of God is of ultimate importance, and if some laws have been replaced by others, one had better know which regulations are still in force and which have been abandoned.

Viewed more cynically, the doctrine of naskh served as a powerful exegetical technique for justifying one's own legal positions and for discrediting the positions of one's opponent. In fact, the doctrine of naskh represents the ultimate triumph of interpretive authority over the text, allowing not just for the reinterpretation of a difficult text, but its complete nullification. Moreover, the criteria for deciding whether a verse is abrogated are all external to the Qur'ān itself—in the hands of the interpreter. And because of the complexities of the science of naskh, only specialists can be fully cognizant of all the information necessary to decide whether a verse is operative or not.

But quite apart from the utility of the doctrine in the economy of knowledge, by accepting the theory of abrogation, Qur'ān commentators and jurists implicitly accepted a particular view of revelation—and a view in tension with official dogma about the nature of the Qur'ān. Naskh encouraged a view of revelation as rooted in particular historical circumstance. In Mahmoud Ayoub's words, naskh is an "expression of the Qur'ān's involvement in the daily life and problems of human society."[15] By contrast, official dogma held the Qur'ān eternal (*qadīm*) and uncreated (*ghayr makhlūq*)—it neither originated in time, nor is it contingent. The revelations transmitted by Gabriel to Muhammad are the eternal word of God, without any hint of human involvement. The Qur'ān is thus immutable and universal. Naskh seems to encourage just the opposite view—that revelation is historically contingent, subject to change with changing circumstances. "What can be of use in one age can be harmful in another," according to Baydāwī (1286). Similarly, according to Zamakhshari, a verse is made to vanish when the common good—*maslaha*— requires it to be eliminated.[16] God, in this view, is like a good doctor. If the patient's condition changes, does the doctor continue the same prescription?[17]

The doctrine of naskh also reflects a view of revelation which does not draw sharp boundaries between the Qur'ān and other sources of authority—particularly the prophetic Sunna. Most commentators draw no clear distinction between scripture and tradition—the boundaries are porous. In this way the doctrine clearly reflects the mature Muslim view of revelation which saw the Qur'ān, the Sunna and the extrapolation of these sources in the various Muslim sciences as a single, unified tradition. Hence most classical commentators came to accept the abrogation of Qur'ān not only by Qur'ān, but also by Sunna.[18]

Finally, naskh involves a frank admission of contradictions in—and possibly even omissions from—revealed texts. The acceptance of the full theory of naskh implies that a good deal may have been revealed to Muhammad that never showed up in the Qur'ān, and that even what is in the Qur'ān was subject to change. The doctrine thus seems to challenge the integrity, completeness and immutability of divine revelation.

Commentators recognized these tensions with official dogma. In fact, the doctrine seemed to play into the hands of those who challenged the eternity of the Qur'ān. Some Mu'tazilite theologians allegedly appealed to the doctrine of naskh to bolster their argument that the Qur'ān had been created in time.[19] There is also some evidence of interreligious polemic on the question of abrogation and its implications.[20] But it was not impossible for clever scholars to explain away the apparent contradictions. Commentators were especially careful to argue that abrogation need not imply any change in the divine will, and thus does not threaten the eternity and immutability of the Qur'ān. The solution was simple and ingenious: God eternally wills for particular rules to be applicable for a given period of time. God does not change his mind. He simply has, from eternity, established expiration dates for commands and he knows all along when a particular rule is due to expire. Thus, what seems to us to be response to circumstance is merely the operation of the eternal will of God. Abrogation, in this view, is nothing more than the revelation that the expiry date of a command has arrived.[21]

Yet perhaps we can see some discomfort at the tensions raised by naskh in the increasing caution with which later Muslim scholars applied the doctrine. Even among those who applied the doctrine most liberally, only a small minority believed that any verse of the Qur'ān could be abrogated. Al-Nahhās, author of one of the chief manuals on naskh, limits its application to commands and prohibitions in the Qur'ān, and whatever has the sense of a command or prohibition.[22] Moreover, the principle was well established that reconciliation of apparently contradictory commands is to be preferred over naskh.[23] At least one scholar, Abu Muslim b. Bahr al-Isfahānī, is reported to have rejected naskh altogether in favor of *takhsīs* (elaboration). Although the majority continued to admit the doctrine, it seems to have invited little enthusiasm. Hence, the fifteenth-century Egyptian scholar Suyūtī only admits to twenty cases of abrogation; the eighteenth-century Indian theologian Shāh Walī Allāh was satisfied with five.

Such tendencies toward caution in the application of naskh may be seen as a reaction to earlier extremes in its application. Perhaps more convincingly, such a trend is a consistent with the increasing hegemony of Sufism in the religious and scholarly lives of Muslims—Sufi tafsīr had little concern for questions of law and little stake in apparent conflicts in the sources.

• • •

Beginning in the mid-nineteenth century, discomfort with naskh gave way to the complete repudiation of the classical theory of naskh by a wide spectrum of Muslim scholars, beginning with the Indian modernist Sayyid Ahmad Khān.[24] Two features of Sayyid Ahmad's position on abrogation are noteworthy: First, he insists that naskh should be applied only as an inter-religious phenomenon; when the Qur'ān talks about abrogation, it is referring not to Islamic revelation, but to prior revelations—the Torah and the Gospels.[25] This departure from the classical exegetes is no surprise: in the context of the colonial Muslim-Christian encounter it was clearly more attractive to emphasize the supersession of the Qur'ān over previous scriptures than to admit internal contradictions in revelation. Second, his rejection of naskh is firmly rooted in a theology of revelation which refuses to countenance any challenge to perfection, consistency and universality of the Qur'ān: "We firmly believe," he writes, "that whatever came down from God is now available in unaltered form in the present Qur'ān, which was actually recorded during the lifetime of the Prophet, that not a single word is omitted, that no verse of the Qur'ān is abrogated." The doctrine of abrogation makes the Qur'ān nothing more than the "scribbling pad of a poet"—an affront to Allah and to Islam.[26]

Sayyid Ahmad Khān's position on naskh might be of little significance on its own, but he proves to have a good deal of company. He is, in fact, simply the first in a line of modernist thinkers in the Subcontinent who have repudiated or questioned the classical theory of naskh.[27] The tendency is especially marked among thinkers associated with anti-hadith tendencies, most notably Aslam Jayrājpūrī[28] and Ghulām Ahmad Parwēz.[29] Their rejection of naskh followed naturally from the sort of Qur'ānic fundamentalism which led them to elevate the Qur'ān at the expense of all other sources of authority. For thinkers like Jayrājpūrī and Parwēz, the doctrine of naskh suggests that the Qur'ān might share all of the same weaknesses that they attribute to hadith. But even Abu'l Kalam Azād, a modernist with more mainstream associations, rejects naskh.[30]

The modernist response has often involved appropriation and reinterpretation of the idea of naskh rather than its complete rejection. Sayyid Ahmad Khān's disciple Chirāgh Alī offers an interesting example: Rather than altogether dispensing with the doctrine of naskh he reinterprets the theory as a means of distinguishing absolute and conditional imperatives of the Qur'ān and giving priority to the former. Chirāgh Alī is alone among modernist theologians, however, in recognizing the potential utility of an adapted and reinvigorated theory of abrogation for the development of a modernist hermeneutic.[31] At quite another level, some modernists have appropriated the idea of abrogation to support general notions of progress and evolution both in nature and in human civilization. Nāsikh and mansūkh, according to Tantāwī Jawharī, reveal the "secret of progress." The natural world models "abrogation"—the abrogation of night by day—in order to instruct humans to put aside old habits in favor of modern ways.[32] Such an exegetical maneuver also fits neatly with pseudo-scientific trends in exegesis of the Qur'ān.

Egyptian modernists, beginning with Muhammad Abduh, have been characteristically more cautious than their counterparts in the Subcontinent. Abduh was unwilling to dispense with naskh altogether, but he was highly reticent about identifying real examples of it.[33] Rashīd Ridā was more openly skeptical of the theory of abrogation. In a discussion of naskh in *al-Manār* he suggests that the early exegetes adopted the technique of abrogation simply as a convenient tool, that they had little or no grounds for their adoption of it, and that they disagreed about almost everything to do with naskh. The end result, in Ridā's argument: Naskh is of dubious value and certainly not to be accepted as an article of faith.[34]

Challenges to naskh have not been limited to modernists. The Pakistani revivalist Mawdūdī rejects the classical theory and, like Sayyid Ahmad Khān, limits naskh to the replacement of previous scriptures by the Qur'ān. To support his position offers his own version of the context for the chief proof-text for naskh, Sura 2: 106. The Jews, he claims, were complaining that the revelations of the Qur'ān contradicted their own scriptures; they asked how, if the earlier scriptures were really from God, they could be superseded.[35] Such a context is useful for contemporary interreligious polemic, but is foreign to the classical exegetical tradition. Mawdūdī is adamant enough in his rejection of naskh to mistranslate another verse. His version of 16:101 reads: "When we send down one verse to elaborate on another...."[36] an accurate translation might read, "When we exchange (*baddalna*) one verse for another...." He is clearly unwilling to allow even the slightest implication of changes in revelation (unless, perhaps, he makes the change himself)!

Mawdūdī is not alone among revivalists in his rejection of naskh. Sayyid Qutb shows no sympathy for the classical theory.[37] Muhammad al-Ghazālī concludes a discussion of naskh with the assurance, "Without doubt the Qur'ān abrogates previous Shariahs...but there is not a single contradiction in the Qur'ān. Every verse has a context in which it is applicable."[38] Thus, much in the same vein as Mawdūdī, he considers naskh to represent nothing more than specification or elaboration (takhsīs) of the particulars of a command.[39]

Rejection of naskh is not universal among modern scholars, but the trend is widespread enough to cause even those who accept the doctrine to treat it conservatively. We have already mentioned Muhammad Abduh's hesitancy to find real examples of it. Mustafa Zayd finds only seven cases of naskh in the Qur'ān. Across sectarian boundaries, the Shi'ite 'alim Abū'l Qāsim al-Khu'ī, although unwilling to dismiss the possibility of naskh in theory, finds no actual instances of abrogation in the Qur'ān.[40]

• • •

The importance of this trend should not be underplayed. A doctrine that found almost universal acceptance among medieval Muslim scholars seems on its way to extinction. How are we to understand the modern repudiation of an exegetical and legal technique that was so widely accepted and that seems to have had enormous utility for exegetes and legal scholars alike? To understand the significance of the repudiation of naskh by such a wide array of modern Muslim thinkers we need to place the problem in the context of the general scripturalist trend with which we began. There are several components to this trend:

1. Distrust for other sources of authority besides the Qur'ān—a sort of Muslim version of the *sola scriptura* of the Reformation. This trend is found in an extreme form only among a small number of Muslims, but as I have argued elsewhere the general tendency is quite widespread.[41]

2. A widespread emphasis on interpreting the Qur'ān by the Qur'ān—that is, putting aside all external aids to tafsir and interpreting the Qur'ān only in light of its own verses. This is the single most consistent trend in modern Muslim tafsir.

3. An emphasis on the universality of the Qur'ān—that is, its independence from any specific context. In its most extreme forms this emphasis on universality

finds expression in pseudo-scientific exegesis—in the claim that the Qur'ān anticipates each new scientific discovery.

4. A continued emphasis on perfection of the Qur'ān as proof of its authority. In classical scholarship the perfection of the language of the Qur'ān was emphasized. In modern times emphasis has shifted to the perfection of its message and structure. The analysis of the Qur'ān by computer to prove its miraculous numerological structure offers a case in point.[42]

Viewed together with these broader scripturalist tendencies, the modern repudiation of naskh serves to illustrate just how large a gap has grown between classical and modern understandings of the Qur'ān. Whereas the doctrine of naskh implies a view of revelation which does not draw sharp boundaries between the Qur'ān and other sources of authority, Qur'ānic scripturalism elevates the Qur'ān at the expense of other sources; whereas naskh assumes the application of external criteria to understand the intent of the Qur'ān, scripturalism emphasizes internal harmonization of the text without external aids; while scripturalism assumes the universal applicability of every part of revelation, the doctrine of naskh assumes the rootedness of the Qur'ān in particular time and place; finally, the doctrine of naskh requires the unabashed recognition that there are contradictions within the text of the Qur'ān, while scripturalism refuses to countenance the possibility of any inconsistency or contradiction within the text. In fact, for scripturalists the absence of contradiction becomes the chief defense of the Qur'ān's authority.

This is all quite the opposite of what we might, perhaps naively, have expected: Where we might have expected "modernity" to lead to greater willingness to subject sources of authority to scrutiny—to usher in more critical approaches to the text of the Qur'ān, for instance—we find instead just the opposite. Among many Muslim thinkers, even among those who are considered modernist in orientation, views of scripture have tended to become more rigid and more doctrinaire. Rather than being "humanized" as we might expect by analogy with modern trends in Christian or Jewish thought, scripture has become even more distant and untouchable.

Why? For explanation we need to look to the socio-historical context—that is, we need to place these trends within the context of the colonial encounter. The context of almost all of modern Muslim treatments of naskh is apologetic.

Virtually all modern treatments of naskh apply the idea primarily to an inter--religious context. The classical understanding of naskh was, frankly, an embarrassment, especially in polemics with missionaries. It implied that the Qur'ān was not consistent, not perfect and perhaps not even complete. But by reemphasizing naskh in its more general sense of the abrogation of Christianity and Judaism by Islam, commentators and apologists could turn a weakness into a weapon. Thus, feeling under attack from Western scholars and missionaries, Muslim thinkers have fallen back on what was perceived to be their strong suit—the integrity of the Qur'ān. In the modern interreligious encounter the Qur'ān has been seen as measuring up favorably to the Bible—but to retain this position required that Muslims avoid the slippery slope that Christians and Jews have encountered. The classical tradition could be jettisoned or rethought; the Sunna might be questioned, but the Qur'ān was a last bulwark. In the words of Shabbir Akhtar, "The Muslim thinker, if he has any wits about him, will resist root and branch any suggestion that the Qur'ān is an amalgam of the divine and human."[43] This is the mistake, according to Akhtar, that Christians have made and he wonders whether Christians (he has in mind Kenneth Cragg) who encourage Muslims (Fazlur Rahman?) in this direction are simply looking for partners in adversity, for "one cannot reasonably accept the authority of a partly fallible scripture."[44]

Such resistance to the application of critical methods to the Qur'ān is often attributed to doctrinal scruples—the persistence of medieval doctrines about the perfection or uncreatedness of the Qur'ān. But there is more to it than that: Muslims have not just continued to hold the same attitude toward the Qur'ān that they always did. Rather, attitudes have changed markedly. But this change has been in the direction of greater rigidity rather than greater flexibility. This is not the persistence of some timeless attitude, but a real change toward scripturalism. And this change is rooted in the particular ways that Muslims have experienced modernity. The distortions of the colonial encounter have made it difficult for Muslims to deal with the Qur'ān in anything but a defensive posture; the distortions of contemporary geopolitics have perpetuated that situation, and there are few signs in modern Muslim scholarship of any significant abatement of this scripturalist tendency.

NOTES

1. Fazlur Rahman, "Concepts Sunnah, Ijtihad and Ijmā in the Early Period," *Islamic Studies* 1, no. 1 (1962) 5–21; *idem*, "Sunna and Hadith," *Islamic Studies* 1, no. 2 (1962): 1–36; *idem*, "Post-formative Developments in Islam," *Islamic Studies* 1, no. 4 (1962): 1–23; These articles were collected and published separately as *Islamic Methodology in History* (Islamabad, 1965). They were also published in both Urdu and Arabic. By his own account Fazlur Rahman was responding through these articles to two quite separate, although interrelated controversies. He was responding, first of all, to the immediate controversy in Pakistan aroused by Ghulām Ahmad Parwēz's radical rejection of Sunna. But he was also responding to the ongoing international, scholarly debate about Joseph Schacht's skeptical views on the authenticity of hadīth which had been published some years earlier in his *Origins of Muhammadan Jurisprudence*.

2. A.T. Welch, "Kur'ān" in *Encyclopaedia of Islam*, New Edition (Leiden: E.J. Brill, 1954), 5:427.

3. Fazlur Rahman, *Islam and Modernity* (Chicago: University of Chicago. 1982), p. 5.

4. In describing classical naskh theory I am heavily indebted to a growing body of secondary literature on the topic, especially John Burton, *The Sources of Islamic Law: Islamic Theories of Abrogation* (Edinburgh: Edinburgh University Press, 1990); Ahmad Hasan, *Early Development of Islamic Jurisprudence* (Islamabad: Islamic Research Institute, 1988), pp. 60–84; and David Powers, "The Exegetical Genre *nāsikh al-Qur'ān wa mansūkhuhu*" in A. Rippin, ed. *Approaches to the History of the Interpretation of the Qur'ān* (Oxford: Oxford University Press, 1988), pp. 117–138.

5. For a list of such verses see Richard Bell, *Introduction to the Qur'ān*. new ed.; revised and enlarged by W. Montogomery Watt (Edinburgh: Edinburgh University Press, 1977), pp. 86–89.

6. John Wansbrough, *Qur'ānic Studies* (Oxford: Oxford University Press, 1977), pp. 193–4.

7. This emergence of abrogation as an exegetical and legal technique has drawn a good deal of scholarly attention during the last couple of decades. There are at least three rival hypotheses to explain the significance of the science of naskh: (1) The doctrine of abrogation is simply what it appears to be—a hermeneutical method to sort out conflicts among the sources; (2) The doctrine of abrogation is a product of the development of theories about the formal sources of Islamic law. These theories often fit rather badly with actual legal practice as it developed, and

naskh was one tool with which to reconcile legal practice with the actual texts of the Qur'ān and Sunna—or perhaps more importantly to explain away discrepancies between revealed authority and legal doctrine. See Burton, *Sources*; (3) Debates over abrogation preserve the vestiges of controversies over the precise boundaries of the revealed text—that is, the emergent science of naskh offers a window into the process by which the Qur'ān achieved canonical status. Moreover, these debates suggest a date and process of canonization much later than Muslim tradition attests. Naskh literature suggests, in other words, that the text of the Qur'ān was not fixed and universally accepted within twenty-four years of Muhammad's death, but rather was still fluid and the subject of controversy into the early eighth Century. See Wansbrough, *Qur'ānic Studies*.

8. The development of literature on naskh may be conveniently divided into three periods: (1) Late eighth century: Views on naskh attributed to early traditionists and exegetes, and the first technical references to naskh appear in the *Muwatta'* of Mālik (d. 795); (2) Early ninth century: The first systematic elaborations of the theory of naskh, e.g., by al-Shāfi'ī (d. 820) and Abū Ubayd (d. 838), coincide with ninth century debates over the sources of Islamic law (*usūl*) as well as with major controversies over the nature of the Qur'ān; (3) tenth and eleventh centuries: "Classical" treatises on naskh by al-Nahhās (d. 949) Hibatullah ibn Sallāma (d. 1020) and others reflect mature development of the doctrine of abrogation and its near universal acceptance by scholars. For fuller discussion of chronology of early naskh literature, see Powers, "Exegetical Genre," p. 119 and Hasan, *Early Development of Islamic Jurisprudence*, p. 61.

9. The earliest mention of wine praises it as a sign of grace (16:67); the next occurrence tells us there is both usefulness and sin in wine, but the sin is greater (2:219); then Muslims are told not to come to prayer drunk (4:43); finally, wine is condemned as an abomination, Satan's work, indicating complete prohibition (9:103). In this example, as in most other cases of abrogation, all the abrogated verses remain in the Qur'ān—but each later revelation is taken as abrogating the former.

10. Powers, "Exegetical Genre," p. 130.

11. Such traditions were suppressed in Sunni circles for the obvious reason that they seem to undermine the incorruptibility of the Qur'ān; the notion that major parts of the Qur'ān were omitted was kept alive among some extremist Shi'ites, and (Modarressi argues) by anti-Shi'ite polemicists seeking to attribute heretical views to Shi'ites more generally. Hossein Modarressi, "Early Debates on the Integrity of the Qur'ān," *Studia Islamica* 77 (1993): 23.

12. Modarressi, "Early Debates," p. 10, n. 20, 21.

13. "The adult male and the adult female, when they fornicate, stone them outright as an exemplary punishment from God. God is mighty, wise." See Powers, "Exegetical Genre," pp. 124–5.

14. Burton, *Sources*, p. 39.

15. Mahmoud Ayoub, *The Qur'ān and Its Interpreters* (Albany: State University Press, 1984), I:19.

16. Helmut Gatje, *The Qur'ān and Its Exegesis* (Oxford: Oneworld Publications, 1996), p. 58.

17. Muhammad Idrīs Kandehlavī, *Ma'ārif al-Qur'ān* (Tandō Allāh Yār: Maktaba 'Uthmaniyya, n.d.), p. 197.

18. John Burton, "Naskh" in *Encyclopedia of Islam*, New Edition, 7:1010.

19. Fakr al-Din al-Razi, *Mafatih al-ghayb* (Cairo: Bulaq, 1872), I:446.

20. Powers, "Exegetical Genre," p. 127; *Encyclopaedia of Islam*, s.v. "*naskh*." Wansbrough, *Qur'ānic Studies*, p. 201.

21. Al-Nahhās, cited in Powers, "Exegetical Genre," p. 126; Nicholas P. Aghnides, *An Introduction to Mohammedan Law* [Reprint] (Lahore: Saug-e-Meel Publications, 1981), pp. 89–93.

22. Powers, "Exegetical Genre," p. 126.

23. Burton, *Sources*, p. 26.

24. Sayyid Ahmad Khān, *Tafsīr al-Qur'ān* (Aligarh: Institute Press, 1980) I:162. Translated by Ernest Hahn, "Sir Sayyid Ahmad Khan's *The Controversy over Abrogation*," *Muslim World* 64 (1974): 124–133.

25. Sayyid Ahmad Khān, *Akhirī Madāmīn* (Lahore: n.p., 1898), pp. 24 ff.; J.M.S. Baljon, *Modern Muslim Koran Interpretation* (Leiden: E.J. Brill, 1961), p. 50.

26. Sayyid Ahmad Khān, *Tafsīr*, 1:162; Hahn, "Controversy," p. 125.

27. For a summary of modernist treatments of naskh, see Hasan, p. 69 and Baljon, *Modern Muslim Koran Interpretation*, pp. 49–50.

28. *Ibid.*, p. 49.

29. Ghulām Ahmad Parwēz, *Mafhūm al-Qur'ān* (Lahore: Idara-i-Tulu'-i-Islam, 1961), I:37; Idem, *Salīm ke nām*, Khut (Karachi: Idara-i-Tulu'-i-Islam, 1984),

II:159.

30. Abū'l Kalam Azad, *Tarjuman al-Qur'ān,* trans. Syed Abdul Latif (Lahore: Sind Sagar Academy, 1978:, II:72.

31. Aziz Ahmad, *Islamic Modernism in India and Pakistan* (Oxford: Oxford University Press, 1967), p. 58.

32. Tantāw Jawharī, *al-Jawāhir fī tafsīr al-Qur'ān al-karīm*, 1:110; cited in Baljon, p. 50.

33. J. Jomier, *Le Commentaire Coranique du Manār: Tendances modernes de l'exegese coranique en Egypt* (Paris: G.P. Maisonneuve, 1954), pp. 196 ff.

34. For discussions of naskh in which Rida participated, see "Kalimāt fī al-naskh wa al-tawātur wa akhbār al-āhād wa al-Sunna," *al-Manār* 11 (1908): 594-8, 688-96, 771-80; "al-Naskh wa'l-akhbār al-āhād" *al-Manār* 12 (1910): 693-99; *al-Manār* 14 (1912), 150 ff.

35. Syed Abul A'la Maudūdī, *Meaning of the Qur'ān*, 9th edition (Lahore: Islamic Publications Ltd., 1988), I:102.

36. *Ibid*. 6:99.

37. Sayyid Qutb, *Fī Zil āl al-Qur'ān* (Beirut: Dar al-Shuruq, 1992), I:136.

38. Muhammad al-Ghazālī, *Kayfa nata āmalu ma'a al-Qur'ān* (Herndon, Virginia: International Institute of Islamic Thought, 1990), p. 83. He is particularly disturbed, for example, by the assertion that the so-called "sword verse" abrogates all the verses which might be taken to encourage a more irenic Muslim missionary method.

39. *Ibid*., p. 80.

40. Mahmoud Ayoub, "A Study of Imami Shi'i Tafsīr" in A. Rippin, ed. *Approaches to the History of the Interpretation of the Qur'ān*, pp. 177-198; Hossein Modarressi, "Early Debates on the Integrity of the Qur'ān," p. 7.

41. Daniel Brown, *Rethinking Tradition in Modern Islamic Thought* (Cambridge: Cambridge University Press, 1996).

42. Rashad Khalifa, *The Computer Speaks: God's Message to the World* (Tucson, AZ: Renaissance Productions, 1981); idem. *Miracle of the Qur'ān: Significance of the Mysterious Alphabets* (St. Louis: Islamic Productions International, 1973); Yvonne Haddad and Jane Smith, *Mission to America: Five Islamic Sectarian Communities in North America* (Gainesville, FL: University Press of Florida,

1993), pp. 138-68.

43. Shabbir Akhtar, "An Islamic Model of Revelation," *Islam and Muslim Christian Relations* 2 (1991): 93-105. 104.

44. *Ibid.*, p. 103.

Chapter 4

FAZLUR RAHMAN'S RESPONSE TO IQBAL

Sheila McDonough

Fazlur Rahman grew up in the milieu of an Indian Muslim culture in which the poetry of Iqbal was a dominating force. Iqbal's poem *The Secrets of the Self* (*Asrar-i-Khudi*) occasioned intellectual and spiritual tumult when he published it in Lahore in 1915.[1] South Asian Muslim culture is one in which poetry is public, read at open gatherings, *mushaira*, and responded to with spontaneous fervor. People shout out their responses in these public poetry sessions. Verses are carried in many peoples' memories, and are recited frequently in reference to various subjects being discussed. Poetry shapes the cultural sense of subtlety and complexity in existence. Since the poetry is recited, literacy is not essential for enjoyment of the poetic tradition.

The arrival in the people's midst of a great new poetic voice, as occurred with the reading of Iqbal's famous poem, is a matter of community rejoicing. In 1915, however, public shock resulted when this new poet attacked the poetic tradition itself. Iqbal challenged his people in a poem which named the mystical poetic tradition of Persian verse as one source of his community's decay. The challenge reverberated throughout the culture. The theme of this provocative poem is that Muslims must recover creative individuality, and break out of the molds of ancestral patterns of thought. Those ancestral molds included the much-loved poetry of writers like Hafiz. Iqbal affirmed that the old poetry which taught people quietest and passive attitudes was a source of cultural sterility. His new poetry carried an appeal to Muslim dynamism; it was another version of the call to Muslim activism first stated by Jamal al-Din al-Afghani in the late nineteenth century.[2] The new poetry appealed greatly to young Muslims of Fazlur Rahman's generation because it offered a critique of their elders as well as a direction for their future thought and action.

When I was a graduate student at the Institute of Islamic Studies at McGill University in the early 1960s Fazlur Rahman taught me Urdu by reading Iqbal's poetry with me. Fazlur Rahman conveyed to me something of his comprehension of Iqbal's poetic genius, yet I was struck by the strength and the ambivalence of Fazlur Rahman's feelings about Iqbal.

Fazlur Rahman wrestled intellectually with Iqbal all his life. He was personally a part of the generation for whom the voice of the new poet had been a life-giving gift of hope and renewal for themselves as Indian Muslims. But he also told me that for some members of his family, poetry was considered mentally unhealthy. There was, he said, a stream of thought in Indian Islam with roots in Wahhabi types of reformism which considered poetry somewhat frivolous and degenerate. For Muslim reformers of this kind, the central focus of Islamic thought was said to be moral seriousness. Light-minded poetry was perceived as distracting and bad for the soul. Fazlur Rahman continued to be caught on the horns of this dilemma; was the joy of Iqbal's rapturous verses likely to distract Muslims from the seriousness of moral purpose?

Fazlur Rahman's later comments on Iqbal, which are spread throughout his writings, are best understood if one realizes that the struggle with Iqbal's thought was very personal for him. He loved the poetry, as did most of his South Asian Muslim contemporaries, and he had responded to the passion that had generated the new style of imagery, a passion for the renewal and revival of Muslim creativity. At the same time he was never entirely sure whether too much poetry of this fiery kind was good for his people.

One facet of this issue is that the intellectual milieu of Islamicists following the death of Iqbal in 1938 was one shaped by distrust of fascism and fear of Nietzsche's alleged "superman" theories. The Nazi use of much of Nietzsche's language made many people fearful of ideas about supermen. W.C. Smith's first book, *Modern Islam in India*, reflects the distrust of fascism characteristic of the Indian socialists, Muslims, Hindus, Sikhs and Christians, whom Smith had known in Lahore in the years immediately following Iqbal's death. Smith wrote that Iqbal had encouraged the Indian Muslim young people to "rush headlong into the arms of the silver-tongued reactionaries."[3] This conclusion was picked up by Gibb in his study of modern Islam.[4] The young Fazlur Rahman, when he went to study in England, was exposed to the ideas of Gibb, and later to Smith when he came to work with him at McGill.

W.C. Smith himself, by the time Fazlur Rahman had come to McGill, had renounced the simple-mindedness of his earlier socialist analysis of Indian Islam. He never again dismissed Iqbal in the simplistic manner of his first book. Most of his later writing was characterized by his effort to talk about how to relate the values of the past to the future, the problem that was central to Iqbal's thought.[5] Fazlur Rahman had an ongoing dialectical relationship with Smith also. He was one of the first Muslims whom Smith had invited to take part in the enterprise he was attempting to establish through his new Islamic Institute at McGill. The idea was to launch a project of studying Islamic history from the perspective of both Muslim and non-Muslim scholars. The aim was at least partially to continue the cooperative effort of studying Islam from both Muslim and non-Muslim perspectives that had been initiated by Shibli Numani and Thomas Arnold at Aligarh in the mid-nineteenth century.[6]

Fazlur Rahman's distrust of Iqbal's poetry thus came to him both from a few Muslim sources, his family tradition of puritan distrust of poetry, and from the warnings expressed by Smith and Gibb against romantic individualism. Many of the Muslim authors writing about Iqbal in the years following the partition of the Subcontinent also indicated a certain nervousness about the alleged superman thrust of Iqbal's ideas. Indians who disliked the Pakistan movement similarly picked up this theme. The socialist milieu of Lahore in which Smith had developed his ideas had been greatly influenced by its hope that Nehru would lead the way to a strong socialist India which they then believed would include the Indian Muslims. These socialists distrusted Iqbal as an alleged conservative reactionary.

Fazlur Rahman, as a Muslim who accepted the creation of the new nation of Pakistan, did not go along with that aspect of South Asian socialist critique of Iqbal. He remained very dedicated to the idea of building a good Islamic society in Pakistan. As is well known, he tried, during the regime of Ayyub Khan, to implement in Pakistan a form of studying Islamic history which he believed would help Muslims to a sounder way of using the values of the past towards creating a better future. But the religious leadership within Pakistan distrusted him, probably at least in part because of his Western education, and drove him out.

Iqbal was a major twentieth-century philosopher as well as the greatest poet writing in Urdu of his generation. The poetry conveyed much of the imperative of his philosophic position to the masses of his people. Those ideas are set forth in prose in his book *The Reconstruction of Religious Thought in Islam* which includes a series of lectures he gave in Hyderabad, India; it was first published in Lahore in 1930. These lectures make difficult reading because they presuppose familiarity with Western philosophical ideas in the 1920s, as well as the Islamic philosophical, theological and legal background.

Fazlur Rahman never wrote a systematic analysis of the philosophical ideas of Iqbal, although these ideas continued to tease his mind. He remained concerned about the impact of the poetry on Indian and Pakistani Muslims, because he came from the generation which had been stimulated and enthused by the poems. In general, in Fazlur Rahman's comments on Iqbal one finds cautionary warnings against getting too "drunk" on the poetry, along with acceptance of much of Iqbal's basic perspective. Fazlur Rahman remained both fascinated by, and suspicious of the power of Iqbal's verses over his people.

An example of his negative critique is found in Fazlur Rahman's comments about Pakistani young people of later generations, namely that "the lay-educated youth, fired by Iqbal's message, became an automatic clientele of Mawdudi."[7] Mawdudi was the exponent of a form of Islamic *intégriste* thought which advocated the implementation of an allegedly Islamic government which would be controlled by a group of Muslim activists who considered themselves the morally sound people.[8] Mawdudi's group maintained that they were the natural heirs of Iqbal because they aimed to implement Islamic law as they understood it in Pakistan. Subsequently, under Zia ul-Haq in Pakistan in the 1980s, much of this implementation actually occurred, with results troubling to many Pakistanis.[9] The eventual disillusion with that period is perhaps reflected in the elections of 1996 in which the Jamaat-i Islami, Mawdudi's followers, did not run candidates.

Fazlur Rahman's use of the phrase "lay-educated" is of central importance to his critique. Fazlur Rahman believed that a better education for Pakistanis in their own religious traditions would enable them to be more enlightened in the choices they made about political and economic leadership for their new nation. He considered improved techniques of moral education the greatest imperative for his people. His idea of moral education included an emphasis on teaching Muslims to appreciate the aspects of the Muslim past as well as the necessity for an ongoing process of devising new structures to implement the Islamic ideals of justice and harmony in Pakistani society, and in the wider world.

In this respect, he did not differ seriously from Iqbal. The latter considered the perspective of Ibn Khaldun crucial for an appreciation of Islamic history.[10] Iqbal emphasized that Muslims must learn from the natural world and from history as well as from their inner selves. They needed to discover how to analyze their past history in order to appreciate the ways in which sound developments had occurred, but they also had to find out why Islamic society had become stagnant. Iqbal was trying to do at least two things at once; first, to stir Muslim hearts out of despair and despondency, and second, to get Muslims to undertake serious and disciplined study of their past in order to appropriate what was good and to abandon what had led them astray. Fazlur Rahman thought that the first goal had been largely successful, but that the second had not been adequately understood, or appropriated.

Iqbal's philosophical position is that reality is process, and that human constructs, institutions, philosophical systems, and social structures, are constantly in flux. He wrote much about time, decay and rebirth. His title *The Reconstruction of Religious Thought in Islam* was intended to convey to Muslims that they must construct their religious thought and practice all over again in order to create new understandings of Islam which would enable them to function effectively as creative persons in the industrialized world of the future. He wrote explicitly for the future; one of his great poems, *Javid Nama*,[11] is addressed to his son as a symbol of the Muslims of the generations yet unborn.

In this poem, the author, guided by the spirit of Rumi, encounters all the significant intellectual options of the age and moves finally beyond them. Young Muslims are urged to encounter the thought of the modern world and to wrestle seriously with it. Iqbal took reason very seriously. He insisted that Muslims study the real world, both in nature and history, and come to terms intellectually with all the challenges coming from reality. Muslims suffered, he argued, from too much absorption in themselves, and insufficient contact with external reality.

Much of Iqbal's poetry contains jibes against Muslim self-satisfaction. He urged that self-righteousness of this kind was a source of decay because Muslim failures to take the ideas and practices of the industrialized world seriously had led to the collapse of Muslim societies.

Iqbal, therefore, undertook to study Einstein himself and to investigate the worldviews of modern science. He did not urge Muslims to separate themselves from the rest of the world, but rather to engage in constructive dialogue and encounter. His philosophy professor at Cambridge, McTaggart, was a personal friend of Alfred North Whitehead. Iqbal understood Whitehead's point that all previous certainties in physics had been overturned by the new physics, and that in mathematics and physics one should expect a continual process of the overthrowing of accepted ideas by new discoveries. Whitehead maintained that dogmatic finality was an error because new data would always be forthcoming. The renowned British mathematician said that he had personally experienced a revolution in his consciousness when all the accepted certainties of the physics he had learned as a young man were overthrown. This experience had taught him that dogmatic finality would always be an illusion in any form of human thought. In Whitehead's words: "The Universe is vast. Nothing is more curious than the self-satisfied dogmatism with which mankind at each period of its history cherishes the delusion of the finality of its existing modes of knowledge. Skeptics and believers are all alike. At this moment scientists and skeptics are the leading dogmatists. Advance in detail is admitted; fundamental novelty is barred. This dogmatic common sense is the death of philosophical adventure. The Universe is vast."[12]

Iqbal began his *Reconstruction* lectures with an insistence that no philosophical ideas, including his own, are final. An indirect reference to Whitehead's experience of a paradigm shift in physics can be discerned in the Muslim philosopher's statement which reads:

> Classical Physics has learned to criticize its own foundations. As a result of this criticism the kind of materialism, which it originally necessitated, is rapidly disappearing; and the day is not far off when Religion and Science may discover hitherto unsuspected mutual harmonies. It must, however, be remembered that there is no such thing as finality in philosophical thinking. As knowledge advances and fresh avenues of thought appear, other views, and probably

> sounder views than those set forth in these lectures, are possible. Our duty is carefully to watch the progress of human thought, and to maintain an independent critical attitude towards it.[13]

One can see from Iqbal's reference to physics that he takes this shattering of traditional ideas as the starting point of his thought. Some Muslims, like Mawdudi, have reacted to this kind of shattering of traditional ideas by affirming that all previous Muslim political and religious thinking has been wrong, and that return to some pristine Islam, as understood by them, is the only solution. Those who hold this attitude tend to dismiss all Islamic history, from the end of the reign of the first four caliphs on, as misguided; they seek political power to impose the ideological system which they believe to be the original Islamic system.[14]

Iqbal did not dismiss all of Islamic history in this manner. He certainly stated again and again that the Muslim society into which he had been born was in a distressed and decayed state. He thought that Ibn Khaldun's analysis of the Muslim decay of the fourteenth century, and the loss of Spain, indicated an earlier failure of Muslim intelligence and nerve. He considered it very important that Muslims learn to think about society in the manner of Ibn Khaldun as a process of decay and rebirth in which each generation should rethink again the structures and values of the past, and consciously make choices as to how to use the past in order to build a better future. Iqbal quoted the Qur'ān to the effect that the challenge is new for each generation.[15] He thought of history as an on-going process in which each generation should make its own decisions in the light of a mature understanding of both the successes and failures of the past. He did not consider all of Muslim history as a failure, but he did emphasize that it was always necessary to move forward.

Fazlur Rahman shared with Iqbal this perspective on the Muslim past. Reading Iqbal's *The Mosque of Cordoba* with him, I became convinced that this is one of the most compelling of Iqbal's poetic statements about the vocation of persons of faith in the world.

> Day succeeding to night—moulder of all time's works!
> Day succeeding to night—fountain of life and of death!
> Chain of the days and nights—two-coloured thread of silk
> Woven by Him that is, into His being's robe!

> Chain of the days and nights—sigh of eternity's harp,
> Height and depth of all things possible, God-revealed.
> You are brought to their test; I am brought to their test—
> Day revolving with night, touchstone of all this world;
> Weighted in their scales you and I, weighed and found wanting, shall both
> Find in death our reward, find in extinction our wage;...
> Yet, in this frame of things, gleams of immortal life
> Show where some servant of God wrought into some high shape
> Work whose perfection is still bright with the splendour of Love—
> Love, the well-spring of life; Love, on which death has no claim.[16]

The Mosque of Cordoba made manifest the insights of its builders, the servants of God bearing witness to their vision of the compelling power of divine love. Muslims in the present need to be stimulated by awareness of the works of the servants of God in the past, and of the great works of art and thought which such devout persons produced. Fazlur Rahman understood Iqbal to mean that the present-day Muslims must also be focused on the demands of witnessing in the present. What is now required is new focusing on ways of implementing perceptions of justice and beauty. The past can and should be a source of inspiration but it cannot provide infallible blueprints for contemporary problems. These require sustained thought, and mutual consultation.

According to Iqbal, the three sources of knowledge are nature, history, and human self-knowledge. Nature includes physics and biology and anything else human beings learn about their universe by observation and systematic thinking. Iqbal insisted that the real world must be studied because the Qur'ān taught that Muslims were to involve themselves with the world as created, and as continuously being recreated. Iqbal believed that the study of history should lead future generations of Muslims to think in the manner of Ibn Khaldun about their failures, and to learn to experiment with social, political and economic structures. There is no one, final Islamic system in Iqbal's thought, because he believed that final systems are not possible. Knowledge of the real world calls into question traditional norms of how to live in society in the same way as new data calls into question intellectual systems in physics. Life must be lived as an ongoing experiment because of the constant impact of the new. To accept finality is to cease to think.

Fazlur Rahman did not criticize Iqbal for these ideas about science and history, and indeed his own thought assumed a similar perspective.[17] What troubled him was the impact of Iqbal's poetry on Muslim minds. He feared that the poetry had been taken as a kind of revelation which many Muslims took as a freedom to cease to think for themselves. It had never been Iqbal's intention to create unthinking followers, but such, Fazlur Rahman argued, had been the result, at least in many cases. Indeed, he maintained that Iqbal's insights had not been worked out systematically enough, particularly with respect to an elaboration of the teaching of the Qur'ān, and an analysis of the structure of the scholarly methods which had shaped Islamic laws. He seems to have thought that much of the misuse of Iqbal, which had resulted in a kind of mindless enthusiasm, had occurred because Muslims had not paid enough attention to study of the Qur'ān and the Sharī'a. Fazlur Rahman made these two projects central to his own endeavors. His important study of the Qur'ān, *Major Themes of the Qur'ān*, was intended explicitly to work out in greater detail the imperatives that he thought were implicit in the approach of Iqbal. Similarly, his study of the structures of thought underlying the Sharī'a, *Islamic Methodology in History*, is another effort to do what Iqbal had not been able to accomplish. Iqbal had said that he had hoped to write an analysis of the history of Islamic religious and legal thinking; Fazlur Rahman was attempting to complete what Iqbal had suggested was necessary.

In addition to being a poet and philosopher, Iqbal was also a practicing lawyer, having been trained at the Inns of Court in London in the years before 1914. His situation in this respect resembled that of the earlier Muslim reformer, Sayyid Ahmad Khan, whose intellectual vigor and toughness of mind Fazlur Rahman also appreciated. Sayyid Ahmad Khan had also the personal experience of dealing in the courts with actual issues confronting Muslims in the modern world. Both Ahmad Khan and Iqbal were aware, through their work in the courts, of many of the actual problems of Muslim people faced with social change. Both of them felt that the traditional Islamic religio-legal system needed to be rethought in the context of the actual social issues of modern life. Indeed, the issue of the reform of Muslim legal thinking which began with Sayyid Ahmad Khan was explicitly carried on by Iqbal and later by Fazlur Rahman.

Iqbal had been a young man when the Russian and Turkish revolutions broke out. As one who responded cheerfully to paradigm shifts and the breaking up of old social and belief structures, he welcomed both revolutions as harbingers of new expressions of value. In both cases, however, he also saw flaws in the assumptions of the revolutionaries as to how the future should be shaped. His poem, *Lenin before God*, acknowledges that Christianity had been so associated in Russia with the dominance of the tsar that it was inevitable that the movement towards greater social justice should deny religion. However, he thought that the fact of one religious group's alliance with an oppressive regime did not disprove the existence of God. The communist dismissal of all religious awareness was simple-minded in his opinion, and did not bode well for the future development of communist society. He also thought that an alliance of religion with politically repressive forces was likely in any society to lead to disillusion with religious teaching in general. He understood his age as one in which the past structures of domination were cracking, and in which new possibilities were latent.

> The Tavern shakes, its warped foundations crack,
> The Old Men of Europe sit there numb with fear:
> What twilight flush is left those faces now
> Is paint and powder, or lent by flask and cup.
> Omnipotent, righteous, Thou; but bitter the hours,
> Bitter the labourer's chained hours in Thy world!
> When shall this galley of gold's dominion founder?
> Thy world Thy day of wrath, Lord, stands and waits.[18]

Iqbal thus saw paradigm shifts not only in new physics but also in reference to new possibilities of social justice. He understood the justice of God within history much as Ibn Khaldun did, namely that the corrupt and exploitative empires eventually collapse. This is an interpretation of Qur'ānic teaching about divine judgement against corrupt societies which Iqbal affirmed strongly. He admired much about the passion for greater social justice created by the Russian revolution, but he feared that the atheism espoused by the revolutionaries would lead to other forms of corruption.

His response to the Turkish revolution led by Ataturk was similarly two-sided. On the one hand, he welcomed the dynamism and energy of the Turkish revolutionaries, and admired their courage and their positive actions in restructuring their society. On the other hand, he thought they, like the Russians, wrongly associated religion with reactionary social forces. It was true that the Muslim religious leaders had supported the Ottoman caliph. But Iqbal thought the structures of life could be changed in the direction of greater social justice without necessarily abandoning religious life and practice. Iqbal, as an Indian Muslim, feared the possibility within India of the Muslims becoming dominated by Hindus who would despise Muslims as impure persons. He therefore said in various ways that some element of the legal thinking of Muslims should be retained in India because equality was a fundamental value of the Islamic tradition.[19] He thought that a reconstruction of legal thought in Islam should lead to a better sense of social and economic justice, and a better idea of how to implement policies to make those forms of justice real. In relation to the intellectual tumult of the 1920s, Iqbal wrote: "We are today passing through a period similar to that of the Protestant revolution in Europe, and the lesson which the rise and outcome of Luther's movement teaches should not be lost on us."[20]

Iqbal thought that the Protestant rejection of the authority structures of medieval Catholicism was similar to the rejections of the medieval Islamic social and political structures which were exemplified by the collapse of the Mughal Empire and the Turkish revolution. However, he did not want Muslims simply to follow the Protestant model. He believed that the ferocious nationalism of Europe, which had resulted, among other disasters, in the outbreak of World War I, was partly caused by the Lutheran reform which he understood to have reduced religiousness to a matter of personal faith only. He therefore thought that Muslims should not opt for reducing religion to personal faith alone, but should continue to think about how to shape social and legal institutions in terms of basic Islamic values.

Fazlur Rahman accepted this idea and likewise warned Muslims not to reduce religiousness to justification by faith alone.[21] Like Iqbal, he urged the rethinking of Islamic religious law through the exercise of ijtihad, independent thinking, on religious and moral questions. They wanted to reform Islamic religious and legal thought and to develop new ways of implementing what they took to be the core values of the Qur'ān. But they both insisted that government should not be directed by national self-interest alone; it should pay heed to questions of how to implement social justice within the nation and in the wider world. At the end of *Islamic Methodology in History*, Fazlur Rahman raises the issue of birth control as an example of a perplexing problem for new Muslim societies like Pakistan. He maintains that traditional ideas on this subject are not adequate because of the new conditions of over-population, and that Muslims must exercise their moral thinking in new ways in order to solve new problems like this one. Birth control is an example of a problem for which the answer of religion as a personal matter only is not an adequate guide since the issues in questions involve the society as a whole.[22]

The idea of creating new values is one which Iqbal brought back from his studies in Europe.[23] He had been exposed to Nietzsche's ideas during his studies of philosophy in Germany not long after the German philosopher's death. He therefore was exposed directly both to Nietzsche's own writings and to the furor occasioned in German intellectual life by Nietzsche's aggressive polemics against traditional European modes of thought and conduct. Since Iqbal's experience in Germany took place before 1914, the young Muslim scholar would have had no idea of the subsequent use of some elements of Nietzsche's thoughts by the Nazis.

Nietzsche's own writings make clear that he intensely disliked the Franco-German war of 1870 which he witnessed, and that he had no sympathy at all with the self-righteous romantic militarism of many of his German contemporaries. His comments on Wagner make these views abundantly clear. Thus, Iqbal understood Nietzsche to be a brilliant critic of Western self-righteous arrogance. Nietzsche thought that late nineteenth-century European civilization was diseased, and Iqbal agreed. He therefore put him on a level with the martyred Muslim mystic al-Hallaj in the poem *Javid Nama*. He perceived Nietzsche as a tormented prophet who outraged his own people. Iqbal undoubtedly experienced that outrage directly in his time in a German university. He considered many Europeans hypocritical because of their unwillingness to face the oppressive nature of their domination over other peoples. He saw Nietzsche's critique as support for his condemnation of European hypocritical self-satisfaction. As he put it,

> In modern Europe, Nietzsche, whose life and activity form, at least to us Easterns, an exceedingly interesting problem in religious psychology, was endowed with some sort of a constitutional equipment for such an undertaking.

> His mental history is not without a parallel in the history of Eastern Sufism. That a really "imperative" vision of the Divine in man did come to him cannot be denied. I call his vision "imperative" because it appears to have given him a kind of prophetic mentality, which by some kind of technique, aims at turning its visions into permanent life forces. Yet Nietzsche was a failure; and his failure was mainly due to his intellectual progenitors such as Schopenhauer, Darwin and Lange whose influence completely blinded him to the real significance of his vision. Instead of looking for a spiritual rule which would develop the Divine even in a plebeian and thus open up before him an infinite future, Nietzsche was driven to seek the realization of his vision in such schemes as aristocratic radicalism. Thus failed a genius whose vision was solely determined by his internal forces and remained unproductive for want of external guidance in his spiritual life. And the irony of fate is that this man, who appeared to his friends as "if he came from a country where no man lived", was fully conscious of his spiritual need.[24]

Iqbal makes very clear here that his own idea of *insan-i kamil*, perfected human being, ought not to be restricted to aristocrats only. This is why Smith and others who discerned fascist tendencies in Iqbal's thought were wrong. The Muslim philosopher's emphasis was on the development of the potentialities of all persons; he explicitly differed with Nietzsche on this issue. He did respond positively to Nietzsche's idea that human beings could become *ubermensch* but he refused to limit this possibility to a few. Iqbal rightly discerned a mystical element in this vision. Nietzsche had said that he liked reading the books of the American author Ralph Waldo Emerson.[25] Emerson had used the term "oversoul" to indicate a greater possibility of human awareness, a notion he perhaps got from his studies of Indian philosophy. It is not unlikely that Nietzsche's *ubermensch* idea is related to Emerson's oversoul. Iqbal seems to have discerned something of this in his recognition of the religious quality of Nietzsche's basic insights.

If we take oversoul, *ubermensch* and *insan-i kamil* as religious terms for the possibility of human personality achieving spiritual depth and wisdom, it becomes apparent why Iqbal would equate Nietzsche with the Muslim mystic al-Hallaj. In the *Javid Nama*, it is the Sufi poet Rumi who guides the questioning Iqbal:

> I said to Rumi, "Who is this madman?"
> He answered: "This is the German genius

whose place is between these two worlds;
his reed-pipe contains an ancient melody.
This Hallaj without gallows and rope
has spoken anew those ancient words;
his words are fearless, his thought sublime,
the Westerners are struck asunder by the sword of his speech.
His colleagues have not comprehended his ecstasy
and reckoned the ecstatic mad.
Alas for the ecstatic born in Europe...
He was a Hallaj who was a stranger in his own city;
He saved his life from the mullahs, and the physicians slew him."[26]

As far as I know, Fazlur Rahman was not aware of the later scholarship which had acknowledged that Nietzsche was not an admirer of German militarism, nor that some Western scholars now thought that Nietzsche had indeed been a religious thinker.[27] Most of the Western scholars do not know that Iqbal had reached that conclusion not long after Nietzsche died. There cannot be much doubt that the "Westerners struck asunder" were the ones Iqbal had encountered in German and British universities. The Muslim philosopher thus saw Nietzsche as a guide to anti-imperialist thinking, a view that would not have been popular in Europe in 1905.

Fazlur Rahman also responded whole-heartedly to Iqbal's understanding of faith. He himself quoted Iqbal in order to explain what he understood as the essential characteristic of faith:

Faith gives the strength to sit in fire like Abraham;
Faith is God-intoxication, self-expending.[28]

This is the key insight of Iqbal's philosophical thought, derived, as he often said, from Qur'ānic imagery. The person of faith sees through a glass darkly, or, as Iqbal quoted from Rumi, follows the scent of the musk-gland of the deer.[29] In our readings of Iqbal, Fazlur Rahman was at pains to convey to me the complex dialectic between faith and reason that characterizes much of Iqbal's writing. In retrospect, I realize that he perhaps wanted to make very sure that I would not fall victim to romantic individualism, or be led astray by mindless enthusiasm. Thus, when we read about *Aql o Dil*, intelligence and heart, I was thoroughly taught to understand that responsible human existence required both, held in proper balance and tension.[30] A similar perspective came to me also from W.C. Smith, who told me to read the Scottish philosopher John MacMurray on *Reason and Emotion.*[31]

The term "self-expending" in this verse explains why Fazlur Rahman and Iqbal did not understand faith as a matter of romantic individualism, nor as an issue of faith set apart from works. Self-expending is a very Qur'ānic phrase which indicates that the person who responds to what he or she discerns of the divine attributes of justice, mercy and goodness must spend himself or herself in working to manifest those attributes in the structures of human existence. Iqbal used another image in his poem, *The Mysteries of Selflessness*; he understands his life as a person of faith to be like a candle consumed by the process of giving light to humanity.[32] Qur'ānic terminology constantly uses the phrase "believe and do right" to characterize the ideal attitudes and practices for believers.[33] For this reason the idea of justification by faith alone is foreign to the Qur'ānic perspective.

This perspective implies what one might characterize as a theology of culture, namely that persons "following the scent of the musk-gland of the deer," responding to their intuitions about the goodness of the Absolute, must work to build better cultural patterns. Much of Iqbal's writings were concerned with delineating different types of cultural patterns. His call for a better future assumes that human beings could do better than they have done, if they would work using reason in the light of faith. Implicit in this appeal is the understanding that the training of reason should come first, because without some form of preparation that could lead believers to be conscious of their own assumptions, the ecstatic experience itself would probably not result in world-transforming creativity.

Iqbal urged that the best cultural pattern would be one which would encourage the development of social, political, economic, religious and educational structures that encourage individuals to be aware of the possibility of grace, and of divine goodness, justice and mercy. Fazlur Rahman insisted in his book on the Qur'ān that *taqwa*, well-formed conscience, was the most basic characteristic that the scripture urged on committed individuals. A lively conscience should be constantly at work in any situation, attempting to discern how the world might be made better.

Fazlur Rahman wrote the article on Iqbal in The *Encyclopedia of Religion*. He said that Iqbal was advocating an "energizing and ethically positive Islam."[34] This should probably be taken as his final comment on the poet-philosopher who was the inspiration of his generation of South Asian Muslims, and whose many provocative and complex ideas engaged him all his life. This conclusion is a refutation of the notion that Iqbal's poetry was ultimately bad for the brains or the morals of the South Asian Muslims. It is also perhaps a note of thanks for the "energizing" power of the imagery that Iqbal had flung in the faces of his surprised people.

One of the issues for which Iqbal was condemned by Smith and Gibb, and many of the others who characterized him as a reactionary, was the matter of changes in the role of women in society. Smith particularly stressed the reactionary nature of the image of the cold, unloving, man-hating Western woman who appears as symbol of evil in the *Javid Nama*. This was taken by many as proof of Iqbal's refusal to advance the cause of women in society. This judgement, however, is too simplistic. It is true that Iqbal in Europe at the turn of century accepted the widespread view that the suffragettes represented a dangerous force of social disruption. However, Iqbal had German women philosophers as his teachers while he was in Germany and his respect for them appears to have run very deep. When he was dying many years later in Lahore, he asked that a German woman be found to take over the responsibility of raising his young children, and this was done. (W.C. Smith was in Lahore soon after Iqbal's death, when the German woman in question would have been looking after the children. Yet he never seems to have been aware of this point. Apparently, Smith did not talk directly with Iqbal's family. The family report is that Iqbal's young daughter was encouraged to learn from her German governess that women should be brave.[35]) Furthermore, by the time Iqbal was writing his *Reconstruction* lectures in the late 1920s, much had changed in the situation of women in the world. Iqbal speaks positively of the contributions of the Turkish poet and social thinker Ziya Gokalp to a rethinking of Muslim attitudes toward women. He quotes the Turkish poet: "There is the woman, my mother, my sister, or my daughter; it is she who calls up the most sacred emotions from the depths of my life! There is my beloved, my sun, my moon and my star; it is she who makes me understand the poetry of life! How could the Holy Law of God regard these beautiful creatures as despicable beings? Surely there is an error in the interpretation of the Qur'ān by the learned?"[36]

Iqbal wrote about the Turkish revolution as an expression of spiritual expansion, of Muslims actively working in the real world to develop new institutions. He understood such expansion as one of the great joys of existence, the awareness of the real possibility of change and the challenge of creating better human institutions. He did not personally agree with all of the elements of the Turkish revolution, as for example in the changes in inheritance laws, but he did affirm very strongly the joy of spiritual expansion occasioned by taking hold of the reins of power and actively changing the conditions of life.[37] The women in Pakistan who have worked to change laws regarding their status have quoted Iqbal to justify their approach. "The teaching of the Qur'ān that life is a process of progressive creation necessitates that each generation, aided but unhampered by the work of its predecessor, should be permitted to solve its own problems."[38]

These women have clearly appropriated Iqbal's approach as a justification for their efforts to work for changes in the legal status of women in their country. A recent commentary on the Qur'ān, which has been written by a Muslim woman, uses many of Fazlur Rahman's insights as a basis for maintaining that Muslim women need to look again at the Qur'ān from their own point of view, and to challenge traditional male interpretations where this seems appropriate.[39] These instances indicate that many Muslim women have appropriated the notion of creative individuality for themselves, and have used this interiorization of the *Secrets of the Self* to affirm their own identity and dignity. I do not think that either Iqbal or Fazlur Rahman would have been offended or dismayed by this development. Each favored the development of active consciences which would work to discover and affirm new and better ways to live, individually and corporately.

NOTES

1. Muhammad Iqbal, *The Secrets of the Self.* Trans. by R. Nicholson (Lahore: Ashraf, 1961).

2. Nikki R. Keddie, *An Islamic Response to Imperialism* (Berkeley: University of California Press, 1983).

3. W.C. Smith, *Modern Islam in India* (London: Gollancz, 1945), p. 133.

4. H.A.R. Gibb, *Modern Trends in Islam* (Chicago: University of Chicago Press, 1947).

5. W.C. Smith, *On Understanding Islam: Selected Studies* (The Hague: Mouton, 1981), p. 113.

6. Sheila McDonough, "Shibli Nu'mani: A Conservative Vision of Revitalized Islam" in Robert Baird, ed. *Religion in Modern India* (Columbia, MO: South Asian Publications, second revised edition, 1989).

7. Fazlur Rahman, *Islam and Modernity* (Chicago: University of Chicago Press, 1982) p. 116.

8. Seyyed Vali Reza Nasr, *Mawdudi and the Making of Islamic Revivalism* (New York: Oxford University Press, 1996).

9. Kemal A. Faruki, "Pakistan: Islamic Government and Society," in John Esposito, ed., *Islam in Asia: Religion Politics and Society* (New York: Oxford University Press, 1987).

10. Allama Muhammad Iqbal, *The Reconstruction of Religious Thought in Islam*, edited and annotated by M. Saeed Sheikh (Lahore: Iqbal Academy Pakistan, revised edition, 1989), p. 125.

11. Muhammad Iqbal, *Javid Nama*. Trans. by A. Arberry (London: Allen and Unwin, 1966), p. 136–41.

12. *Dialogues of Alfred North Whitehead as Recorded by Lucien Price* (Boston: Little, Brown and Company, 1954), p. 7.

13. *The Reconstruction of Religious Thought in Islam*, p. xxii.

14. Sheila McDonough, *Muslim Ethics and Modernity* (Waterloo, Ont: Wilfred Laurier University Press, 1984) pp. 55–80.

15. *The Reconstruction of Religious Thought in Islam*, p. 40.

16. V.G. Kiernan, trans. *Poems from Iqbal* (London: John Murray, 1955), pp. 37, 38.

17. Fazlur Rahman did not teach that something like an "Islamization of knowledge" was possible; he rather argued that Muslims must learn to think, and be left free to work their ideas out. The Muslim philosopher, Ismail al-Faruqi, spent several years at the McGill Institute of Islamic Studies when Fazlur Rahman

was there. It was the practice then to have many faculty members present during seminars, so these two Muslim scholars often debated one other. The issue of the Islamization of knowledge was something about which they had a clear disagreement. Al-Faruqi was in favor of a self-conscious Islamization of knowledge, whereas Fazlur Rahman was not. The Pakistani scholar basically agreed with Iqbal that knowledge can and often does lead in unpredictable directions. We have to expect that new knowledge will upset our convictions precisely because we are challenged by a universe that is much more complex than we know. Fazlur Rahman, "Islamization of Knowledge; A Response" in *The American Journal of Islamic Social Sciences* (Herndon, VA: The International Institute of Islamic Thought), 5/1 (1988): 3–11.

18. *Poems from Iqbal*, p. 43.

19. Hafeez Malik, ed. *Iqbal: Poet-Philosopher of Pakistan* (New York: Columbia University Press, 1971), p. 386.

20. *The Reconstruction of Religious Thought in Islam*, p. 14.

21. Fazlur Rahman, *Islamic Methodology in History* (Karachi: Central Institute of Islamic Research, 1965), p. 99.

22. *Islamic Methodology in History*, p. 190.

23. Muhammad Iqbal, *Stray Reflections*, ed. by Javid Iqbal (Lahore: Ashraf, 1960), p. 88.

24. *The Reconstruction of Religious Thought in Islam*, pp. 194, 195.

25. F. Nietzsche, *On the Genealogy of Morals*. Trans. by Walter Kaufman (New York: Random House Vintage Books, 1967) p. 339.

26. *The Javid Nama*, pp. 111–12.

27. Irena Makarushbin, *Religious Imagination and Language in Emerson and Nietzsche* (New York: St. Martin's Press, 1994).

28. Fazlur Rahman, *Islam* (Chicago: University of Chicago Press, second edition, 1979), p. 225.

29. *The Reconstruction of Religious Thought in Islam*, p. 73.

30. *Poems from Iqbal*, pp. 61–62.

31. John MacMurray, *Reason and Emotion* (London: Faber, 1935). See also Roberta Cameron, unpublished doctoral thesis in the Religion Department of

Concordia University, Montreal, "The Making of Wilfred Cantwell Smith's *Towards a World Theology*," 1997.

32. Muhammad Iqbal, *The Mysteries of Selflessness*. Trans. by A. Arberry (London: John Murray, 1953).

33. Sheila McDonough, "Iman and Islam in the Qur'ān" in *Iqbal Review* (Karachi: Iqbal Academy, 1971) pp. 81–88.

34. Mircea Eliade, ed. *The Encyclopedia of Religion* (New York: MacMillan, 1987), 7: 275–76.

35. Javid Iqbal, "Iqbal: My Father" in Hafeez Malik, ed. *Iqbal: Poet Philosopher of Pakistan*, p. 62.

36. *The Reconstruction of Religious Thought in Islam*, p. 128.

37. *The Reconstruction of Religious Thought in Islam,* editor's note on note 42, p. 195.

38. Khawer Mumtaz and Farida Shaheed, eds. *Women of Pakistan: Two Steps Forward, One Step Back?* (London: Zed Books, 1987), p. 4.

39. Amina Wadud-Muhsin, *Qur'ān and Woman* (Kuala Lumpur: Pererbit Fajar Bakti, 1992).

PART III.
HERMENEUTICS AND CONTEMPORARY ISSUES

Chapter 5

QUR'ĀNIC INTERPRETATION AND MODESTY NORMS FOR WOMEN

Valerie J. Hoffman

In the course of a lifetime of research and teaching in Islamic intellectual history, Fazlur Rahman frequently pointed out how far Muslims had strayed from their roots in their interpretations of the Qur'ān, and the stultifying manner in which alleged prophetic Sunna enshrined in Hadith altered the teaching of the Qur'ān and restricted society's capacity to adapt the teachings of the Qur'ān to its own needs.[1] In his later works he addressed the need to build new Islamic laws and institutions by deducing the general principles of Qur'ānic teaching and moving from there toward the creation of laws suited to contemporary society.[2] Of all the issues in Islamic law in need of re-examination in light of contemporary needs and changes in modern society, perhaps none are more sensitive and critical than those that relate to women. This is also an area where, according to Fazlur Rahman, the original intention of the Qur'ān was consistently bypassed in favor of prevailing social convention.[3] The discussion of Islamic modesty norms for women is one of those moral and practical questions that highlight various Muslim approaches to the interpretation of the Qur'ān and its application to daily life, and it illustrates Rahman's point very well. On the other hand, it is an issue that is perhaps more emotionally laden than most others, since it is so closely linked to the traditional Arab values of manliness, honor and chastity, and has come to symbolize the confrontation between the Muslim world and Western imperialism.[4]

The approach taken by traditional Qur'ānic exegesis is to analyze Qur'ānic verses phrase by phrase or word by word; to ascertain the meaning of individual words by their root meanings and usage in Arabic poetry from the time of the Prophet; and to use Hadith to provide interpretations of the legal import of verses and the historical circumstances (*asbāb al-nuzūl*) in which a verse was revealed.[5] The priority of Hadith in the interpretation of the Qur'ān has grave consequences in that it establishes an alleged historical precedent that should be normative for all future generations of Muslims. Such was the authority of Muhammad's example that his Sunna and the Qur'ān came to be regarded as having equal authority, from the time of the second century A.H., and the saying became common: "Sunna is judge of the Qur'ān, and not the Qur'ān of the Sunna."[6] That is, the Qur'ān is interpreted by the actual practice (*sunna*) of Muhammad and the pious ancestors (*salaf*) as reported in the narrative accounts (Hadith, *āthār*); any apparent discrepancy between the meaning of the Qur'ān and the contents of the Sunna is to be resolved in favor of the latter, because of the inherent difficulty of understanding the Qur'ānic text without its clarification or exemplification by the Prophet. Furthermore, on many questions related to women's issues, Hadith has decidedly altered the tenor and import of the Qur'ān, as Fazlur Rahman noted.[7] However, since the late nineteenth century some Muslims have questioned the authenticity and applicability of much of the Hadith literature, and call instead for other bases of understanding the Qur'ān.

Muslim modernists say that the Qur'ān must be understood as a whole and not in piecemeal fashion. Muhammad 'Abduh (1849–1905) insisted on interpreting the Qur'ān by its own context, or by means of other Qur'ānic verses (*tafsīr al-Qur'ān bi'l-Qur'ān*) rather than by means of extraneous material, since the Qur'ān, by its own explicit statement, is a clear book that coheres in all its parts.[8] Fazlur Rahman goes further by contending that certainty belongs not to the meanings of particular verses of the Qur'ān and their content but to the Qur'ān as a whole, that is, as a set of coherent principles or values where the total teaching converges.[9] Modernists tend to distinguish the eternal or essential aspects of the Qur'ān—its spiritual teachings—from its social regulations, which responded only to particular situations.[10] They often insist that the Prophet never intended his judgments on particular matters to be the final literal authority for all time, but that specific laws should develop to meet the needs of changing societies.[11] The idea that Islamic legislation is progressive is based either on a belief in evolution as positive change or in social change as an inevitable though possibly morally neutral fact of life.[12]

This way of thinking runs counter to the traditional Sunni idea that the generation of the Prophet is itself the most perfect model for all Muslims to follow in all aspects.[13] The question of whether Muslims ought to follow the interpretation of Qur'ānic verses on modesty norms provided in Hadith, or derive from the Qur'ān general principles that should be applied in a manner consistent with the exigencies of modern life, is obviously crucial and controversial. However, we would be mistaken if we were to assume that Muslims in the pre-modern period interpreted the modesty requirements for women in a consistent fashion. Indeed, rather than taking literally the Hadith commands to let the women go to the mosques, or for a man to look at the face of his prospective fiancee, or taking at face value the equal Qur'ānic treatment of men and women on matters of religion and moral responsibility, medieval Muslims tended to interpret the Qur'ān in light of their own social situations and prevailing concepts of the competence and danger of women. Thus, rather than letting the Qur'ān or even Hadith shape the authoritative doctrine on women's modesty norms, medieval exegetes such as al-Tabari, al-Zamakhshari, al-Baydawi and Ibn Kathir let prevailing practice and cultural perceptions mold their interpretation of the appropriate application of these norms. An examination of their commentaries on this issue reveals that it is not the Qur'ān that dictates appropriate practice, but prevailing social convention that molds Qur'ānic interpretation.

Nonetheless, many Muslims today insist that one can derive a very precise definition of modesty norms for women from the Qur'ān, and in view of the popularity of this view an examination of the verses in question must be undertaken.

Much of the debate over this subject revolves around the interpretation of a number of terms and phrases contained in Sūrat al-Nūr (chapter 24 of the Qur'ān), verses 30–31, which read as follows:

> Tell the believing men to avert their eyes and to preserve their chastity [literally, protect their pudenda, *yahfazū furūjahum*]; that is purer for them. God knows what they are doing. And tell the believing women to avert their eyes and

preserve their chastity and not to show their adornment (*zīna*) except that which is apparent (*mā zahara minhā*), and to draw their head shawls (*khumur*) over their bosoms (*juyūb*) and not to show their adornment except to their husbands, their fathers, their fathers-in-law, their children, their husband's children, their brothers, their brothers' children, their sisters' children, their women and servants, male dependents who have no need of women, or children who have no knowledge of the pudenda (*'awrāt*) of women. And tell them not to stamp their feet so people will know what ornaments (*zīna*) they have hidden. Repent to God, all you believers; perhaps you will prosper.

This verse contains a number of key concepts that need to be defined in order to understand exactly what is required of women: the definition of *zīna* (ornament, beauty, adornment) and that *zīna* which is "apparent" or may show; the *khimār* (plural: *khumur*) which must be drawn over the *juyūb* here translated as bosom; what are considered to be the private parts or pudenda (*'awrāt*) of women; and from whom must women hide their *zīna*. Other aspects of these verses are clear enough: both men and women are commanded to avert the eyes from looking at provocations to lust—with the obvious implication that the possibility of looking at such sources of temptation existed—and to preserve their chastity. Women need not fear displaying their adornment and beauty to those who are close relatives—either their husbands or close relatives whom they cannot marry—or in front of children and male dependents who have no sexual interest.[14]

The commentators agree that averting the eyes means avoiding looking at things that are prohibited but desirable, "because looking corrupts the heart."[15] The protection of the pudenda (*hifz al-farj*) may refer either to the avoidance of adultery or to covering them so they would not be seen.[16]

Many of the early commentators interpret *zīna* as referring primarily to the adornment a woman might put on herself. Al-Zamakhshari (1075–1144 A.D.) says *zīna* is the jewelry, *kuhl*, or dye with which a woman adorns herself.[17] The "hidden adornment," says Ibn Jarir al-Tabari (839–923 A.D.), consists of such things as anklets, bracelets, earrings, and necklesses. Concerning "that which is apparent," he offers several possible interpretations: the outer clothing, *kuhl* on the eyes, the ring on the hand, bracelets, and the face. He quotes the Prophet's cousin Ibn 'Abbas, a frequently cited early authority on Qur'ān interpretation, who said that the adornment which is apparent is "the face, the *kuhl* of the eye, the dye on the palm of the hand and the ring, for these the woman shows in her house to whoever enters." This is a good example of how current practice determined the interpretation of the verse. A hadith from the Prophet on the authority of Qatada is also offered: "The woman who believes in God and the Day of Judgment may not show her hand except to here"—and he grasped the middle of his forearm.[18]

Zamakhshari, however, points out that it is not the ornamentation itself which needs to be hidden, but the part of the body which is being adorned with such ornamentation: indeed the prohibition of seeing the ornamentation is entirely dependent on the part of the body it adorns. God's concern, he says, is with covering the place of ornamentation, not with the ornamentation itself.[19]

Fakhr al-Din al-Razi (d. 1209) also applies the word *zīna* to natural beauty, although he feels constrained to defend that interpretation: "Many women have nothing but their natural beauty, and this must be included in the general rule." He feels this is indicated by the words "let them draw their head shawls over their bosoms," because the intention of the head shawl is to cover the beauty of the body.[20]

Zamakhshari allows a woman's hair to show, because it falls over the clothes, which may be seen unless the clothes are too fine or transparent to cover the body adequately. A woman's face, hands and feet may also be shown despite any ornamentation (make-up or jewelry) that might adorn them, because "to cover them causes difficulty [*haraj*: oppression, distress], for the woman has no recourse but to work with her hands, and she must show her face, especially to give testimony and to appear in court and to marry, and she must walk in the streets showing her feet, especially if she is poor. This is the meaning of 'except what is apparent,' i.e., except what it is customary and natural to show."[21]

Zamakhshari's commentary indicates that the Qur'ānic modesty code must be practical as well as moral, and must consider the needs of the poor as well as the concerns of the wealthy. A wealthy man may be able to afford to seclude his women entirely, and might think that his honor demands such seclusion, but the Qur'ānic modesty norms are assumed not to cater to the privileges of the wealthy. Zamakhshari does not expect the Qur'ān to impose prohibitions that are unreasonable or make it difficult for a woman to go about her normal duties.

Ultimately it is custom itself which determines what *zīna* must be hidden and what may be shown.

As Razi says of the "apparent zīna": "It means whatever a person ordinarily shows....They are allowed to uncover what they are used to uncovering, and what necessity requires them to uncover, because the laws of Islam are true, easy, and liberal." Women customarily show their hands and face, he wrote. However, the prohibition of displaying the "hidden *zīna*" is not without considerations of status: it applies only to free women, not slaves, since slave women are considered property which must be seen in order to be bought or sold.[22]

Ibn Kathir (1301–1373 A.D.) agrees with Razi in defining the *zīna* that may be shown to "strange" (i.e., non-*mahārim*) men as the face and hands, because, he says, they often cannot be hidden. This, he adds, is the accepted interpretation. On the other hand, al-Baydawi (d. 1282 or 1291 A.D.) says that although the exegetes exclude the face and hands from what must be covered because they are not *'awra* (pudendal), this interpretation must apply only to prayer (which has its own rules for covering), because the entire body of the free woman is *'awra*, and none of it may be seen by anyone other than her husband and *mahārim* except in cases of necessity, such as medical treatment or giving testimony."[23] *Zīna* may include all natural and artificial beauty with the exception of the face and hands, because they are not *'awra*. Baydawi apparently sees giving testimony as an exceptional activity necessitating bending ordinary modesty requirements, whereas Zamakhshari cited the giving of testimony as an ordinary activity of women, proving the necessity of showing the face in public on a regular basis. This idea that the permission to uncover the face and hands of a woman applies only to prayer is found also in the writings of Ibn Taymiyya (d. 1328 A.D.). The ever-more stringent demands for what is perceived to be proper modesty for women is striking between the more lenient views of Tabari (d. 923) and Zamakhshari (d. 1144) and the stricter views of Baydawi (d. 1282) and Ibn Taymiyya (d. 1328). Historians have also found that sexual segregation and restrictions on women increased during the 'Abbasid period (750–1258) and subsequent centuries into Ottoman times, but socio-historical information about women is scanty for this period, and we cannot know for certain whether modesty standards grew progressively stricter over the course of these centuries.[24] The opinions of the exegetes, which claim to reflect standard practice and agreed-upon interpretation, suggest that the twelfth to fourteenth centuries may have been pivotal on this issue, but it is the eleventh-century writer al-Ghazālī (d. 1111) who states that the trend toward secluding women began in the generation after Muhammad and his Companions, and that women in his day did not generally go out with their faces unveiled.[25]

The *khimār* is a type of head covering; the *jayb* (plural: *juyūb*) is an opening or hollow, and the verse is commonly thought to refer to the cleavage between the breasts. The verse (24:30–31) is commonly thought to command women to cover their bosoms. Zamakhshari comments that before the revelation of this verse women had wide openings in their clothing from which one could see their necks and breasts, and the women would let their *khumur* fall down their backs, exposing the front. The intent of this verse then is that women draw their *khumur* over their front and cover themselves with their head shawls.[26] The *khimār*, says Tabari, should cover the woman's hair, neck and earrings.[27]

Older women who are, in a sense, desexualized, no longer menstruating or able to give birth, are allowed more freedom than other women, as indicated by 24:60: "Those women who have ceased giving birth (*al-qawā'id min al-nisā'*), who have no hope of marriage, may remove their outer clothing, without shameless display of their adornment (*ghayr mutabarrijīn bi zīna*), although it is better for them to remain modest."

The idea of *zīna* and the beauty or adornment which must be covered is clearly linked to the definition of *'awra* (pl. *'awrāt*, pudenda), the genital or pudental parts of the body which must be covered. The root meaning of *'awra* is a weak spot, imperfection, deficiency, or ugliness. The word appears in three verses in the Qur'ān, only one of which (in its plural, meaning pudenda) pertains to women, and that is in the verse we have been analyzing (24:31). One of these passages is in 33:13, where some of Muhammad's followers asked leave to return to their homes, arguing that their homes were defenseless (*'awra*)—a claim that the Qur'ān rejects. The other verse is 2:57, where *'awrāt* refer to times of day when the privacy of the believers was not to be violated by the intrusion of servants or children without permission. These may be considered times of particular vulnerability and defenselessness, when a greater measure of protection is in order. The *Lisan al-'Arab* defines *'awra* as "weak spots from which one fears being struck (for example, harbors during war), anything which causes embarrassment if it shows, such as the pudenda of men and women or the entire body of a woman, as it says in Hadith, "Woman is *'awra*." Uncovering *'awra* (the pudenda of men, the entire body of women except the face and the hands, and possibly the soles of the feet) causes shame.[28]

The entire discussion of modesty and the segregation of the sexes in the legal sources revolves around the interpretation of *'awra*. In men *'awra* is limited to the area between the navel and the knee. A free woman's *'awra* in the company of other women is like the *'awra* of a man, but in the company of men the entire body is considered to be *'awra*, with the exception (according to most interpretations) of her face and hands. Razi wrote that some jurists went so far as to say that the back of a woman's hand is *'awra*, because a woman's business transactions require only the palm of her hand to show. Razi stipulates that a man should look at the hands and face of a woman only if he has a justifiable purpose, such as intending to marry her, or making a bargain with her, or if she is giving testimony, or if he is buying a slave girl. (Concerning slave girls the jurists disagree: some limit their *'awra* to what lies between the navel and the knee, while others say it is everything that need not show for work.) There are also occasions when the *'awra* may be seen by a man: by a physician examining a woman for treatment; by a circumciser during circumcision; by a witness of adultery, that he might testify against her; by a witness of childbirth, to give testimony of the birth; or by a witness of nursing, to give testimony that a particular woman has nursed the baby—a relationship that has legal implications in Islam.[29] Looking at the body of a woman requires justification, and if it can be avoided, it should be. One legal scholar held that a man should not purposely look at a woman's body in order to provide testimony regarding adultery, childbirth, or nursing, because adultery is best left concealed, and the testimony of women is adequate in the other cases. However, if a woman is drowning or burning, a man must look at her body in order to rescue her.[30]

Such is the shamefulness of looking at *'awra*, that it is even considered reprehensible for a man to look at the pudenda of his wife or even his own pudenda. And it is not permitted for a man to sit naked in an empty house if he has something with which to cover himself, because the Prophet said, "God is even more deserving (than humans) of our embarrassment."

While *'awra* is often defined according to context, Razi says that the body of a woman is *'awra* in and of itself. This is proven, he says, by the fact that the prayer of a woman is unacceptable if her body is not covered, whereas the body of a man is otherwise.[31]

The public appearance of the female body is shameful, while covering it confers honor on both the woman and her family. The *Lisan al-'Arab* quotes Muhyi al-Din ibn al-'Arabi (1165–1240) as saying that *'awra* is covered not because it is vile, but to give it honor."[32] This idea that what is weak and vulnerable is invested with greater honor by being hidden is the rationale behind the segregation of the sexes and the seclusion of women: because women are both beautiful and likely to produce harm and corruption among men, and because they are vulnerable, weak spots that must be protected from shameful exposure, they are in their whole persons considered to be *'awra*, a term that with men refers only to their pudenda. Their seclusion and covering is regarded as honorable treatment, an honor which also confers nobility on their men.

These definitions of *'awra* and their application to the modesty code for women like the definitions of that adornment which may show, are based on the customs and practices of the Muslims of seventh-century Arabia and later Muslim society, and not on any explicit definition in the Qur'ānic text itself. If *'awra* is indeed what causes embarrassment if it shows, would the removal of embarrassment in the modern context, in which the unveiling of women in the public sphere has become commonplace, entail a re-definition of *'awra* in relation to women? Many Muslims do not feel free to ask this question, given the hadith indicating that "woman is *'awra*." There are books of Islamic jurisprudence stating that the whole body of a woman is *'awra* and must be covered except her face and hands and that is the standard that must remain. What began as an application of Qur'ānic principles of modesty to the customs and mentality of the early Muslim community became the imposition of those customs as the unquestioned norm for all Muslim communities for all time. To deny the priority of those norms is to deny the superiority of the early Muslims over the degraded present-day society that has been corrupted by the infiltration of Western values.

These ideas are reiterated in contemporary Islamic writings. Sayyid Qutb (d. 1966), the most important writer of the Muslim Brotherhood, wrote that the meaning of *zīna* varies from age to age according to what is regarded as beautiful in women. But his discussion of modesty requirements for women reflects no such flexibility and is entirely based on hadiths and the traditional interpretation of Islamic modesty norms.[33]

There are several Qur'ānic verses addressed specifically to Muhammad's wives, urging them to exercise particular restraint in behavior and modesty in dress:

> Wives of the Prophet, you are not like other women. If you fear God, do not be too complaisant in your speech, lest the lecherous-hearted lust after you. Show discretion in what you say. Stay in your homes[34] and do not display yourselves as women did in the first Jahiliyya. Perform your prayers, give alms and obey God and His Messenger. God only wants to remove uncleanness from you [masculine plural], family of the Prophet, and to purify you. Remember [feminine plural form] the revelation and wisdom of God that you recited in your homes. (33:32–34)
>
> You who believe, do not enter the Prophet's houses unless he gives you permission.... And if you ask his wives for anything, ask from behind a curtain (*hijāb*); that is purer for your hearts and theirs. You are not to speak ill of the Messenger of God or marry his wives after him.... Prophet, tell your wives, your daughters, and the women of the believers to draw their cloaks (*jalābīb*) around them. That is better, so they will be recognized and not molested. (33:53, 59)

The first passage and the first part of the second concern only the Prophet's wives, and some have suggested that complete covering was meant for them only, as a distinction from other women, but that their status as exemplars for the women of the community led ultimately to the veiling and seclusion of all free Muslim women. Verse 33:59, however, quickly shifts the context to all "women of the believers," telling them to draw their cloaks around them in order to be recognized as free Muslim women and not molested. The commentators tell us that men in Medina used to sexually assault slave women in public, and that any woman who went out at night to relieve herself was vulnerable to such attacks. The verse counsels free Muslim women to distinguish themselves from slave women by covering themselves, thereby protecting themselves from assault. The implications of creating the veil as a status indicator will be discussed shortly. The traditional Qur'ān commentators, however, are more interested in defining the words and concepts relevant to modesty norms that are introduced in these passages.

The Qur'ān's order to the Prophet's wives that they "not be too complaisant" in their speech signals that modesty was to include proper modulation of the voice to avoid tones that would arouse the interest and passions of men; discretion is also enjoined in what they say. This verse is probably behind the commonly quoted hadith that says that a woman's voice is *'awra*. The wives of the Prophet are urged to stay at home, and not to display themselves (*lā tabarrajna*) in the manner (*tabarruja*) of the first Jahiliyya. The definition of the first Jahiliyya is a matter of some dispute, but all interpretations point to a time before the coming of Islam, a time when women had exhibitionist habits. (Some of the commentators offered accounts of the manner in which they displayed themselves. This can only be seen as fanciful descriptions of the tantalizingly flagrant alleged violations of Muslim moral sensitivities committed by pre-Islamic Arabs—an indulgence in sensationalism supposedly sanctioned by the meticulously comprehensive task of exegesis.[35])

The word *tabarruj* implies both shameless display and coquettish behavior, and it is the latter sense that Razi sees as the primary target of the verse. The command to stay at home is supported in Ibn Kathir's exegesis by a hadith which applies to all women: "Woman is *'awra*; when she leaves her home, Satan looks at her. She is closest to her Lord when she is ensconced in her house."[36] Even the freedom women have to attend prayers at the mosque, guaranteed by a sound hadith from the Prophet, was countered by another hadith: a woman's prayers in her courtyard are better than her prayers at the mosque, and her prayers in her home are better than her prayers in her courtyard, and her prayers in her own room are better than her prayers in her house.[37]

Although we are dealing here with Sunna rather than the Qur'ān, al-Ghazali's discussion of this issue is worth quoting because it illustrates the extent to which interpretation is conditioned by cultural norms and expectations. Al-Ghazali says, "The Messenger of God permitted women to go to the mosques, but now it is correct to forbid them, unless they are old." Indeed, he says, this was correct even in the time of the Companions.

> 'A'isha said," "If the Prophet had known what women would do after his death, he would have forbidden them to go out." When Ibn 'Umar said, "The Messenger of God said, 'Do not forbid the women servants of God to go to the mosques of God,'" one of his sons said, "Indeed, we will forbid them!" His father beat him and was angry with him and said, "Listen to me! I tell you that the Messenger of God said, 'Do not forbid them,' and you say, 'We will forbid them'?" The son insisted on disagreeing with his father because the times had changed, and he (Ibn 'Umar) was angry with him because he disagreed with the apparent meaning of the command without offering an excuse. Likewise the Messenger of God permitted them to go out on festival days, but only with their husbands' consent. Going out now is permissible for the virtuous woman with her husband's consent, but staying home is better. She should not go out except for an important task, for going out to see things or for unimportant matters diminishes her husband's manliness and may lead to corruption. When she does go out, she must avert her eyes from looking at men. We do not mean to say that men's faces are *'awra* for women as women's faces are *'awra* for men,...but looking is forbidden when there is danger of temptation. If there is no such danger, then there is no problem, for men have always gone out with their faces exposed, whereas women go out veiled. If the faces of men were *'awra* for women, men would have been commanded to veil, or women would have been commanded not to go out when not necessary.[38]

This passage is a blatant admission that the interpretation of modesty norms is subjected to purely cultural considerations. A clear permission for women to pray at the mosque is discarded in consideration of "changed times"; the reason why women should not be allowed out is that this diminishes their husbands' manliness, a high cultural value for which the Qur'ān has little regard; and the definition of *'awra* itself is based on actual practice rather than textual analysis.

The implication in verse 33:33 is that the modest behavior enjoined by the Qur'ān would result in the greater purification of the Prophet's wives, although the change in gender in the Qur'ān's address in that passage has permitted the Sufis and Shi'a to develop the idea that God has purified the descendants of the Prophet (*ahl al-bayt*) by protecting them from sin and placing them at a level above other Muslims, worthy of special love and devotion.

Verse 33:53 is known as "the verse of the *hijāb*," and hadiths from 'A'isha indicate a sharp distinction between the time "before the *hijāb*" and the time after the command was revealed. *Hijāb* means a veil, covering, barrier or protection, and is not used exclusively to pertain to the separation of women from men: the Qur'ān refers to the *hijāb* as a barrier between the saved and the damned (7:46, 41:5, 17:45) and to the veil of darkness behind which the sun sets (38:32). In contemporary usage the *hijāb* is also an amulet to protect against evil spirits. It is the word used in contemporary Egypt for women's Islamic dress, although at the turn of the twentieth century Qasim Amin used the word to refer to the entire system of the secluding and covering of women. Whatever the specific meaning of the word, after the revelation of the "verse of the *hijāb*," the Prophet's wives were less free to mingle with men than before.

The contemporary Moroccan feminist and sociologist Fatima Mernissi has examined the historical context of the revelation of this verse in detail. The Prophet, she says, had experimented with the merger of public and private spheres by having his house and his wives' apartments directly face the courtyard of the mosque, so that the public life of the mosque literally intruded into his own domestic life. As the political situation in Medina grew more tense, including an accusation of adultery leveled against his favorite wife, 'A'isha, the "descent of the *hijāb*" served to give order to a confused and complex situation—but at a cost. Mernissi sees the *hijāb* as concealing not only Muhammad's wives from public view, but the ruler's private domain from public access, a trend that culminated in the 'Abbasid custom of seating the caliph behind a veil, remote and inaccessible to the public.[39]

The verse commanding the "women of the believers" to go out only covered by a cloak (*jilbāb*, pl. *jalābīb)* follows shortly thereafter, and both Mernissi and the traditional commentators link it to the "revelations [or descent] of the *hijāb*." Although the amount of covering is quite unspecific in the Qur'ān —Zamakhshari says that the *jilbāb* is a wider garment than the *khimar*, beneath the outer cloak—the commentators tell us that women wore it over their heads and bodies, and Ibn Kathir tells us that God ordered women to show only one eye."[40] Razi also assumes that the women covered their faces, and that the meaning of "that they would be recognized [or known]" is that it would be known that they are free women and not to be followed or that it was known that they would not commit adultery.[41]

The purpose of covering the breast, hair, neck and ears, says Ibn Kathir, was to distinguish Muslim women from non-Muslim women, who used to show all of these.[42] This interpretation is indicated by the Qur'ān itself, which tells the women of the believers to draw their cloaks (*jalābīb*) around them so that they would be recognized and not molested. (33:59) But Ibn Kathir also relates a story on the authority of al-Suddi that emphasizes that the *jilbāb* was primarily a symbol of class, distinguishing the free Muslim woman from the slave.

> Some immoral people of Medina used to go out at night when the streets were dark and make advances toward the women; for the houses of Medina were small, so when the women went out at night to relieve themselves, these immoral men would force them to have sexual relations. But if they saw a woman wearing a *jilbāb*, they would say, "This is a free woman," and would leave her alone. But if they saw a woman who was not wearing a *jilbāb*, they would say, "This is a slave girl," and attack her.[43]

Therefore, although contemporary Muslims interpret the rationale behind the *jilbāb* to be modesty—and the contemporary American exegete Amina Wadud-Muhsin is clearly offended by the idea that modesty could be linked to social status[44]—early Muslims interpreted the *jilbāb* as a status marker. Mansour Fahmy, an Egyptian writing in Paris in 1913, insists that the original purpose of the veil was to distinguish free women from slaves rather than Muslims from non-Muslims. He heartily endorses the opinion of Snouck Hurgronje, who wrote that "this passage is speaking neither of the veil nor of Muslim women taken as a group."[45] Fahmy points out that 'Umar ibn al-Khattab forbade slave women to wear the veil of the free woman, and that as the demarcation between classes became more profound, the veil and seclusion took on a growing importance.[46] This identification of the veil and seclusion with class status has an interesting parallel in the ethnographically documented Islamization of the Hausa people of Nigeria: women who had previously played key roles in the Hausa economy by their work in agriculture preferred, upon the abolition of slavery, to adopt the more prestigious seclusion of the wealthy Muslim woman. Although they do not necessarily veil, Muslim Hausa practice a segregation of the sexes and seclusion of women not found among non-Muslim Hausa.[47]

Fatima Mernissi believes that the command for free Muslim women to wear the *jilbāb*, like the descent of the *hijāb* separating the Prophet's wives from the public, represented a grave setback for the Prophet's original project of an egalitarian and open community in which each individual was responsible to regulate his or her own behavior. Muhammad had experimented with egalitarianism among the believers, she says, encouraging the freeing of slaves and the autonomous decisions of individuals to convert to Islam. But the lack of public security in Medina led him to adopt "a slaveholding solution" by protecting only free women, and leaving slave women vulnerable to sexual assaults.

> This was an implicit acknowledgement that they could be approached and attacked...[t]he *hijāb* incarnates, expresses and symbolizes this official retreat from the principle of equality. Symbolically, regression on social equality became entangled and implicated in regression on sexual equality in the case of the female slave. The *hijāb*/curtain descended on them both, mingling and confusing the two ideas in the consciousness of Muslims during the fifteen centuries that followed.[48]

Mernissi says that the *hijāb* represented "the exact opposite of what he had wanted to bring about. It was the incarnation of the absence of internal control; it was the veiling of the sovereign will."[49] She attributes the Prophet's ultimate failure to achieve his original vision to a combination of old age and external circumstances—challenges to his authority, rampant insecurity, and his inability to instill his moral vision in his followers.

Ibn Taymiyya, however, clearly believed the purpose of Qur'ānic modesty prescriptions was avoidance of temptation (*fitna*), not class distinctions. Although he recognizes that the veil was restricted to free women in the time of the Prophet, and admits a distinction between the definition of the *'awra* of a free woman (her entire body) and that of a slave girl (what lies between the navel and the knee), he vehemently rejects the idea that in his day it would be permissible for slave women to go about unveiled. He enunciates the principle that "anything from which *fitna* is feared should be covered."[50] Like Ghazali, he speaks of the corruption of morals which necessitated a greater covering in his day than in the day of the Prophet:

> The slave girls in the time of the Companions used to walk in the streets with their heads uncovered and serve men with soundness of heart. But now, if a

> man wanted to let his pretty Turkish slave girls walk in public in these lands and times,...that would be a corruption.[51]

Ibn Taymiyya defines the distinction in the dress of free women from slave women as custom, not indicated expressly by the Qur'ān or Hadith.[52] Following the principle of avoiding *fitna* (temptation), Ibn Taymiyya says that "beardless, good-looking youths should not be allowed to go to places and alleys where *fitna* is feared, except in case of need. The good-looking, beardless youth should not show his body, by sitting in the bath with strange men or dancing among the men, for in that there is *fitna*, as in looking at him."[53] Since "the principle is that whatever is the cause of *fitna* is not allowed,"[54] a woman should not be allowed to be alone with anyone who is not one of her relatives who are within the degrees of marriage prohibition (the *mahārim*); she should not even be allowed to be with an animal, such as an ape, that the woman may desire or that may desire her.[55]

According to Ibn Taymiyya, responsibility for keeping women chaste lies with their close male relatives. Responding to a question regarding a woman with grown children who committed adultery, Ibn Taymiyya stated that it was not permitted to invoke the legal penalty of death against her or to deprive her of her children's company or her basic needs, because the fault lay not with the woman but with her children and paternal relations. They are obliged to prevent her from engaging in forbidden acts by confinement or even by literally binding her within the house.[56]

Although the Qur'ān specifies that both the adulterer and adulteress should be given one hundred lashes, and Hadith specifies that non-virgin adulterers should be stoned, cultural notions of the weakness of women had led to the prevalent idea that the guardianship (*qiwāma*) of men over women (a principle articulated in the Qur'ān 4:34) includes taking responsibility for their behavior, especially their sexual behavior.[57] Ghazali, too, enunciated the principle that the chastity of women is the responsibility of men. Men must keep their wives chaste by having regular sexual intercourse with them, no less than once every four days. It seems that he regarded the Sharī'a prohibition against having more than four wives to reflect women's need for sexual intercourse no less than every four days.[58]

Perhaps the most astonishing example of reading cultural norms into the Qur'ānic text is Ibn Taymiyya's interpretation of 33:59, which commands women to draw their cloaks around them so that they would be recognized and not molested. In his discussion of the meaning of the *'awra* of a free woman, he says that the majority of the Hanbali school, in contrast to the Hanafi and Shafi'i schools, hold that it is not permissible to look at the face and hands of a woman, even without passion. He says that Ahmad ibn Hanbal and Malik ibn Anas both held that "all of (the body of a free woman) is *'awra*, even her fingernails."[59]

> It says in the book of sound Hadith, "Women shall not cover their faces or wear gloves during the pilgrimage." Since they [women] were commanded to cover themselves with the *jilbāb*, so they would not be known, which means covering the face, or covering the face with the *niqāb*, then the face and hands are part of the *zīna* which may not be shown to strangers. What remains permissible for strangers to look at is only the outer clothing.[60]

Most other fiqh scholars, however, do not interpret the *jilbāb* as a garment that performs the function of the *niqāb*. The prohibition against covering faces or wearing gloves on the pilgrimage indicates only that the custom of covering these was known, not that it was commanded or even commonly observed. In fact, there are other hadiths that give the opposite impression. But what is truly amazing is that Ibn Taymiyya misquotes the Qur'ān, for he says, "They were commanded to cover themselves with the *jilbāb*, *so they would not be known*" [emphasis mine], which means covering the face, whereas the Qur'ān actually says, "Tell your wives and daughters and the women of the believers to draw their *jalābīb* over them. That is better, *so they may be known* and not harmed" [emphasis mine]. As Ibn Kathir explains, "That is, if they did this it would be known that they are free women, not slaves or prostitutes." It seems that it had become customary for women to cover their faces, and Ibn Taymiyya felt constrained to find justification from the Qur'an and Hadith for the idea that the entire body of the woman is *'awra*, "even her fingernails."

Fahmy documents the increasing severity of the veiling and seclusion of women through Islamic history, including the introduction in the first and second centuries after the Hijra of the *niqāb* and the *burqu'*, which are for the purpose of covering the face. The covering of the face, long endorsed by Islamic religious scholars, has no origin or justification in the Qur'ān, and the exegetical works generally admit that a woman's face and hands may be left uncovered. However, by the time of al-Baydawi and Ibn Taymiyya, many religious scholars clearly felt that the entire body of a woman—even her fingernails—should be covered. Fahmy believes this opinion is derived solely from cultural values, not religious texts, but adds that one can hardly separate religious dictate from custom: "If you ask Islam to justify the prescription of the veil, the response is: by the agreement (*ittifāq*) or consensus *(ijmā')* of the Muslims. Hence one can hardly distinguish between custom and religion."[61]

MODERN QUR'ĀN EXEGESIS

Just as the evolution of customary practice in the Muslim world influenced the interpretation of the meaning of *'awra* and the stipulations for female modesty, so it was a change in the social conditions of the Muslim world that caused Muslims to re-evaluate this interpretation. Qasim Amin's famous book, *Tahrīr al-Mar'a* (The Emancipation of Women), which was published in 1899 and launched what is arguably the most heated debate of the century in the Muslim world, is an obvious product of changing social conditions. Egypt and the Muslim world as a whole had fallen under the sphere of Western imperialism, through colonialism or cultural impingement. Muslims were searching for answers to their loss of worldly power, and many of them felt their setbacks had to do with a lack of faithfulness to the true religion or with adherence to faulty interpretations of Islam that failed to allow for modernization and new ways of thinking and living. Western missionaries, scholars and visitors critical of Muslim culture targeted the plight of the Muslim woman, which many felt to be one of the reasons for the backwardness of the Muslim world. It was largely Western criticisms and the challenge that European lifestyles presented to the Muslim world that brought the issue of the status of women and veiling of women to the forefront of public debate. Leila Ahmed argues that Qasim Amin's arguments for the removal of the face veil and the customs of sexual segregation reflect the internalization of a colonialist discourse on the veil promoted by Europeans with the intent of justifying European colonialism, while hypocritically maintaining patriarchy at home.[62] Amin was a judge in the secular court system, not trained in the Sharī'a or in Qur'ān interpretation, and some believe that his book was actually written by his mentor, Muhammad 'Abduh.[63] Amin's interest in the emancipation of women was linked to both the social concern that women's ignorance and isolation from the world of men perpetuated the inculcation of superstition in children, and the economic concern that women's productivity was required for Egypt to develop into a modern nation-state. On the other hand, those who upheld the seclusion of women were those who were most likely to feel economically threatened by the massive introduction of women into the work force.[64] Thus the interpretation of Islam is as likely to be based on social conditions and cultural constraints as a reasoned analysis of the Qur'ān and Sunna.

In the modern period discussion of the subject of women has tended to become much more polemical in nature. Whereas the medieval authors wrote for a male audience at a time of Muslim self-confidence, modern authors address a much wider audience that includes women and Westerners, and they are writing at a time of Muslim self-examination in the face of weakness. In the face of European criticism of Islam on the basis of its treatment of women, modern authors of differing persuasions almost always feel constrained to indicate the superiority of the status of women in Islam over their status in other religions, whereas medieval authors freely discussed the superior status of men over women in Islam.[65] If women have been treated badly, say modern expositors, it is Muslims who are at fault for failing to give them their rights that have been guaranteed by the Sharī'a.[66] But Islam itself offers women all their rights, if it is rightly interpreted.[67]

Qasim Amin's arguments are based on the imperatives of social evolution, and only secondarily on analysis of the sources. He predicates his appeals on two statements he takes as axiomatic: 1) that woman is the key to the progress or backwardness of nations, and 2) that change and evolution are part of the natural order that the Muslims resist at their own peril.[68] He argues for an end to the face veil and seclusion and that women are to be educated and work in order to overcome the problems of ignorance, superstition, and dependency that he saw crippling the nation. He points out that the Sharī'a does not require covering of the face of women or the secluding women in their homes. He is careful not to advocate unbridled modernity or the wholehearted embrace of European customs. Indeed, he says that if there were a single text in the corpus of Islamic law that required the customs of the *hijāb* as they were then practiced, he would have felt compelled to refrain from discussing the issue at all.[69] What he desires, he says, is simply the dress called for by the Sharī'a, *al-hijāb al-sharʻī*, which allows women to show their face and hands. The veil, he says, is merely "an historical phase in the life of women in the world," and one that is not even unique to Muslims.[70] He scoffs at the prevalent idea that the appearance of women is the cause of temptation (*fitna*), which is the main reason given by advocates of veiling in the modern period. He points out that the Qur'ān commands men and women equally to avert their eyes from that which is forbidden, and finds unacceptable the implication that it is men's weakness that necessitates the covering of women.[71]

The Tunisian reformer Tahir al-Haddad (d. 1935) similarly argued that society has deprived women of their rights, and the veil as practiced was never advocated by the Sharī'a, and that the practice itself was applied unevenly. He criticizes the practices of seclusion and veiling on psychological grounds: they give women psychological complexes, raise barriers between husbands and wives, and deprive women of the company of their own families. Like Amin, he states that the questionable religious practices in which women participated were due to their exclusion from proper religious instruction. Religion itself, therefore, would benefit from the removal of the customs of veiling and seclusion.[72] He points out that the Qur'ānic command addressed to both men and women to lower their eyes assumes that there is no such physical impediment as the veil guarding women from the view of men.[73] It is interesting that the French translation of Haddad's book (for which the author, having died more than forty years before, could in no way be responsible) takes the opposite approach from those who interpret the "apparent *zīna*" as that which cannot be hidden without difficulty; according to the French translation, Haddad says "the apparent *zīna*" is everything *except* that which necessarily cannot be hidden.[74] Haddad specifies that what is intended in this verse is display with the intention of provocation. "What is to be understood is not dress itself but its relation with the intention to licentious profligacy denoting bad manners." He also states that the ambiguity of the Qur'ānic stipulations regarding modesty indicate that they are to be applied evolutionally—that is, the meaning of the apparent *zīna* should reflect the standards of the time. He says that were the veil one of the pillars of Islam, as

Muslims so often claim, the imams of the law would not be in such disagreement concerning the definition of what must be hidden.[75]

Advocates of new roles for women and the new interpretations of female modesty requirements that such roles would necessitate, look not only to the legal texts but also to the historical precedent of women who were actively involved in public life in early Islam. Rashid Rida (d.1935) wrote a short article in *Al-Manār* about the participation of women in early Islam, and even authors whose platforms and goals are not primarily inspired by Islam are careful to follow suit.[76]

But if changing social conditions call for a re-examination of the Islamic sources, this can also take the form of appealing to the authority of earlier interpretations of the Qur'ān. The search for inspiration in the early Muslim community can limit available options to what existed at that time. The same standards and texts that appeared progressive to reformers of the late nineteenth and early twentieth centuries are still used to define the roles women should play and the dress they should wear. Advocates of social evolution from the 1930s to the present have often ignored the early Islamic texts and the standards they offer, and they have difficulty justifying their alternatives by analysis of the Islamic sources. With the wave of interest (already building in the late 1970s, but firmly established in the 1980s) in establishing an Islamic basis for society, the legal texts and hadiths have taken on a role that appears to be the reverse of the trend we previously noted: rather than changing the interpretation of modesty norms to harmonize them with social conditions, for the first time it is traditional Qur'ānic and legal interpretation that are defining the dress of women involved in the contemporary Islamic movement. Women are being taught that their bodies are *'awra* and must be covered, that their voices are *'awra* and should not be heard except under certain conditions. Women are turning from a Western-inspired lifestyle and dress to one that is consciously based on traditional interpretation of Islamic texts. This may be the first time since the revelation of the "verse of the *hijāb*" that Qur'ānic interpretation is indeed influencing practice.[77]

But the adoption of the medieval interpretations is selective. In a society that has abolished slavery, the theoretical distinction between slave and free no longer pertains, and the standards of cover for free Muslim women are enjoined for all. In practice, the *hijāb* still serves as a marker of status, for it is worn almost entirely by educated young women of the middle or upper class. Daughters of Egyptian peasants who attend university discard their traditional black garment in favor of this new marker of status. And like the Qur'ānic *jilbāb* that offered status recognition to women and thereby protected them from molestation, the new *hijāb* also serves not only to protect men from the danger of *fitna*, but perhaps more importantly to protect women from molestation. Polemicists who call Western attire "naked dress" say that by turning to Islamic dress women find new dignity and power.[78] Some observers have even called this a type of "Islamic feminism." To the extent that, by creating a portable protection the *hijāb* has allowed women to enter public space freely, even defiantly,[79] it may indeed be a form of empowerment—but an empowerment based on capitulation to traditional attitudes regarding the inherently sexual nature of the entire female body and male dominance of public space.

The definitions of *'awra*, the hidden *zīna*, the *khimar* and *jayb*, as presented in the modern Islamist literature, are all taken from the traditional interpretations of the Qur'ān exegetes and legal scholars. But the tone of the writings in the modern period is polemical. The exegesis of Muhammad 'Abduh and Rashid Rida, and Sayyid Qutb's exegetical work, *Fī Zilāl al-Qur'ān*, are sermons rather than an exposition of terms. Qutb's discussion of Qur'ānic modesty norms is an attempt to find philosophical justification for the segregation of the sexes rather than an elucidation of the meanings of words and verses in detailed fashion. The definitions, after all, are already there in the literature. What is needed for today is a rationale for their continued application in the modern age in the face of so much change that appears to be going in the contrary direction. It is the strength of sexual attraction that needs to be discussed, and the voracity of sexual passions once aroused. It is the debauchery of the West and of Western-inspired lifestyles that needs to be exposed and contrasted with the security offered by adherence to Islamic modesty standards. The danger of women is emphasized: they have "hungry, stealthy glances, which call and provoke, arousing temptation in the breasts of men."[80] The disintegration of traditional social customs and values in the face of modernization has led to a sense of alienation that can only be relieved by adherence to traditional Islamic values. Among the most important of such values is the modesty of women.

We will not discuss the modern polemical literature at length here, as this has been done elsewhere,[81] and the discussions have, in any case, little to contribute to Qur'ānic exegesis, since they make no attempt at new definitions, only new justifications. Much of it has more to do with anti-Western sentiment and horror at the conditions of modern life than with intellectual activity inspired by an examination of the Qur'ān.

The one modern Arab woman who has made a name for herself in Qur'ānic exegesis, the Egyptian literary scholar 'A'isha 'Abd al-Rahman, who writes under the name Bint al-Shati', has limited her exegetical work to the short, non-legal chapters at the end of the Qur'ān, which do not touch on the subject of women.[82] We do, however, have a short booklet, the transcript of a lecture she delivered at Umdurman Islamic University, in which she discusses "the Islamic understanding of women's liberation." In this lecture, she does not address the issue of women's dress, but she does challenge the traditional understanding that the "guardianship" (*qiwāma*) of men over women (Qur'ān 4:34) implies male responsibility for women's moral behavior—the rationale behind the seclusion of women. "The guardianship of the father or husband over the woman does not mean in the least that he bears her responsibilities before the Law.... 'No soul bears the burden of another'"(35:18).[83] This new understanding of the competence of women to oversee their own moral behavior is generally accepted.

Fatima Mernissi examines the vocabulary behind women's status and seclusion in Muslim society in her works,[84] but she does so in order to analyze the many facets of its historical implications and expose the misogyny of Muslim societies, not to advocate a new interpretation of the Qur'ān.

Only Amina Wadud-Muhsin, a North American scholar consciously adopting the hermeneutic method of Fazlur Rahman, has picked apart the meaning of the Qur'ānic terms traditionally used to justify women's subordination, in order to liberate those terms from the social biases of the medieval commentators. [See as well Chapter 6 herein.] But she does not do this on topics of women's modesty. She finds the detailed analyses of the meaning of the hidden *zīna*, *'awra*, *hijāb*, *khimār* and *juyūb* irrelevant by her reading of 24:31 because the modesty standards indicated by these terms are intended to be defined by any given society according to its own sense of propriety:

> In Arabia at the time of the revelation, women of wealthy and powerful tribes were veiled and secluded as an indication of protection. The Qur'ān acknowledges the virtue of modesty and demonstrates it through the prevailing practices. The principle of modesty is important—not the veiling and seclusion which were manifestations particular to that context. These were culturally and economically determined demonstrations of modesty. Modesty is not a privilege of the economically advantaged only: all believing women deserve the utmost respect and protection of their modesty—however it is observed in various societies. Modesty is beneficial for maintaining a certain moral fibre in various cultures and should therefore be maintained—but on the basis of faith: not economics, politics or other forms of access and coercion. This is perhaps why Yusuf Ali translates verse 24:31 "what (must ordinarily) appear" (with regard to uncovered parts), to indicate that (ordinarily) there are culturally determined guidelines for modesty.[85]

For Wadud-Muhsin, the "hidden *zīna*" is something that ought to be defined by social convention. The medieval exegetes, by implication, were therefore correct to revise their understanding of Qur'ānic modesty standards to conform to social convention—but so may we. The modesty standards of seventh-century Arabia or ninth-century Iraq are not suitable for today, and should certainly not be coercively enforced.

As flexible and sensible as Wadud-Muhsin's approach may seem to us, we must note that it seems sensible to us because we live in a society where cultural relativity, broadmindedness, and flexibility are laudable values. Wadud-Muhsin is very much an American in her insistence on an almost infinite number of possible interpretations of appropriate modesty, and her insistence that modesty should never reflect status or privilege may well reflect the struggles of the African-American community to which she belongs. In today's scholarly world, when we are increasingly aware that science is never entirely "objective" but is conditioned by cultural values, it is no surprise to find that the reading of something as important and maleable as sacred texts is likewise so conditioned.

CONCLUSION

The Qur'ānic verses that enjoin modesty for women do not clearly define how women are to dress and the extent to which they may participate in public life. They contain a number of terms and phrases that require detailed interpretation in order to establish their specific requirements. The initial revelation of the "verse of the *hijāb*," according to Hadith, resulted in a radical change in women's dress, but women continued to participate in the religious and public life of the community. Increasing severity in the social practice of sexual segregation and female modesty led, in turn, to stricter interpretations of the Qur'ānic stipulations. The meaning of the *'awra* and "hidden *zīna*" of women was extended in later interpretations to include the face and hands, although it was admitted that these are not included in the legal definitions of earlier scholars. Ghazali's belief that women should be secluded for the sake of public morals and male honor led him to overrule the Prophet's permission for women to go to the mosque, and Ibn Taymiyya's belief that the face of women is *'awra* actually led him to misquote the Qur'ān and thereby misinterpret the apparent intention of the Qur'ānic verse commanding Muslim women to wear the *jilbāb*.

In the modern period, changing social conditions prompted Muslims to reclaim the earlier, less severe standards of Qur'ān exegetes and legists. Ultimately, however, the impulse for social change led many Muslims to disregard the legal texts altogether in their quest for modernity. The disjunction between the modernizing, largely secular, sectors of society and the religious values that continued to be maintained in traditional sectors of society led, with the expansion of secular education into those sectors, to the "Islamic awakening" *(al-sahw al-islāmī)*, as it is called in the Arab world, among educated young people. This "awakening," begun in the Arab world in the 1920s and in India/Pakistan in the 1940s, became a major social movement in the 1970s and 1980s. It reverses previous tendencies to interpret the Qur'ānic modesty standards in light of social convention, by consciously remodeling dress and behavior in conformity with the standards set by the early Qur'ān exegetes.

The type of reinterpretation of modesty norms advocated by Fazlur Rahman is represented only by the few lines Wadud-Muhsin has devoted to the subject, which, on their own, stand little chance of challenging the sway currently held by traditional interpretations. The polemics on women's modesty remain polarized between those who seek an "Islamic interpretation" that is invariably conservative or even reactionary, and the contemporary "modernists" who, unlike those of the turn of the century, neglect the vital issue of Qur'ān interpretation.[86]

Fazlur Rahman's complaint that the original intention of the Qur'ān was consistently bypassed in favor of social convention, and Fahmy's assertion that it is impossible to separate religious dictate from standard custom, may appear to be overturned by the current move to model behavior on traditional texts. But cultural values and social concerns remain the dominant factor in Qur'ānic exegesis. Muslims seeking an anchor in the disquieting anomie of modern society embrace the security of a solid moral code and adopt the literal interpretations of medieval exegetes. Muslims who embrace the changes modernity brings seek a flexible approach to scriptural interpretation and application. Exegetes in a privileged position in a slaveholding society had little difficulty seeing Qur'ānic modesty norms as intended to affirm their status as free, privileged males. An African-American woman, however, not surprisingly rejects the idea that modesty should connote status or privilege. The reading of texts is always culturally conditioned, even when the intention is to find an unbiased, "original" meaning.

NOTES

1. Fazlur Rahman devoted an entire book to elucidating the flexibility inherent in the original application of the concept of Prophetic Sunna and how as the principles of Islamic jurisprudence were developed by al-Shafi'i, the scope for reasoned adaptation of Qur'ānic principles was considerably narrowed. *Islamic Methodology in History* (Karachi: Central Institute of Islamic Research, 1964).

2. Most explicitly in *Islam and Modernity: Transformation of an Intellectual Tradition* (Chicago and London: The University of Chicago Press, 1982); see especially p. 20.

3. Fazlur Rahman "Status of Women in the Qur'ān," in *Women and Revolution in Iran*, ed. Guity Nashat (Boulder, CO: Westview Press, 1983), pp. 37–54.

4. See Valerie J. Hoffman-Ladd, "Polemics on the Modesty and Segregation of Women in Contemporary Egypt," *International Journal of Middle East Studies* 19, 1(1987); 23–50, and Leila Ahmed, *Women and Gender in Islam: Historical Roots of a Modern Debate* (New Haven and London: Yale University Press, 1992), ch. 8.

5. I use Hadith, with a capital H, to refer to the corpus of literature containing the accounts of the sayings and deeds of the Prophet and his Companions. When referring to individual reports, I use hadith, with a lower-case h.

6. Ignaz Goldziher, *Études sur la tradition islamique*, trans. Léon Bercher (Paris: Adrien Maisonneuve, 1952), p. 2.

7. Fazlur Rahman "Status of Women in the Qur'ān," p. 41. See also Barbara Freyer Stowasser, *Women in the Qur'ān, Traditions, and Interpretation* (New York and Oxford: Oxford University Press, 1994).

8. J.J.G. Jansen, *The Interpretation of the Koran in Modern Egypt* (Leiden: E.J. Brill, 1974), pp. 25–27. The Qur'ān frequently proclaims itself to be a "clear book" (5:15, 12:1, 15:1, 26:2, 27:1, 28:2, 36:69, 43:2, 44:2). The claim that the Qur'ān coheres in all its parts is based on 39:23, which describes the Qur'ān as *kitāban mutashābihan*, translated by Kenneth Cragg as "a Book which is self-consistent." Cragg, *Readings in the Qur'ān* (London: Collins, 1988), p. 278.

9. Fazlur Rahman, *Islam and Modernity*, p. 20. This approach may be contrasted with that of another contemporary scholar, 'A'isha 'Abd al-Rahmān (also known under the pseudonym Bint al-Shati'), who says that "before anyone can understand the Qur'ān in either a general or specific way, he must understand the words and styles of the Qur'ān in a detailed literary fashion." *Al-Tafsīr al-bayānī li al-Qur'ān al-karīm*, 2nd ed., 2 vols. (Cairo: Dār al-ma'ārif, 1966), 1:11.

10. This is boldly set forth by Asaf A.A. Fyzee, *A Modern Approach to Islam* (Bombay: Asia Publishing House, 1962), pp. 85–96, 98–108, portions of which are reproduced in *Islam in Transition: Muslim Perspectives*, eds. John J. Donohue and John L. Esposito (New York and Oxford: Oxford University Press, 1982), pp. 188–193. He states outright that verse 4:34, which lays down the principle of male guardianship over women, is "purely local and applicable only for the time being," and is "no longer applicable in modern life." *Islam in Transition*, p. 192.

11. Fazlur Rahman demonstrates through a discussion of specific legal issues in the Qur'ān that Qur'ānic legislation was gradual, piecemeal, "*experimental* legal tackling of problems *as they arise*" (emphasis in the original). He goes on to assert: "Whereas the spirit of the Qur'ānic legislation exhibits an obvious direction towards the progressive embodiment of the fundamental human values of freedom and responsibility in fresh legislation, nevertheless the actual legislation of the Qur'ān had partly to accept the then existing society as a term of reference. This clearly means that the actual legislation of the Qur'ān cannot have been meant to be literally eternal by the Qur'ān itself." *Islam*, 2nd ed. (Chicago and London: The University of Chicago Press, 1979), pp. 37–39.

12. E.g., Tāhir al-Haddād, *Imra'atuna fī'l-Sharī'a wa'l-mujtama'* [first published 1930] (Tunis: Al-Dār al-Tūnisiyya li'l-Nashr, 1972), p. 24, who sees society in positive evolution. Fazlir Rahman sees social change as inevitable though not necessarily morally progressive. But as a consequence of social change, "The

process of questioning and changing a tradition—in the interests of preserving or restoring its normative quality in the case of its normative elements—can continue indefinitely and...there is no fixed or privileged point at which the predetermining effective history is immune from such questioning and then being consciously confirmed or consciously changed." *Islam and Modernity*, p. 11.

13. This is either explicitly or implicitly stated in modern writings. Sayyid Qutb (d. 1966), the prominent ideologue of the Muslim Brotherhood, describes the generation of the Prophet as "the age of purity most favored of humanity in all ages," as contrasted with "our sick, defiled, fallen age." *Fī zilāl al-Qur'ān*, 30 vols. (Cairo: 'Īsa al-Bābī al-Halabī and Co., 1953), 2:13–14.

14. The list of *mahārim*, the male relatives who are permitted to see a woman, does not include uncles. The commentators say this is because the woman may marry her first cousin (in fact this is the traditionally preferred marriage), and the uncle could describe her to his son. Abu'l-Qasim Jar Allah Mahmud ibn 'Umar al-Zamakhsharī al-Khawarizmī, *Al-Kashshāf 'an haqā'iq al-tanzīl wa 'uyūn al-aqāwīl fī wujūh al-ta'wīl*, 4 vols. (Beirut: Dār al-Kitāb al-'Arabī, 1947), 3:232–3.

15. 'Imād al-Dīn Abū' l-Fadā Ismā'īl ibn Kathīr al-Qurashī al-Dimashqī, *Tafsīr al-hāfiz ibn Kathīr*, 9 vols., ed. Muhammad Rashīd Ridā (Cairo: Matba'at al-Manār, 1924/25–1928/29), 6:96; Abu Ja'far Muhammad ibn Jarīr al-Tabari, *Jami' al-bayan 'an ta'wīl ayy al-Qur'ān*, 2nd ed., 30 vols. (Cairo: Mustafa al-Bābī al-Halabī and Sons, 1954–68), 18:116.

16. Ibn Kathīr, 6:96.

17. Zamakhsharī, 3:230.

18. Tabarī, 18:118–19.

19. Zamakhsharī, 3:230.

20. Al-Fakhr al-Rāzī, *Al-Tafsīr al-kabīr* (Cairo: Mu'assasat al-matbū'āt, 1934), 23:205.

21. Zamakhsharī, 3:231.

22. Rāzī, 23:205–06.

23.'Abd Allah ibn 'Umar al-Baydāwī, *Beidhawii Commentarius in Coranum* (*Anwār al-tanzīl wa asrār al-ta'wīl*), H.O. Fleischer (Leiden: F.C.W. Vogel, 1846–48), 2:20.

24. See Ahmed, *Women and Gender in Islam*, ch. 5 and 6; James A. Bellamy, "Sex and Society in Islamic Popular Literature," in *Society and the Sexes in Medieval Islam*, ed. Afaf Lutfi al-Sayyid Marsot (Malibu, CA: Undena Publications, 1979), pp. 40–41; and Barbara Freyer Stowasser, "The Status of Women in Early Islam," in *Muslim Women*, ed. Freda Hussain (London and Sydney: Croom Helm, 1984), pp. 11–43.

25. Abū Hāmid Muhammad al-Ghazālī, *Ihyā' 'ulūm al-dīn*, 5 vols. (Cairo: Matbā'at lajnat nashr al-thaqāfa al-islāmiyya, 1937), 4:142.

26. Zamakhsharī, 3:231.

27. Tabarī, 18:120.

28. Ibn Manzūr, *Lisān al-'arab*, 2nd ed., eds. 'Abd Allah 'Ali al-Kabīr et al. (Cairo: Dār al-ma'ārif, 1981), 4:3166–7.

29. Mainly involving the prohibition of marriage between a nursing woman and her foster child, and between foster-siblings.

30. Rāzī, 23:202–4.

31. Ibid., p. 204.

32. *Lisān al-'arab*, 4:3167. This idea is echoed in a very different context in the first letter of St. Paul to the Corinthians: "The parts of the body which seem to be weaker are indispensable, and those parts of the body which we think less honorable we invest with the greatest honor, and our unpresentable parts are treated with greater modesty, which our more presentable parts do not require." (1 Cor. 12:22–4) On Ibn 'Arabi's unique (though subsequently influential) ideas concerning women and sexuality, see Valerie J. Hoffman-Ladd, "Mysticism and Sexuality in Sufi Thought and Life," *Mystics Quarterly*, XVIII, 3 (Sept. 1992): 82–93.

33. Qutb, *Fī zilāl al-Qur'ān*, 18:95.

34. Barbara Stowasser and others doubt that this really means "stay in your homes." ("The Status of Women in Early Islam," p. 39, n. 24.) She favors the meaning of "walking noiselessly on the sides of your feet," because the sound of the jangling of anklets arouses the passions of men.

35. Tabarī, 22:4–5; Zamakhsharī, 3:537; Ibn Kathīr, 6:545.

36. Ibn Kathīr, 6:545.

37. Ghazālī, 4:162.

38. Ibid., pp. 142–3.

39. Fatima Mernissi, *The Veil and the Male Elite: A Feminist Interpretation of Women's Rights in Islam*, trans. Mary Jo Lakeland (New York: Addison-Wesley Publishing Co., 1991), ch. 10.

40. Ibn Kathīr, 6:612. Such an extreme interpretation is not favored in contemporary Egypt, even among most proponents of "Islamic dress" for women. I was present during a conversation between Shaykh Muhammad al-Ghazālī, the prolific writer of the Muslim Brotherhood, and Shaykh Muhammad Zakī Ibrāhīm, head of the Muhammadiyya Shadhiliyya Sufi Order. The latter told the former that he saw a young woman walking in the street with only one eye uncovered, to which Ghazālī retorted, "That is exactly the kind of extremism that will make unbelievers of many."

41. Rāzī, 25:230.

42. Ibn Kathīr, 6:100.

43. Ibid., p. 471.

44. Amina Wadud-Muhsin, *Qur'ān and Woman* (Kuala Lumpur: Penerbit Fajar Bakti Sdn, Bhd., 1992), p. 10.

45. *Bijdragen tot de taal en landen kunde van Nederlandsch-Indie*, vols. 5 (May 1896); quoted in Mansour Fahmy, *La condition de la femme dans la tradition et l'évolution de l'Islamisme* (Paris: Librairie Felix Alcan, 1913), p. 49.

46. Fahmy, *La condition de la femme*, p. 58.

47. M.F. Smith, *Baba of Karo: A Woman of the Muslim Hausa* (London: Faber & Faber, Ltd., 1955), p. 22.

48. Fatima Mernissi, *The Veil and the Male Elite*, pp. 178–9.

49. Ibid., p. 185.

50. Taqī al-Dīn Ahmad ibn Taymiyya, *Hijāb al-mar'a al-muslima wa libāsuha fi al-salāt*, ed. Muhammad Nāsir al-Dīn al-Albānī (n.p., n.d.), p. 38.

51. Ibid., p. 42.

52. Ibid., pp. 35–6.

53. Ibid., p.42.

54. Ibid., p. 43.

55. Ibn Taymiyya, *Kitāb al-ikhtiyārāt al-'ilmiyya* (Cairo: Matba'at Kurdistan al-'ilmiyya, 1329/1908), p. 54.

56. Ibn Taymiyya, *Al-Fatāwā al-kubrā*, ed. Hasanayn Muhammad Makhlūf (Cairo, 1966), 4:288.

57. For a modern Muslim's understanding of the meaning of male guardianship over women, see Wadud-Muhsin, *Qur'ān and Woman*, pp. 70–74.

58. Ghazālī, 4:148-9

59. *Hijāb al-mar'a al-muslima*, pp. 13–14.

60. Ibid, pp. 16–17.

61. Fahmy, *La condition de la femme*, p. 57.

62. Ahmed, *Women and Gender in Islam*, ch. 8.

63. Māhir Hasan Fahmī, *Qāsim Amīn* (Cairo: Al-Mu'assasa al-misriyya al-'āmma li al-ta'līf, ca. 1962), p. 5; Afaf Lutfi al-Sayyid, *Egypt and Cromer: A Study in Anglo-Egyptian Relations* (London: John Murray, 1968), p. 187.

64. This point is well-argued in Juan Ricardo Cole, "Feminism, Class, and Islam in Turn-of-the-Century Egypt," *International Journal of Middle East Studies* 13 (1981): 387–407.

65. Ibn Kathīr, 1:536.

66. For example, Muhammad 'Abduh says this in Muhammad 'Imāra, *Al-Islām wa al-mar'a fi ra'y al-Imām Muhammad 'Abduh* (Cairo: Matba'at 'Abidin, 1975), p. 62.

67. For example, Zaynab al-Ghazālī, the leading woman of the Muslim Brotherhood in Egypt, told me she left Hudā Sha'rāwī's Feminist Union at the age of 18 and founded the Muslim Women's Association, because Islam "gave women everything—freedom, economic rights, political rights, social rights, public and private rights. Islam gave women rights in the family granted by no other society. Women may talk of liberation in Christian society, Jewish society, or pagan society, but in Islamic society it is a grave error to speak of the liberation of women. The Muslim woman must study Islam so she will know that it is Islam that has given her all her rights." See Valerie J. Hoffman, "An Islamic Activist: Zaynab al-Ghazali" in *Women and the Family in the Middle East: New Voices of Change*, ed. Elizabeth Warnock Fernea (Austin: University of Texas Press, 1985), pp. 234–5.

68. For a more detailed discussion of Amin's arguments, see Valerie Hoffman-Ladd, "Polemics on the Modesty and Segregation of Women in Contemporary Egypt," pp. 23–50.

69. Muhammad 'Imāra, *Qāsim Amīn: Al-A'māl al-kāmila*, 2 vols. (Beirut: Al-Mu'assasa'l-'arabiyya li'l-dirāsāt wa'l-nashr, 1976), 2:45.

70. Ibid., pp. 44–45.

71. Ibid., p. 50.

72. Haddād, *Imra'atunā fi'l-sharī'a*, pp. 182–7.

73. Ibid., p. 31.

74. Tahar Haddad, *Notre femme. La législation islamique et la société*, translator unnamed (Tunis: Maison tunisienne de l'édition, 1978), p. 38.

75. *Imra'atunā fi'l-sharī'a*, pp. 32–33.

76. E.g., Rashid Rida, "Ishtirāk al-nisā' ma'a al-rijāl fi al-'ibādāt wa al-mu'amalāt," *Al-Manār*, January 2, 1922, p. 112; Nawal El Saadawi, *The Hidden Face of Eve: Women in the Arab World*, 2nd ed., trans. Sherif Hetata (Boston: Beacon Press, 1981), pp. 125–31.

77. I do not mean to imply that the motive for wearing Islamic dress is always religious. In the mid-1980s Islamic dress became fashionable in the lower middle class in Cairo, and the impetus for wearing it often has less to do with religious concerns than with social pressures and the desire to present oneself as respectable in a society where economic exigencies require women to enter unconventional roles. See Arlene Elowe MacLeod, *Accommodating Protest: Working Women, the New Veiling, and Change in Cairo* (New York; Columbia University Press, 1991).

78. Mahdiyya Shihāda al-Zamīlī, "Libās al-mar'a wa zīnatuhā fi'l-fiqh al-islāmī," M.A. thesis, al-Azhar University, Islamic College for Girls, 1978, pp. ii–iii.

79. A point insisted on by Fadwa El-Guindi, "Veiling *Infitāh* with Muslim Ethic: Egypt's Contemporary Islamic Movement," *Social Problems* 28 (1981):481.

80. Qutb, *Fī zilāl al-Qur'ān*, 18:94.

81. Hoffman-Ladd, "Polemics on the Modesty and Segregation," p. 40

82. *Al-Tafsīr al-bayānī li'l-Qur'ān al-Karīm* [*The Rhetorical Exegesis of the Noble Qur'ān*], 2 vols.; Vol. I: Cairo, 1962; Vol. II, Cairo, 1969. On Bint al-

Shati', see my article, "'Abd al-Rahman, 'A'isha" in *The Oxford Encyclopedia of the Modern Muslim World*, New York: Oxford University Press, 1955).

83. *Al-mafhūm al-islāmī li tahrīr al-mar'a* (Omdurman: Jami'at Umm Durmān al-Islāmiyya, 1967), p. 9.

84. Besides *The Veil and the Male Elite*, Mernissi has written a number of other books. *Beyond the Veil: Male-Female Dynamics in Muslim Society*, now in a revised edition (Bloomington: Indiana University Press, 1987), has become a classic in the study of Islamic gender ideology.

85. *Qur'ān and Woman*, pp. 9–10. A. Yusuf Ali's translation, *The Holy Qur'ān: Text, Translation and Commentary*, U.S. ed. (Elmhurst, NY: Tahrike Tarsile Qur'ān Inc., 1987) is popular among Muslims in the United States.

86. See Hoffman-Ladd, "Polemics on the Modesty and Segregation of Women."

Chapter 6

FAZLUR RAHMAN AND ISLAMIC FEMINISM

Tamara Sonn

INTRODUCTION

Fazlur Rahman often characterized modern Muslims as fitting into four categories: conservatives "interested in preserving Islam's religious and cultural heritage;" fundamentalists who "absolutize Islamic laws contained in the Qur'ān;" modernists "who believe that the Qur'ān produced certain solutions for certain problems in a certain place but say the responsibility of the contemporary Muslim is to get behind the letter of these laws to the spirit that animated them;" and secularists "who make no appeal to religion at all."[1] He believed secularism is atheism, and therefore, of course, hopelessly misguided. Conservatives, he held, are well-intentioned but ineffective because they are out of touch with the needs of the modern world. He believed fundamentalists, among whom he classified Ayatollah Khomeini, are likewise out of touch with the world, but go beyond the conservatives' simple ineffectiveness, actually propagating positions that are detrimental to the health of the Muslim world. He believed their approach was poorly thought out, defensive, and ultimately doomed to failure. "This fundamentalism will not last long. It's a phase in the internal dynamics of Islamic society. The modernist trends in Islam are irreversible," he concluded.[2]

By modernism, Fazlur Rahman meant the recognition that revelation took place in specific times and places, as did interpretations of revelation for subsequent times and places. Therefore, revelation and interpretations of revelation—such as those in traditional *tafsīr* (Qur'ānic exegesis) and the Islamic laws based on them—must be re-examined in light of the specific circumstances from which they emerged, and reformulated in ways appropriate to present circumstances. This entire undertaking must be based on a clear understanding of the overall spirit of the Qur'ān as well as the dynamics of today's complex society.[3] It is that essence of revelation to which every generation must aspire anew, through fresh study and determined intellectual and spiritual effort, both in understanding and application.

Among the positions developed by the fundamentalists that Fazlur Rahman criticized was the prohibition of interest. "The fundamentalists have a hang-up about this," he said. "The Qur'ān, it is true, banned a system of usury that was terrible. Interest rates were then 60, 70, 80 per cent. Banking practices have changed, however, since the Industrial Revolution. And faith has to take into account such changes."[4] Accordingly, he judged that the Qur'ānic injunction was against usurious interest rates, not against moderate or reasonable interest rates. Insofar as moderate interest rates are essential to the working of today's economy, and Muslims must participate in the global economy or risk further marginalization, Fazlur Rahman concluded that the fundamentalists' rejection of all forms and levels of interest was detrimental to Muslims' economic and political well-being, and therefore not only foolish but un-Islamic. He similarly reasoned regarding some of their views on women's status, such as the controversial issue of rules of evidence. As is well known, the Qur'ān indicates that the court testimony of one male is equivalent to that of two females, an inference generalized into law in *fiqh* (Islamic jurisprudence). In Fazlur Rahman's words, the Qur'ānic passage in question (Surah 2:275–78) "emerged at a time when few women engaged in financial transactions and when women did not deal with business affairs in general. How can you deduce from this a general law which says that under all circumstances and for all purposes a woman's evidence is inferior to a man's?"[5]

Fazlur Rahman's insistence on rethinking Islamic views of women was a recurrent theme in his insistence on the modernist approach to Islamic reform. In this chapter I will focus on this aspect of Fazlur Rahman's work and its effect in engendering a systematic feminist critique of Islamic tradition in North America, that of Lebanese-born American legal scholar, Azizah al-Hibri. I will begin with a description of Fazlur Rahman's overall approach to Islamic reform and his specific ideas on Islamic interpretive methodologies (hermeneutics) before examining al-Hibri's work.

FAZLUR RAHMAN'S INTERPRETIVE METHODOLOGY

When analyzing various approaches to Islam in the modern world, we are talking about interpretations of Islamic principles, whether conscious or unconscious. It is important to distinguish between those who simply interpret Islam for application in the modern world and those who both interpret Islam and discuss the methodology according to which they interpreted. Scholars such as Jamāl al-Dīn al-Afghānī (d. 1897 c.e.), Muhammad 'Abduh (d. 1905), and Muhammad Iqbal (d. 1938), for example, are generally called modernists because they call for the application of Islamic principles to new or changed circumstances. Like conservatives and even fundamentalists (I am using that term here in the sense in which Fazlur Rahman used it, to mean those who call for a return to sociopolitical and economic systems which were effective in Islam's history, without trying to determine whether or not those systems are still likely to be effective), these modernists scarcely concerned themselves with the mechanics of Islamic exegesis or interpretation. Rather, they generally accepted the legacy as received, calling for and frequently engaging in interpretation or reinterpretation, particularly in areas that had not been treated in classical sources.[6] Therefore, although Fazlur Rahman characterized himself as a modernist, he actually belongs in a subcategory of modernists, those who call for reassessment of the entire Islamic legacy in hermeneutical terms. This subcategory includes such noteworthy scholars as Hasan Hanafī, Muhammad Arkūn, Muhammad al-Jābirī, 'Abd Allāh al-'Arwī (Abdallah Laroui) and Abdullahi an-Na'im, all of whom consciously address the interpretive methodology by which the Islamic legacy has been produced.[7]

This approach stands in stark contrast to the "Islamization of knowledge" approach to revitalization of Islam, widely popular in North America today.[8] The "Islamizers" call for the incorporation of modern science and technology into the traditional Islamic educational system. Fazlur Rahman saw this approach as essentially fundamentalist as well; it was based on the assumption that Islamic revival will be achieved by replacing Islam in those areas of society from which it has allegedly been removed, such as politics, law, and scientific or technological education. It is further based on the assumption that the "Islam" that will energize society when it is put back into operation is the same or virtually the same "Islam" that so spectacularly empowered the Islamic community of the Salaf (the "pious ancestors," or model Muslim community of Prophet Muhammad and his immediate successors). Islamic institutions and legal codes were sufficient then and they will be sufficient now, so the thinking goes, if only they are conscientiously applied.

By contrast, Fazlur Rahman is specifically and primarily interested in hermeneutics. He agrees with conservatives, fundamentalists and modernists of all kinds that society has deviated from "the straight path", but he believes that is at least partly due to a misunderstanding from the outset of what the straight path was. He believes, in other words, that Islam began its deviation over 1000 years ago by failing to adequately understand the nature and role of revelation. Therefore, he calls for a critical assessment of the intellectual legacy of Islam, with a view to (1) understand how it happened to assume the form in which it has been inherited, (2) distinguish in the process between essential Islamic principles and their particular formulation as a result of the needs of specific—and probably now outmoded—socioeconomic and political contexts, and (3) determine how best to apply the essential principles of Islam in contemporary circumstances (which themselves must be critically assessed).

Indeed, all efforts to understand the meaning of the Qur'ān are efforts at interpretation according to Fazlur Rahman, since, as he paraphrases Gadamer, "all experience of understanding presupposes a preconditioning of the experiencing subject."[9] Overall, he rejects the idea that interpretations are utterly predetermined. However, it is essential to his reasoning that socioeconomic and historical factors, such as one's education and one's political and economic concerns, affect interpretation. Similarly, he rejects the implication that truth as such is inaccessible to humans. For him, the Qur'ān is truth, unquestionably, the revealed word of God. Yet this does not preclude his recognition that even the Qur'ān is an interpretation. In Fazlur Rahman's words, "[C]ertainly, in the case of the Qur'ān, the objective situation is a *sine qua non* for understanding, particularly since, in view of its absolute normativity for Muslims, it is literally God's response through Muhammad's mind...to a historic situation...."[10]

It should be noted that Fazlur Rahman did not believe that any one interpreter or group of interpreters (i.e., any *mujtahid, faqīh, 'ālim* or body of *fuqahā'* or *'ulamā'*) could achieve a perfect understanding of essential Islam that would be suitable for all time. If such a perfect formula were accessible, revelation would cease to be relevant, a position Fazlur Rahman would have found heretical. He stated explicitly that asking of any interpreter(s) an eternally applicable formula for social justice would be like asking a physician for an eternally effective cure when, in fact, people must continually seek cures as new ailments arise. Instead, he believed every generation has the responsibility to return to revelation, the source of divine inspiration, engage in concerted effort to understand its overall principles, and determine ways to apply those teachings which are appropriate to contemporary circumstances:

> [T]he process of questioning and changing a tradition—in the interests of preserving or restoring its normative quality in the case of its normative elements—can continue indefinitely and...there is no fixed or privileged point at which the predetermining effective history is immune from such questioning and then being consciously confirmed or consciously changed. This is what is required for an adequate hermeneutical method of the Qur'ān....[11]

Overall, he believed this task involved distinguishing between the accidents of the historical circumstances in which the Qur'ān was revealed, and the essential principles being implemented in those circumstances; only when Islamic principles have thus been derived from the body of Islamic revelation can the truly prescriptive elements be applied, and the merely descriptive be properly jettisoned.

Many scholars currently interested in Islamic hermeneutics are influenced by the European post-structuralist concern with principles of interpretation. Muhammad Arkūn, for example, and 'Abd Allāh al-'Arwī, mentioned above, refer to the work of French post-structuralists Jacques Derrida and Michel Foucault. However, Fazlur Rahman described his methodology in a purely Islamic idiom, based on what he considered essential features of Islamic hermeneutics. As I have written elsewhere, he believed that at its core Islam incorporates an historicist awareness.[12] He believed that Islam, uniquely among the monotheistic traditions, is aware of its historic contextualization. This was symbolized to Fazlur Rahman in such important ways as the institutionalization of the Islamic calendar. The significance of the hijra (the emigration from Mecca to Medina in 622 c.e.) for him is that the long process of revelation of the covenant, beginning with Prophet Abraham, was completed with Prophet Muhammad. Humanity had all the revelation it needed: it was enjoined with the task of recreating in society the equality all humans share in the eyes of God. That is at once the challenge and the purpose of human existence, the *amāna* or trust accepted by humanity at creation. It is the measure according to which we will be judged; a just society is one reflecting that equality, and to the extent that each of us contributes or at least attempts to contribute to the creation of a just society, we will be rewarded in the afterlife. Yet there is no eternal formula in the sense of specific social, economic or political institutions that can guarantee social justice. Instead, there is the example established by Prophet Muhammad himself of how the principle of human equality in fact was made the *raison d'être* of a society. Humans must continually return to the record of that example, the Qur'ān, for inspiration. Although that example does not give the specific details of how all just societies will operate, it does provide a perfect example, and—to the sincere heart—the motivation to implement the same principles in changed and changing historical circumstances.

Several other elements of revelation also revolve around Islam's inherent historicism, in Fazlur Rahman's opinion. The notion of abrogation (*naskh*), for example, whereby the Qur'ān claims that it creates verses to supersede (or abrogate) earlier verses as it sees fit: "For whatever verse We abrogate or cast into oblivion, We bring you a better or the like of it; don't you know that God has power over everything?" (Surah 2:100; see Chapter Three above for another view of naskh.) Successive verses dealing with the consumption of wine (first limiting it and then prohibiting it altogether), and those concerning the nature and extent of jihad, are examples. According to a traditional understanding of the principle of abrogation, earlier verses pertain only to the particular circumstances in which they were revealed, while the later verses are taken to be the ultimate word on the subject. In Fazlur Rahman's opinion, the later verses are likewise responses to changing circumstances, so that the Qur'ān itself gives the model for continual flexibility and dynamism in the effort to create a just society. He also rejected the interpretation according to which those verses believed to be the most recently revealed provide the final verdict on a given issue. In the historicist perspective, virtually all verses dealing with specific issues are subject to historical interpretation.

Another component in what Fazlur Rahman saw as the Qur'ān's inherent historicism is its distinction between *muhkam* and *mutashābihāt* texts. The Qur'ān states, "He it is Who sent down to thee the Book. In it are verses that are *muhkamāt*, and—those are the source [or essence] of the Book, and others are *mutashābihāt*. As for those in whose hearts is perversity, they follow the latter seeking discord, and seeking its inner meaning; and none knows its interpretation except God." (Surah 3:5–7) The question is, of course, what do the terms muhkamat and mutashabihat mean? Here again, Fazlur Rahman takes issue with traditional interpretations. In general, the distinction is between unequivocal verses, not subject to interpretation, and equivocal or possibly metaphorical texts, those which are open to interpretation. But as Jane McAuliffe has described, the classical tafsir of al-Tabiri and Ibn Kathir severely limits both the process and scope of those portions of scripture which are open to interpretation.[13] Unequivocal texts are taken, at least in Sunni Islam, to be those whose interpretations have been established by the 'ulamā' and institutionalized by the fuqahā' (jurisprudents) in Islamic law, and those without such established interpretations are interpretable only by God. Thus, there is little, if any, interpretation left to the ordinary believer. For Fazlur Rahman, on the other hand, as noted above, the process of interpretation is not subject to finalization, nor is its practice limitable to a specific or official group of scholars. Furthermore, for him there are relatively few verses of the Qur'ān which are not open to ongoing efforts of interpretation and application. As he repeatedly stressed, the Qur'ān "is not a legal document."[14] It "exhibits an obvious direction towards the progressive embodiment of the fundamental values of freedom and responsibility in fresh legislation," but the key to understanding it is in looking behind the historic details surrounding the verses in order to grasp the essential principles involved.[15]

Undoubtedly, the most important element in Fazlur Rahman's interpretive methodology, however, is his emphasis on *ijtihād*, or intellectual jihad, as he was fond of calling it. For him ijtihad is the key to Islamic hermeneutics. The foregoing elements—the Qur'ān's historicism, its ultimately practical nature, its gradualism, the notions of abrogation and the muhkamāt/mutashābihāt distinction, and others, such as the Qur'ān's insistence that humans use their intellects in the service of God—all point to the need for interpretation of the Qur'ān's message in the light of current circumstances in order to most effectively carry out "the Qur'ān's goal of an ethical, egalitarian social order."[16] Ijtihād is the name given to such interpretive efforts overall. It is, in Fazlur Rahman's words, "the effort to understand the meaning of a relevant text or precedent in the past, containing a rule, and to alter that rule by extending or restricting or otherwise modifying it in such a manner that a new situation can be subsumed under it by a new solution."[17] He blames the stagnation that has characterized the Islamic world since the Middle Ages, in fact, on the limitation and eventual cessation of ijtihād:

> Most modern Muslim thinkers have laid the blame...on the destruction of the caliphate in the mid-thirteenth century and the political disintegration of the Muslim world. But...the spirit of Islam had become essentially static long before that; indeed, this stagnation was inherent in the bases on which Islamic law was founded. The development of theology displays the same characteristics even more dramatically than does legal thought.[18]

Although the early Muslim leaders clearly exercised independent judgement regarding how best to implement Islamic principles and achieve the Islamic goal of social justice, they failed to stress the need for continued ijtihād, much less to institutionalize it:

> There is no doubt that early scholars of Islam and leaders of the community exercised a good deal of freedom and ingenuity in interpreting the Qur'ān, including the principles of ijtihād (personal reasoning) and qiyās (analogical reasoning from a certain text of the Qur'ān and arguing on its basis to solve a new case or problem that has certain essential resemblances to the former). There was, however, no well-argued-out system of rules for these procedures, and early legal schools sometimes went too far in using this freedom. For this reason in the late eighth century c.e., al-Shāfi'ī successfully fought for the general acceptance of "traditions from the Prophet" as a basis of interpretation instead of ijtihād or qiyās. Yet the real solution lay only in understanding the Qur'ānic injunctions strictly in their context and background and trying to extrapolate the principles or values that lay behind the injunctions of the Qur'ān and the Prophet's Sunna. But this line was never developed systematically, at least by Sunni Muslims.[19]

Accordingly, Fazlur Rahman set himself the task of outlining the procedures for an adequate ijtihād-based Islamic hermeneutic, essential, he believed, for the success of the Islamic imperative.

FEMINIST IJTIHĀD

As noted above, among the examples most commonly used by Fazlur Rahman in demonstrating the kind of interpretation he called for were those areas of Islamic law dealing with women: "In understanding the Qur'ān's social reforms, however, we will go fundamentally wrong unless we distinguish between legal enactments and moral injunctions. Only by so distinguishing can we not only understand the true orientation of the Qur'ānic teaching but also solve certain knotty problems with regard, for example, to women's reform. This is where the Muslim legal tradition, which essentially regarded the Qur'ān as a lawbook and not the *religious source* of the law, went so palpably wrong."[20] Besides the question of the relative weight of women's legal testimony, he frequently discussed polygyny. Having discussed the relevant Qur'ānic verses (allowing up to four wives under specific circumstances, but advocating monogamy as "the safest course"), he goes on to note, "There is apparently a contradiction between permission for polygamy [sic] up to four; the requirement of justice among co-wives, and the unequivocal declaration that such justice is, in the nature of things, impossible."[21] He then describes the institutionalization of multiple wives in Islamic law as a clear deviation from Qur'ānic principles of justice, human equality, and the model of a mutually nurturing marriage relationship established by the Qur'ān and the Sunna. He attributed that deviation specifically to a confusion between the muhkamat and mutashabihat verses in this regard. "The traditionalist interpretation was that the permission clause has legal force while the demand for justice, though important, is left to the conscience of the husband...."[22] Overall, however, the fault lay with the early Muslim community's failure to base its legal rulings on an understanding of the spirit of the Qur'ān. Rather than recognize the overriding themes of human equality and dignity, and then legislate regarding marriage accordingly, the formulators of Islamic law frequently legislated on an ad hoc basis, and this is clearly an example.

Azizah al-Hibri has taken this line of thinking and developed it into the beginnings of a full-scale Islamic feminism. Like Fazlur Rahman, al-Hibri demonstrates that Islamic law regarding polygyny deviates from both the overall values and specific injunctions in the Qur'ān. Her treatment is based on a survey of Islamic interpretation, beginning with a description of Islamic law. In her view, very much like that of Fazlur Rahman, the Qur'ān "contains two kinds of rules, general and specific."[23] Also like him, she claims that the majority of Qur'ānic teachings are general; specific rules are relatively few, dealing primarily "with matters of worship or with matters relating to family, commercial or criminal law."[24] And like Fazlur Rahman she focuses on ijtihād as the vehicle of Qur'ānic interpretation and the key to reform. "Since general rules, by their very nature, require interpretation before they can be applied to a specific context, they are the source of a fair amount of flexibility."[25] She then goes even further than Fazlur Rahman, although still in the spirit of his teaching, claiming that "any capable Muslim who engages seriously in the process of interpreting Islamic texts and Islamic law" is engaged in ijtihād.[26] Again, "[T]he field of ijtihād, which is based on serious scholarship, is open to all qualified Muslims." [27]

Clearly speaking from a Sunni context, al-Hibri is here arguing against the privileged position of any scholar or body of scholars in interpreting the Qur'ān, as did Fazlur Rahman, although her rationale differs slightly from his. She bases hers on an analysis of the role of the Sunna, the traditional record of Prophet Muhammad's extra-Qur'ānic words and behavior and a source of Islamic law. Al-Hibri recounts evidence demonstrating general agreement that it was not recorded during the Prophet's lifetime. As a result, the credibility of various reports had to be demonstrated through "chains" of authenticity:

> For this reason, it became necessary for Muslim scholars to develop, in connection with the sunna, a sophisticated science of attribution in order to minimize the problems associated with hearsay. As a result, claims regarding the sayings or behavior of the Prophet were divided into numerous categories including claims that were judged to be false, weak, truthful or completely trustworthy. All claims, however, were collected in books which discussed in detail why each claim was judged as it was.[28]

The next step in al-Hibri's treatment is somewhat more controversial. Basing herself on an analysis of Islamic legal texts, she claims (completing the foregoing quote), "The final decision on these matters was left to the reader." This is how al-Hibri accounts for the fact that Sunni Islam rejects the idea of clergy as mediators between God and people. "A Muslim may rely on the analysis of a scholar, or may discuss the matter at length with other Muslims, but in the final analysis, a Muslim has to take personal responsibility for her or his own actions."[29] In other words, all of Islamic law is interpretation: "Islam has no clergy...Islam has only mujtahids [interpreters]."[30] Once again, all Muslims may engage in ijtihād. Indeed, basing her view on a hadith according to which the Prophet said, "The best of religious practice is the easiest and the best worship is engaging in *fiqh*" al-Hibri concludes, "[I]n Islam ijtihād is not only a right but the duty of every qualified Muslim."[31]

Having established that interpretation of the sources is incumbent on Muslims, al-Hibri goes on to describe what interpretation entails, and the results of failing to engage in it. The chore of interpretation, she says, involves both distinguishing between general and specific Qur'ānic injunctions, and deriving "from the general rules of the Qur'ān and sunna the Islamic laws best suited to the relevant epoch and community."[32] Thus, again, there is no privileged interpretation for all time. Nevertheless, al-Hibri continues, around the tenth- century Sunni jurists assumed for themselves just such a privileged position by stifling ijtihad. "Instead, Sunni scholars were encouraged to confine their ijtihad within the boundaries of the established schools. The intention was to limit the uncontrolled proliferation of ideas, some of which, it was feared, were tainted with foreign influence. This policy undoubtedly contributed to, if not significantly accelerated, the decline in intellectual activity that had begun to manifest itself during that time."[33]

Finally, al-Hibri discusses the nature of Islamic revelation as it impacts legislation, in support of her view of Islamic hermeneutics: "Gradualism is an important feature of Islamic law."[34] On basic issues such as monotheism, of course, there could be no gradualism, for monotheism is the central source of all Islamic values. But on other issues, there is room for gradualism, given the practical nature of Islam as a medium of continual socio-moral reform. "[S]ome jurists have discouraged an abrupt change in the system of government, even for a good cause, if it results in chaos and divisiveness among the people." Thus, "a major principle of Islamic jurisprudence is that laws may change with the passage of time and the change of place or circumstances. Properly understood, this principle permits a mujtahid to examine a specific ayah [verse] in light of both the attendant circumstances of its revelation as well as its meaning to determine the scope and significance of the ayah in general, or with respect to a specific situation at hand. A corollary of this principle is that a change in law is permitted whenever a custom on which such law is based changes."[35] Quite logically, gradualism is associated with abrogation in al-Hibri's analysis. Like Fazlur Rahman, she interprets abrogation as the superseding of earlier verses by later ones according to the needs of the times: "The justification for these changes was that the latter injunctions were not suitable for the people at the earlier time. Even the Qur'ān clearly states: 'It is part of the Mercy of God that thou does deal gently with them. Wert thou severe or harsh hearted, they would have broken away from about thee.'"[36]

These are the bases upon which Azizah al-Hibri establishes her well-reasoned and highly challenging development of Fazlur Rahman's thought. For her, the decline of the Muslim world was not just due to a failure to establish and legislate in the context of an overall Qur'ānic *weltanschauung*, as in the analysis of Fazlur Rahman. Nor is she concerned only with interpretation of verses dealing with women. Instead, al-Hibri is critical of the overall patriarchal approach of Islam: "The Qur'ān and Islamic law have been interpreted for centuries by patriarchal men."[37] She believes that among the most profound reforms wrought by Islam was the transcendence of the patriarchal system that dominated pre-Islamic (or *jāhilīya*, the age of *jahl* or "ignorance") Arabia. However, it was that very reform which was almost immediately reversed in the power struggles following the death of Prophet Muhammad. For that reason, she believes, "Islam *as it is practiced today* is utterly patriarchal...."[38] The time has come, she believes, for Islam to reverse its patriarchalism, to return to—or more precisely, in her view—to develop an authentically non-patriarchal Islam. As she completes the foregoing quote, "*true* Islam is not [patriarchal]."

Al-Hibri begins her analysis with a description of the patriarchalism of pre-Islamic Arabia. Pre-Islamic Arabia knew highly-developed civilizations, like the southern Arabian kingdom of Sheba over 1000 years before the coming of Islam. By the dawn of Islam, a number of civilizations had come and gone. The records we have of the civilization dominant in the North in the centuries just prior to the rise of Islam show a complex society consisting of sophisticated commercial and trading centers surrounded by a predominantly nomadic desert hinterland. Al-Hibri notes that there were some female deities in the region, probably remnants of an earlier matriarchal society.[39] She finds further evidence of ancient matriarchalism in the fact that some tribes were matrilineal and matrilocal. Furthermore, some women seem to have engaged in dominant cultural activities such as poetry reading, combat, and commercial enterprises. Some even seem to have made independent decisions regarding sexual matters. Nevertheless, al-Hibri contends that these examples are exceptions, for pre-Islamic Arabia was, in her terms, "viciously patriarchal."[40] Evidence is seen in the fact, noted even in the Qur'ān, that female infanticide was widely practiced. Whether this was a result of poverty, demonstrating that women were in general economically defenseless, or fear of shame, demonstrating that women were not highly regarded, it seems clear that society was not as hospitable to females as to males.

Al-Hibri notes that there is evidence of a decline in the frequency of female infanticide just prior to the rise of Islam. Yet that was due, she argues—following Mahmasani—to the institutionalization of the dowry. "[B]y that time many Arab men had discovered that selling their daughters for a large dowry was much more profitable than burying them in the ground."[41] Related to this devolution of women from economic liability to chattel value was the fact, reported by al-Hibri on the authority of Said al-Afghānī, that there was virtually unlimited polygyny in pre-Islamic Arabia, and wives were considered part of a man's property. Sons could then marry from among the inherited wives, except for his mother; exchange them for dowry with other men; or allow them to buy their freedom from him if they had any property of their own.

Thus al-Hibri constructs a picture of pre-Islamic society in which some women were free and independent, but the majority were virtual slaves, private property of men. She believes this historical evidence indicates that at the dawn of Islam, Arabia was experiencing the end of transition from an earlier matriarchy to a patriarchal system. She believes, furthermore, that the transition was a function of the introduction of technology, particularly weaponry (arrows and swords), into the desert, via the trading routes developed under Byzantine and Persian influence. "There is some evidence to indicate that Arab men adopted these tools and developed them while limiting the women's access to them. So that while women were busy weaving, herding and rearing, men were developing and expanding the material basis for their later takeover through the technologies of war and trade."[42]

Al-Hibri next turns to the implied question, why would men prevent women access to the advanced weaponry? After all, they had been effective warriors, often, as al-Hibri recounts, using only tent poles. Would they not have been considered of greater value had they been better armed? It seems to al-Hibri, based on evidence that some women had been renowned warriors, that men considered women a threat, and that explains why men deprived them of access to advanced weaponry. Al-Hibri considers it important in this context to point out that "rarely in the annals of ancient Arab history have I seen stories attributing physical or mental inferiority to women."[43] Indeed, this seems to be further evidence of an ancient matriarchy in the process of being eclipsed. Had women been considered weak or inferior, they would not have been considered a threat. That advanced technology, furthermore, proved crucial to the consolidation of patriarchal order in pre-Islamic Arabia:

> Within the family unit, the father became the uncontested and absolute ruler. The wives and daughters were referred to interchangeably as slaves....The tribe as a whole was itself defined on the basis of patrilineage....Since the tribe was the highest political, economic, military and legal authority, without which the individual had no significance whatsoever, it followed that the 'paternal bond' became the supreme bond in the society of Jahiliyyah, permeating all its facets and founding all power within it. It became the core and essence of that patriarchal system.[44]

As is well known, Islam brought many reforms, and prominent among them were those dealing with the dignity and rights of women. Al-Hibri lists fourteen such reforms, including the best known, the prohibition of female infanticide, restriction of polygyny, and allowing women the right to divorce and inherit.[45] However, she insists that the list is incomplete without including the end of patriarchy. "[T]he major contribution of Islam towards the ultimate defeat of Patriarchy [sic] does not lie in any such list of reforms. Rather, it lies in the fact that Islam replaced the 'paternal bond' of Jahiliyyah totally by the religious bond within which everyone—male or female, black or white, young or old, rich or poor—is equal. By doing that Islam struck at the heart of the patriarchal system."[46]

It is here that al-Hibri sees the greatest gap between "true" Islam and Islam "as it is practiced". The tribal paternal bond and the patriarchal mentality, not to mention the power structure and vested interests therein, were too well entrenched to be readily replaced.

In al-Hibri's reading, the return to patriarchalism commenced almost immediately upon the Prophet's death. The Wars of the Riddah, as they are known in Islamic history, wherein many Arab tribes renounced their affiliation with the Muslim community in the absence of the Prophet's personal leadership, were a part of this process. The rebels were brought in line through military force. But these overt challengers were not the only ones who effectively renounced the teaching of Islam; they were just the only ones who were caught. "Almost simultaneously, the patriarchal takeover of Islam commenced from inside its male ranks. Since women were still at the early stages of building their power base, they were ultimately unable to stop this turn of the tide. And the whole process of co-optation unfolded in broad daylight."[47] There were occasional efforts to sustain the reforms wrought by the Prophet. Al-Hibri recounts the story of 'Umar ibn al-Khattab's suggesting at the mosque that dowries be reduced to a symbolic sum, whereupon an elderly woman objected, "You shall not take away from us what God has given us." 'Umar accepted this correction, saying, "A woman is right and 'Umar is wrong."[48] But they were not sufficient to overcome the momentum of entrenched patriarchalism. Ultimately, women were deprived of most of their personal rights, as well as access to economic and political power: "[A]nd till this very day," she concludes, "in some Arab countries women may not engage in business or travel without their husbands' written approval. Women were shrouded in black from head to toe and segregated from men....And this was done in the name of Islam!"[49]

The time has come, however, in this age of Islamic reform, to reverse these trends and return to authentic Islamic teachings concerning women. Al Hibri focuses on several areas of traditional practice concerning women which she considers obviously un-Islamic: the imposition of the veil, the practice of polygyny, limitation of women's right to initiate divorce, institutionalization of men as guardians of women, diminution of the weight of women's legal testimony, and limitation of women's rights of inheritance. She treats the issues of polygyny, divorce, and guardianship in detail. In all cases, she demonstrates that the legal institutionalization is at odds with the overall spirit and, in some cases, the direct teaching of the Qur'ān, especially given changed and changing economic and social conditions which inevitably impact the status of women.

To begin, al-Hibri claims that the legalized practice of polygyny "has caused much misery for women," with the clear implication that it therefore could not be in accord with Islamic principles. She debunks the argument that the Prophet's polygyny constitutes a model for emulation by ordinary believers. Citing the Qur'ān (Surah 33:3 and 50), she claims that in this respect, at least, the Prophet was not like other men.[50] Overriding that example are Qur'ānic verses with clear instructions regarding marriage. Fazlur Rahman concludes that the Qur'ān's allowance of polygyny, while at the same time envisioning a time when monogamy would be the norm, is a function of its gradualism. Al-Hibri goes further; she claims that the conditions placed upon polygyny by the Qur'ān are such as to preclude its practice altogether. Analyzing logically the relevant verses, she states that the Qur'ān's position is unequivocal: "[Y]ou may marry only one wife."[51] Thus she judges the classical legalization of polygyny: "It seems rather evident that the whole issue of polygamy is the result of patriarchal attempts to distort the Qur'ān in the male's favor."[52]

Al-Hibri reaches a similar conclusion in her discussion of rights of divorce. Acknowledging that women have always had the right to impose conditions in their marriage contracts, such as the demand for monogamy or her right to divorce, she recognizes that exercising the right to impose such conditions has generally been the prerogative of upper class women with economic alternatives to marriage. She then predicts that, with more and more women working outside the home, they will gain economic freedom "and this form of modified contract will become the rule rather than the exception."[53] Again, this eventuality will be a necessary corrective to the aberrant form of marriage standardized by patriarchy.

Al-Hibri devotes the most attention to deconstructing the institutionalization of male supremacy over women. The Qur'ānic verse in question is: "Men are *qawwāmīn* over women in matters where God gave some of them more than others, and in what they spend of their money." (Surah 4:34) She claims that the traditional interpretation of *qawwāmīn* as "protectors" and "maintainers," and neglect of the phrase "some of them", has led to an inflexible institutionalization of females as necessarily obedient to males. This, she believes, is both unwarranted and inconsistent with Islamic principles. She believes the verse is not restrictive to men alone, for one thing; whenever one is materially responsible for another, one must care for and maintain the dependent and has a right to expect reciprocal respect. This, she believes, applies to males as well as females, in accordance with the abundant Qur'ānic verses regarding the equality of all human beings. Like Fazlur Rahman, she believes that there is no denying that in the majority of cases at the time of the Prophet, males were materially responsible for females and children. But it is only a confusion between those specific historic circumstances of revelation and the basic principles of human equality and justice that allows the verse to be interpreted as a requirement that women always be economically dependent upon, and therefore submissive to, males. Like many other aspects of patriarchy, this interpretation has led to a distortion of the Qur'ān's spirit and undermined its mission. She concludes her treatment with an approving quotation of Nazirah Zein Ed-Din, an early 20th century Arab feminist:

> What is this unjust law (of veiling) which is permeated with the spirit of tyranny and oppression? *It is in violation of the book of God and his Prophet*, may God bless his soul. This law is the law of the victor, the man who subdued the woman with physical force. *Man tampered with God's book* to make this law. He prided himself on his tyranny and oppression, even as those hurt him, too. He made the law independently, not permitting the woman to share in a single letter. So it came out *in accordance with his desires and contrary to the will of God*."[54]

CONCLUSION

Azizah al-Hibri's conclusions regarding the status of women in Islam are similar in spirit to those of Fazlur Rahman, and in some cases, as noted, go even further than his. Clearly, she agrees with Fazlur Rahman that "the most important legal enactments and general reform pronouncements of the Qur'ān have been on the subjects of women and slavery....But the later Muslims did not watch the guiding lines of the Qur'ān and, in fact, thwarted them."[55] But al-Hibri expands the argument to include the entire structure of patriarchy. It seems fair to speculate that the reforms wrought by the rejection of patriarichalism will not be limited to those issues discussed above, directly reflecting the status of women in society.

Patriarchalism is associated with a number of social features, such as those having to do with political and economic structure (authoritarian and hierarchical vs. consultative and cooperative); humanity's relationship to the environment (exploitive vs. nurturing), and approaches to conflict resolution (militarist vs. cooperative). As such, it affects all members of society. As she quoted Zein Ed-Din, the tyranny and oppression of patriarchy hurt men, too.[56]

Of perhaps even greater significance, however, is the fact that al-Hibri's analysis is, she is convinced, an Islamic one. Unlike the many critics of Islam's orientation toward women who are unconcerned with the religious orthodoxy of their methodology, Azizah al-Hibri is very concerned. She consciously strives to work within an Islamic idiom: "It would have been easier to dismiss the whole question on the basis that religion is a patriarchal tool. However, this is (a) giving too much to Patriarchy [and] (b) ignoring the sentiments of feminist Muslim women who find the problems raised above very real...."[57] Besides, as she says elsewhere, "Islam encourages such interpretation. And fighting within Islam can give women a powerful weapon. If you can argue that God is on your side, even the most misogynist of men, if they are devout, will have to take heed."[58] Azizah al-Hibri is not the only Islamic feminist to develop views in reliance on Fazlur Rahman's Islamic methodology. Amina Wadud-Muhsin's work on women in the Qur'ān also makes use of Fazlur Rahman's methodology.[59] No doubt, further works will appear in the same vein, for the goal is not a definitive interpretation, but as he repeatedly stressed, an ongoing effort "towards the progressive embodiment of the fundamental values of freedom and responsibility in fresh legislation"—for which Fazlur Rahman hoped to articulate an adequate hermeneutic.[60]

NOTES

1. *Chicago Sun-Times*, "Collapse of Islamic Fundamentalism Seen," 3/31/79.

2. *Ibid*.

3. As he put it in an interview in Chicago in 1979: "All the passages in the Qur'ān came out of a concrete situation. Whenever a special problem arose, Muhammad made a reply. The background for his reply is contained in the 'occasions of revelation.' It is my firm belief that modern Muslims must study the 'occasions'

because it is there that the dynamics of faith are found. The rationales, the reasons behind the laws, are the essence of the revelation." *Ibid.* Fazlur Rahman's fullest treatment of this approach may be found in his *Islamic Methodology in History* (Karachi: Central Institute of Islamic Research, 1965) and *Islam and Modernity: Transformation of an Intellectual Tradition* (Chicago: The University of Chicago Press, 1982).

4. "Collapse of Islamic Fundamentalism Seen," *Chicago Sun-Times*, 3/31/79.

5. *Ibid.* See also Fazlur Rahman, *Major Themes of the Qur'ān* (Minneapolis: Bibliotheca Islamica, 1980), pp. 40–41.

6. Despite occasional usage of the terms "interpretation" and "hermeneutic" interchangeably, there is a difference between the two. When, for example, C. du P. le Roux discusses "Hermeneutics—Islam and the South African Context" (*Journal of Islamic Studies* 8 [1988]: 23–28 and 9 [1989]: 48–54), he uses the term in the same way that Seyyed Vali Reza Nasr uses "interpretation" in "Islamic Opposition to the Islamic State: The Jama'at-i Islami, 1978–1988" (*International Journal of Middle East Studies*, 25 [1993]: 261–83). Both discuss specific interpretations and issues that have influenced those interpretations, but neither discusses the actual interpretive methodologies involved, that is, the formal elements or mechanics of interpretation.

7. See, e.g., 'Abd Allāh al-'Arwī, *Al-'Arab wa al-Fikr al-Tārīkhī* (Beirut: Dār al-Haqīqa, 1973) and *The Crisis of the Arab Intellectual: Traditionalism or Historicism?* (Berkeley: University of California Press, 1976), translated from French by Diarmid Cammell as Abdallah Laroui, *La crise des intellectuels arabes: traditionalisme ou historicisme?* (Paris: Librairie François Maspero, 1974). See also Mohammed Arkoun, *La Pensée arabe* (Paris: Presses Universitaires de France, 1979), translated from French by Ādil al-'Awwā as Muhammad Arkun, *Al-Fikr al-'Arabī* (Beirut: Manshūrat 'Uwaydāt, 1983); and Mohammed Arkoun et Louis Gardet, *L'Islam: Hier-Demain* (Paris: Editions Buchet/Chastel, 1978), translated from French by 'Alī al-Muqallid, Muhammad Arkun and Louis Gardet, *Al-Islam: al-Ams wa al-Ghad* (Beirut: Dār al-Tanwīr, 1983). Hasan Hanafi, *Les Methodes d'exégese: Essai sur la science de Fondements de la Comprehension 'Ilm Usūl al Fiqh* (Cairo, Conseil Superieur des Arts, des Lettres et des Sciences Sociales, 1965) and *Al-Turāth wa al-Tajdīd: Mawqifunā min al-Turāth al-Qadīm* (Beirut: Dār al-Tanwīr, 1981).

8. "Islamization of Knowledge" is the approach generally attributed to Isma'il al-Faruqi (d. 1986) and carried on by the International Institute of Islamic Thought, Herndon, Virginia. See I.R. Faruqi, *Islamization of Knowledge* (Herndon, VA: International Institute of Islamic Thought, 1982) and F. Rahman, "Islamization of

Knowledge: A Response" *The American Journal of Islamic Social Sciences*, 5/1 (1988):3-11.

9. Fazlur Rahman, *Islam and Modernity*, p. 9. Here he is describing what he believes to be the essence of Gadamer's hermeneutical theory, in his notion of an individual's "effective history, that is, not only the historical influence of the object of investigation, but the totality of other influences that make up the very texture of my being."

10. *Ibid.*, p. 8.

11. *Ibid.*, p. 11.

12. See Tamara Sonn, "Fazlur Rahman's Islamic Methodology" in *Muslim World*, 81/3–4 (1991): 212–230, *Interpreting Islam* (Oxford: Oxford University Press, 1996).

13. See Jane Dammen McAuliffe, "Quranic Hermeneutics: The View of al-Tabari (d. 1323 c.e.) and Ibn Kathir (d. 1373 c.e.)" in *Approaches to the History of the Interpretation of the Qur'ān*, ed. Andrew Rippin (Oxford: Clarendon Press, 1988), pp. 46–62.

14. See, for example, Fazlur Rahman, *Islam*, Second edition (Chicago: The University of Chicago Press, 1979), pp. 37ff.

15. *Ibid.*, p. 38.

16. Fazlur Rahman, *Major Themes*, p. 38.

17. Fazlur Rahman, *Islam and Modernity*, pp. 7–8.

18. *Ibid.*, p. 26.

19. *Ibid.*, p. 18.

20. Fazlur Rahman, *Major Themes*, p. 47. Emphasis in the original.

21. *Ibid.*

22. *Ibid.*

23. Azizah Y. al-Hibri, "Islamic Constitutionalism and the Concept of Democracy" in *Case Western Reserve Journal of International Law*, 24/1 (1992). Reprinted as pamphlet by the American Muslim Foundation, p. 3.

24. *Ibid.*

25. *Ibid.*, p. 4.

26. *Ibid.*

27. *Ibid*, p. 5.

28. *Ibid.* Fazlur Rahman does discuss the question of ijtihad in collecting the various reports that ultimately comprised the record of the Sunna, but in a different context from that of al-Hibri. See his *Islamic Methodology in History*, chapters 1 and 2, "Concepts *Sunnah, Ijtihad* and *Ijma'* in the Early Period" and "Sunnah and Hadith."

29. Azizah Y. al-Hibri, "Islamic Constitutionalism," p. 5.

30. *Ibid.*

31. *Ibid.*, p. 7: Al-Hibri further cites the traditionally recognized qualifications of a mujtahid—rationality, maturity, morality, piety and knowledge of the literature, the facts and the applicable modes of reasoning. She also notes that the Shi'i views on ijtihad differ from the Sunni, but claims, "At this level of discussion, there are no significant differences between the two views that are worth focusing upon, nor do these differences alter the conclusions reached in this article."

32. *Ibid.*, p. 6.

33. *Ibid.*, p. 7.

34. *Ibid.*, p. 10.

35. *Ibid.*, p.8.

36. Azizah al-Hibri, "A Study of Islamic Herstory: Or How Did We Ever Get into this Mess?" *Women's Studies International Forum*, 5/2 (1982): 214.

37. Quoted in Judith Miller, "Women Regain a Kind of Security in Islam's Embrace." *New York Times*, 12/27/92.

38. Azizah al-Hibri, "A Study of Islamic Herstory," *op. cit.*, p. 207. Emphasis in the original.

39. Here al-Hibri expresses agreement with arguments developed in Sobhi Mahmassani, *Al-Awdā' al-Tashrī'īyya fī'l-Duwal al-'Arabīyyah* (Beirut: Dar al-'Ilm li'l-Malayin, 1965).

40. Azizah al-Hibri, "A Study of Islamic Herstory," *op. cit.*, p. 208.

41. *Ibid.*, p. 209.

42. This argument is more fully developed in Azizah Y. al-Hibri, "Capitalism Is an Advanced Stage of Patriarchy; But Socialism Is Not Feminism," *Women and Revolution*, Lydia Sargent, ed. (Boston: South End Press, 1981).

43. Azizah al-Hibri, "A Study of Islamic Herstory," *op. cit.*, p. 211.

44. *Ibid.*, p. 212.

45. *Ibid.*, pp. 212–13.

46. *Ibid.*, p. 213. Before continuing, it is important to clarify what we mean by patriarchy. Al-Hibri does not define it, but her analyses seems consistent with those of one of the foremost scholars of patriarchalism, Gerda Lerner. In *The Creation of Patriarchy* Lerner describes patriarchy as "the manifestation and institutionalization of male dominance over women and children in the family and the extension of male dominance over women in society in general." Gerda Lerner, *The Creation of Patriarchy*, (Oxford: Oxford University Press, 1986) p. 23. Lerner is careful to point out that patriarchy "implies that men hold power in all the important institutions of society and that women are deprived of access to such power. It does *not* imply that women are either totally powerless or totally deprived of rights, influence, and resources." (*Ibid.* Emphasis in the original.)

47. Azizah al-Hibri, "A Study of Islamic Herstory," *op. cit.*, p. 215.

48. *Ibid.*, 215. Al-Hibri is here quoting from Widad Sakakini, *Insāf al-Mar'ah (The Equality of Women)* (Damascus: Thabat Press, 1950), pp. 12–30.

49. Azizah al-Hibri, "A Study of Islamic Herstory," p. 215.

50. *Ibid.*, 216.

51. *Ibid.* The Qur'ānic verses in question: "Marry women of your choice, two or three or four; but if you fear that you shall not deal justly [with them], then only one...." (4:3) and "You are never able to be fair and just among women, even if you tried hard...." (4:129)

52. *Ibid*, p. 217.

53. *Ibid.*

54. *Ibid.*, p. 219. Al-Hibri cites Nazirah Zayn al-Din, *al-Sufūr w'al-Hijāb* [Unveiling and the Veil] (Beirut n.p., 1928) and adds the emphasis.

55. Fazlur Rahman, *Major Themes*, p. 38.

56. Al-Hibri has expanded on some of these issues, particularly political organization, in "Islamic Constitutionalism and the Concept of Democracy."

57. Azizah al-Hibri, "A Study of Islamic Herstory," p. 219.

58. Quoted by Judith Miller, "Women Regain a Kind of Security."

59. Amina Wadud Muhsin, *The Qur'ān and Woman* (Kuala Lumpur: Penerbit Fajar Bakti SDN.BHD., 1992).

60. See Fazlur Rahman, *Islam*, p. 38.

Chapter 7

INTERPRETATIONS OF FAMILY PLANNING: RECONCILING ISLAM AND DEVELOPMENT

Donna Lee Bowen

The need for economic and social development has brought policies first conceived in Western nations to the Muslim world. Adapting Western programs to Middle Eastern and Muslim needs has at times seemed an uneasy fit. Spokesmen for Islam argue that care for the moral well-being of society should be a paramount concern. They emphasize that the West, by adopting wholescale secularization and emphasizing individual rights to the exclusion of community needs, has compromised the welfare of families. Muslims have asserted that in the long run they can develop their societies more effectively than the West because of the religiously-derived strength of the social and moral fabric. Implicit in this argument is the sense that Islam is adaptable to modern exigencies and that Muslims would adopt programs which guaranteed a better life for their families.

This raises the conundrum of whether development and modernization are compatible with religious values and practice. Can religions revealed centuries or millennia ago respond to contemporary needs? What if the contemporary needs run against the grain of long-accepted community practice? Can adherence to the principles found in the Qur'ān and elaborated in Islamic law ease these adjustments? In this paper I wish to discuss one area of development planning that has proven crucial for the economic well-being of many Muslim states, and one that was of particular interest to Fazlur Rahman—family planning—and the fit of family planning with Muslims' pro-natalist expectations and the cultural norms to which Muslims adhere. Some citizens of Muslim countries have been highly resistant to family planning; others have approached family planning programs with caution. One method of resistance was to condemn the practice as un-Islamic or declare that Islam prohibited the practice. Over time, Western economic planners and development experts have wondered to what extent Islam itself was a factor in popular resistance against family planning.

This paper takes up the question of how individual Muslims resolve the issues brought up by development—here narrowed to the question of family planning—and their religion. During my research on family planning in Morocco from 1993 to 1995, I met and discussed family planning with Moroccan professionals, all Muslims, none of them graduates of specialized study programs in the Islamic sciences. These men and women supplied their perspective on the role of Islam in development, especially in terms of family planning programs. In particular, they formulated a method which enables a Muslim to extrapolate from principles of his/her religion to analyze a subject not specifically dealt with in revelation. Family planning is an appropriate area of study in this context because of the inherent contradictions between the traditional pressures to procreate, the love of parents for children and desire to have progeny, and contemporary financial pressures to limit family size to two or three children. The pressures which individuals address also operate on a national level. Each country needs a strong, trained work force, but also can face economic and social difficulties when population numbers overpower the ability of the state to provide expected services for its citizens.

Population growth rates in Muslim countries range from 1.9% in Tunisia to 4.9% in Oman.[1] The need of some countries to lower their growth rates has spurred interest in family planning programs. Bilateral and multilateral international associations have worked with Middle Eastern administrators to develop feasible and cost-effective programs to enable men and women to understand the concept of family planning and to have access to the means of avoiding pregnancy if it fits their family needs. Some countries, such as Tunisia, Egypt, Morocco, Indonesia and Iran, have seen a need to foster family planning programs. Other countries, such as Saudi Arabia, Syria, Iraq, Yemen and Palestine, have not built a national family program and leave dispersal of contraceptives solely to the private sector. For the most part, nations with populations that are large in relation to their resource bases and with a large prospective labor force have been more likely to develop family planning programs than those with a small labor force and healthy economies who often need to import labor. Since family planning programs were introduced in the Muslim world over a quarter of a century ago, many nations—including Tunisia, Algeria, Morocco, Egypt, Turkey, Lebanon and Indonesia—have shown a marked increase in the number of families employing family planning methods. However, these countries are still working to bring their population growth rates down further to targeted goals.

The slow growth in contraceptive prevalence among Muslims has given rise to a number of questions: Given the traditional pro-natalist stance in the Muslim world, does the religion itself forbid use of family planning measures? Do Muslims believe that Islam forbids use of family planning measures and therefore hesitate to utilize them? To what extent can the low contraceptive usage figures and high population growth rates in Muslim countries be attributed to Islamic beliefs? Are Muslims influenced by the statements of local religious leaders regarding family planning use? Do education programs have any impact on people's understanding of how Islam relates to contemporary issues?

This paper takes up these questions from the point of view of Moroccan Muslim professional men who deal both explicitly and implicitly with questions of the application of Islamic principles to practical issues which concern personal health and family well-being in their work. In their discussions, they take on the interrelationship of Islam and development by addressing the issue of Islam and family planning.

FAMILY PLANNING AND ISLAM

Questions raised by use of family planning provide an opportunity to apply Islamic values to development issues. At first glance, family planning and the use of contraceptives challenge long-held customs of both the Muslim community and Muslim families. Islamic law supported the Middle Eastern customary practice of encouraging large families. The strength of any political community was and is determined to a large extent by population numbers. Likewise, family vitality centers on procreation; the status of both the husband and the wife depend upon production of children, specifically sons. Failure of the wife to bear children traditionally has resulted in her repudiation or the husband taking an additional wife. Contrary to popular beliefs, however, Islamic law does not require a man to marry or a couple to bear children if the husband is unable to support that responsibility financially. Religiously, both marriage and children are strongly recommended, and in social terms the pressure to marry and have children is intense. But it is social and economic considerations, as well as cultural expectations and human desires, rather than religious teaching, that emphasize the necessity of marriage and children for both men and women.

Various studies have traced Islam's position on family planning.[2] The practice of *wa'd* (female infanticide) was banned in the Qur'ān. A study of the fiqh (legal) literature demonstrates that contraceptive methods were known and condoned before the time of Prophet Muhammad. Islamic jurisprudence, drawing on the hadith (traditional) literature, establishes the precedent of *'azl (coitus interruptus)* which was used among the Arabs and was not prohibited by the Prophet.

Reasoning from the fiqh precedents, many contemporary 'ulamā' have held that just as 'azl is permitted, methods developed by modern science which have the same effect as 'azl, the temporary avoidance of impregnation, are also permitted.[3] Most 'ulamā' agree, however, that any measures which permanently prevent childbirth (such as methods of male or female sterilization) or which are considered as killing the fetus (abortion) are prohibited by Islam.

Support of the 'ulamā' has been welcome, if not crucial, for nations like Morocco which are working to lower their birth rate. 'Ulamā' support, however, has not eliminated all concerns as to the religious permissibility of contraception. While the 'ulamā' speak to the well-educated and, in essence, set the policy position of official Islamic pronouncements, local Muslim leaders in towns and villages speak to the less well-educated rural populations. These less-educated religious leaders feed beliefs that family planning is un-Islamic and religiously prohibited by their strident opposition to contraception measures. As a result of their cursory education in Islamic sciences and lack of experience with the complex sources of Islamic fiqh, they draw conclusions diametrically opposed to those of the 'ulamā'. Reasoning from ahadith such as, "Marry, have children and multiply so I may be proud of you on Judgement Day," many local religious leaders hold that family planning—or preventing pregnancy—is forbidden by Islam.

Some men pick up on the ideas of local religious leaders. Few rural villagers, or even urban residents packed into lower-class housing tenements around the edges of large cities, have recourse to scholars of religion to advise them on technical aspects of religious permissibility. This grants local religious leaders inordinate power in influencing opinions. In rural areas opposition is still more pronounced than in urban areas where contraceptive use is increasingly common. Many men, but few women, would tell family planning workers that contraception is forbidden in Islam. According to one professional I interviewed, who is currently involved in family planning in Morocco, "They say that contraception kills the fetus—thus contraception is murder—just as abortion is. We tell them it isn't, but they don't accept it. When we explain family planning thoroughly to a woman and show how it applies to her life, she usually says 'Fine. Give me some.'" Also, while women are more inclined to experiment with contraception in general, they seek the approval of their husbands. When visiting nurses offer contraceptive pills to rural women whose circumstances indicate their use may be welcome, I found that many answer, "I don't know. You'll have to speak to my husband." (This has become far less prevalent in recent years although the excuse of deference to husbands is still common in rural areas.) These areas of customary practice and belief, whether termed religious or not, can prove to be decisive in determining contraceptive usage patterns.

MOROCCAN REALITIES

The need for family planning has become particularly urgent as the "Moroccan baby boomer" segment of the population has reached adulthood and begun their families. The problem is bound to become worse in the future. Of 30 million Moroccans, 40% are under the age of 15. Even if Morocco reduces its birth rate further, population estimates for 2020 range from a low of 40.5 million to a high of 54.5 million.[4] Currently, unemployment rates run around 30%. Up to 98% of university graduates in the humanities and social sciences experience a year or two of unemployment before finding a position—often one not commensurate with their educational preparation. Provision of an infrastructure which will address the needs of this growing population already levies considerable demands on the government which it is not able to provide satisfactorily.

Morocco has recently achieved noteworthy results in increasing family planning usage. For many years it was regarded as a slow-starter, and many felt religion was a factor in popular disinterest in family planning. From the mid- to late-1960s to the early 1970s Morocco's population growth ranged from 3.0% to 3.3%. This level of growth spurred technocrats and development experts into emphasizing the relevance of family planning to Moroccan development planning. For political reasons, the national government was hesitant to pursue a national program, but individuals working with both Moroccan health services and international groups began laying the groundwork for nationwide family planning services. By 1995, the Moroccan Family Planning Office, working within the context of Maternal and Child Health programs in the Ministry of Public Health, succeeded in increasing public awareness and acceptance of family planning, bettering both infant and maternal health, bringing down infant mortality rates and lowering the rate of natural increase to 2.2%. By 1995 50% of Moroccan women between 15 and 49 years of age used contraceptives. The effect of family planning programs has been felt notably in urban areas where the contraceptive prevalence rate reached 64%. The rural contraceptive use rate rose to 39%.[5]

Much of the success in increasing family planning use is not only due to increased availability and publicity, but to attention given to cultural sensibilities. The Moroccan health infrastructure carefully designed the family planning program to be sensitive to Moroccan feelings about Islam, family and procreation. Rather than presenting family planning as preventing births, the government emphasized its use in spacing children. It also promulgated religious rulings that both abortion and sterilization were contrary to Islam and not acceptable means of family planning, while contraception was.

FOUR PERSPECTIVES ON RELIGION AND FAMILY PLANNING

Fazlur Rahman once observed that education systems operate as a considerable detriment to the possibility of developing programs which both facilitate development but also reflect Islamic values. Most educational systems in the Muslim world operate along either of two tracks, he said: secular education for professional (Western) styles of training, and the traditional Islamic system for training in Islamic sciences. The educational program which trains an engineer or an economist, for example, is sufficiently heavy to preclude having time for classes in religious studies. The opposite is also true. To become learned in religious sciences requires full time study through graduate school in order to utilize the sources with skill and ability. Thus, Fazlur Rahman concluded we will see few engineers or physicians with sufficient background in religious sciences to allow them to synthesize both areas of study with real expertise. While Fazlur Rahman's argument has important ramifications for the spread of Islamic activism, my interviews for this article indicate that there are exceptions to his argument. At least in the case of highly educated Moroccans, Muslims with specific interests in Islam's relation to social problems demonstrate considerable expertise in applying Islamic principles to their specialized fields of concern.

For this article, I discussed demographic and social issues with Moroccan physicians, administrators, demographers, nurses and university professors. In many cases, the discussion moved to the permissibility of family planning and the place of contraceptive programs in the Muslim community. These discussions centered on the definition of family planning and whether Islam permits its use.

Four principles pertaining to the relation of Islam and development emerged from the interviews. First, Islam is a religion responsive to social needs and individual welfare. Second, Islam is both implicitly and explicitly committed to development, in the sense of working for the best interests of Muslims. Third, while the texts of Islam are vital points to work from, the application of reason is critical in working through contemporary questions. Fourth, Islamic principles must be separated from traditional cultural practices; what has been practiced over the years should not be taken necessarily as religious truth.

In the following section, I present the views of four professional Moroccan men—none with ties to any Islamist group—who work in areas related to family planning: family law, medicine and administration. All four were trained in secular institutions, and none received any specialized religious educational training. Dr. Moulay Taher Alaoui, currently the Dean of the College of Medicine in Rabat, began working with family planning issues as a young physician in the mid-1960s. He headed the Moroccan Family Planning office in the mid-1970s. Dr. Rachid Amiry, a physician in Tetouan, heads the local branch of the Moroccan Association for Planned Parenthood, an affiliate of the

International Planned Parenthood Federation. Moheiddine el-Fartakh, a recent university graduate, is an administrator for the Tangier office of the Moroccan Association for Planned Parenthood. Dr. Ahmad Kamlishi is a professor in the College of Law at Mohammad V University, Rabat. The interviews were conducted separately, over the time span of four months. For the purpose of this article I have interspersed comments from each and organized their points by subject matter.

WHAT IS FAMILY PLANNING?

When asked to evaluate family planning (*tanzīm al-'usra*[6]), Kamlishi focused on the term *tanzīm* (planning or organization) and answered with a question: "What do you mean planning? If there isn't order there is chaos." Kamlishi emphasized that order is a concept integral to Islam. Other Moroccans have stressed that the terminology used was crucial to public acceptance of family planning. Amiry noted that the concept of imposing order on a family came naturally to Muslims. For example, Muslims are enjoined to perform their prayers in a given order and at certain times of the day. Likewise, families can benefit from a sense of planning or order. Muslims see families as the means of structuring society into orderly units. Threats to families are indicative of disordering of society which explains why any matter which involves family make-up becomes controversial. Individual actions such as adultery trigger heavy penalties because they undermine family structure and threaten to replace social order with chaos.

Amiry emphasized the importance of family in Islam. "Families are sacred in Islam. As they are vital, we need a system to care for families." A reference for ordering families comes from the verses in the Qur'ān which enjoins mothers to nurse infants for two whole years (2:233). Many 'ulamā' take this injunction as advocacy of natural means of birth control—preventing pregnancy while the infant takes nourishment from the mother and while the mother regains strength.

Alaoui argued further legal analogies based upon classical Islamic jurisprudence. He drew on the Sunna of the Prophet Muhammad wherein Muhammad indicates that *coitus interruptus* or *'azl* is acceptable practice for Muslims. Thus, reasoning by analogy *(qiyās)* family planning methods are acceptable. This position summarizes the rationale used by the 'ulamā' in permitting non-permanent contraceptive usage. Working from this position, they hold that it is for the wife and husband to determine their needs and that of their family and act accordingly, employing family planning as a means to further the welfare of the family.

Kamlishi took a different tack and argued from a societal perspective that Islamic permission for family planning is not set in stone—that it is impossible to state whether family planning is prohibited or permitted without investigating specific national cases. In his reasoning, permissibility is keyed to time and place. As the condition of Muslims and of Muslim communities differs in Bangladesh and in Saudi Arabia, so should their response to family planning. "In Bangladesh we cannot say that family planning is not necessary, because it is, given their conditions of life." Given other circumstances, say in Saudi Arabia, it may not be. Following wars, he added, often nations emphasize pro-natalist policies to rebuild a devastated community. He added that there is no basis for people to say it is forbidden. Instead, people should ask what is in the best interests *(maslaha)* of the community in this time and place. As for Morocco, there is no question that its use is appropriate, given Moroccan circumstances of low literacy, unemployment and high birthrates. "Family planning is necessary in Morocco."

The Moroccan health infrastructure has been careful to delineate the scope of family planning, defining it as a means to better the health of the mother, and to space, not limit births. At the same time that contraceptive methods are advocated, abortion and sterilization are not considered means of family planning and are only prescribed when the mother's health is endangered. Alaoui noted that both the religious and health systems agree that the life of the mother is given precedence to the life of the child. The importance of life and the possibility of giving birth are balanced by concerns for parental rights and traditional family structure. An example is that, according to Alaoui, *in vitro* fertilization is permitted, but only if the sperm of the husband and the egg of the wife are employed. In Islam, conception is to be restricted to the family unit in an absolute sense, whether within or outside the womb.

RIZQ AND GOD'S WILL

Two of the most effective theological arguments used by opponents of family planning concern *rizq* and the will of God. The two are intertwined in many minds. Rizq refers to the idea that God will provide sustenance for humankind if they trust sufficiently in His power. "God will provide for whom He will" (3:37). Reliance on God's will (*'irāda*) often prompts deterministic thinking. Many debates over the meaning of rizq question the form and extent of God's rizq and to what degree God's will determines our actions. Local religious leaders *(tolba)* generally assert that use of family planning is unlawful because people deny the efficacy of God's will by attempting to circumvent God's desire that a woman be impregnated. In addition, contraceptive measures used for economic reasons repudiate God's promise to care for all his creations.

In an attempt to better educate local religious leaders on issues of family planning, 'ulamā' have organized information sessions and seminars on family planning. They are designed to counter traditionalists' opposition to family planning. El-Fartakh and Amiry attended the sessions held in the Tangier and Tetouan regions and reported on the discussions. They reported that traditionalist tolba believe Islam forbids contraception, and that they have their belief on the hadith, "Marry, procreate and multiply, that I will be proud of you on Judgment Day." Three points emerge from this hadith. First is the importance of marriage and having children. The second point is the question of God's will being observed; and third, the question of God's approbation on Judgment Day. A related issue, inherent in the hadith but undetermined by its content, is the question of what is meant by multiply. Should a certain number of children be produced by a given family?

At the beginning of a seminar, a group of tolba attacked the primary reason for the seminar as a justification for family planning and asserted that bearing children is dependent upon God's will. The 'alim directing the seminar countered with an agricultural argument bearing on questions of order which implicitly concern issues of God's will. "Your gardens and fields benefit from irrigation. But God himself didn't make dams and block up streams of water for this purpose, man did. Following your reasoning, we shouldn't build dams since it is not God's will. If you maintain that it is against God's will to imprison man's sperm so it cannot reach the egg to prevent pregnancy, why should man be permitted to imprison water—another gift of God's *baraka* [blessing]—for his own purposes?"

Different definitions of the meaning of rizq are critical to this debate. Does God's promise to provide for humankind mean that no effort on people's part is necessary? Or are people to contribute to their sustenance through the God-given abilities of physical strength, speech, and reasonable sensibility? Proponents of family planning argue that children cost money and the expense of providing for children is sufficient reason to limit the size of one's family. Opponents of family planning would contend that no economic excuse is sufficient to limit one's family size. God has promised to sustain his creations and faith in his so doing is necessary. Amiry recounted an argument with a faqīh (legal scholar) who quoted him the above hadith. He then said that this hadith tells us to have children. "But you tell us to have fewer children. What is the answer?" Amiry quotes his reply: "Have children with some order, with some planning. The Prophet doesn't give us any fixed number of children to have. If we have two children we produced an increase *(takāthur)*. Even to have one child is to increase by one person."

These points are argued often and heatedly whenever family planning is discussed. Family planning proponents suggest various arguments to undermine the anti-family planning position. Alaoui addressed this problem with a popular story from the hadith literature. "An Arab comes to the Prophet Muhammad after visiting a mosque to pray. He says, 'I came to pray and left my camel outside, trusting in God. The camel has wandered off. Will God compensate me?' The Prophet replies, 'Trust in God, but tie your camel.'"

QUANTITY OF CHILDREN VERSUS QUALITY OF CHILDREARING

Other economic arguments come up frequently. One that is deeply imbedded in Islam is the importance of providing sufficiently for one's family. Just as marriage is not obligatory in Islam and is predicated upon a man's having sufficient means to marry, neither is having children an obligation. Instead, parents are expected to be financially able to support a family. Alaoui, Amiry and el-Fartakh observed that if we read the verses in the Qur'ān which speak of children closely, we see that in each instance where we are told of the value of children, the importance of wealth is also mentioned. For example, "Property and children are the beauty of earthly life." (18:46) In this verse, the order of the subject clause is noteworthy: wealth precedes children. Amiry stated, "If one has ten children, but lacks the means to take care of them, this is against religion." The professionals stressed that the intent of these verses is not to emphasize materialist values above human concerns. The message is rather to underscore the importance of providing for children as well as giving birth to them. Alaoui insisted that Muslims must be able to live in security—physical, financial, and economic. El-Fartakh recounted a telling analogy which was introduced by the 'alim giving the major address at the family planning seminar for tolba. He spoke as if to a married couple: "Here is an apple. Both you and your wife divide the apple and take one-half each. A year passes and you are blessed with a child. I present you with another apple. This time we divide the apple in thirds. You won't eat as well, but still have enough. Next year, with the addition of a second child we divide the apple in fourths; the next year in fifths. Soon, as your family increases to six or seven children, you've divided the apple into such small slices that no one eats well."

In the 1960s, Mahmoud Shaltout, the rector of al-Azhar University, was one of the first prominent 'ulamā' to support the use of family planning. His rationale was akin to that presented by Kamlishi above, that Islam should respond to the needs of the Muslim community. Shaltout observed that a nation already burdened by the costs engendered by a large population would be weakened by additional births. He explained that a nation's strength can be measured by numbers as long as the numbers contribute to the well-being of the community. The situation in Egypt had passed that point; additional numbers sapped community might instead of strengthening it. The upshot of his argument was the question he posed of whether the quantity of the population was undermining the quality of the population. Kamlishi, Amiry, and el-Fartakh each separately pursued this argument. El-Fartakh quoted the hadith, "Marry, procreate and multiply that I may be proud of you on Judgement Day." He then asked, "Did the Prophet say here that he is going to be proud of the number of children we produce? Is he going to be proud of the children if their parents can't rear them well? Is he going to be proud of thieves, of drug users if we don't bring them up well? The Prophet wants Muslims who are well brought up, who do good work, who are schooled well. So why are we having so many children? Isn't it better to have two or three children and train them, school them, bring them up well? Is not that better than twenty children who end up in prison?" He continued, "Any blessing needs to be appreciated in moderation. Too much of a good thing can become a problem for us. For example, we need rain this year in Morocco, so rain for us is very important. But if we have too much rain, then it ceases to be a blessing and becomes a curse. So it is with children. They are a blessing, a wonderful thing for us to enjoy. But if we have so many that we cannot care for them, what do we do? Just as we channel rain into canals and dams in order to use it well, so we need to see birth control pills or IUDs as dams to regulate births so neither reaches flood stage."

Amiry and el-Fartakh brought up two final components of an economic analysis which are little mentioned in scholarly discussions but spoken of often in general conversation. The first concerns the staying power of families. In the past decade, with the lowering of infant mortality, the conventional wisdom of keeping the husband with the family has changed. Amiry notes that children used to be the means of keeping marriages together. "Now they are becoming a cause of divorce. In the past, a woman who did not bear her husband sons could expect divorce or perhaps a second wife. Accordingly, women bore children unceasingly, wanting to both have sons and to ensure that whatever children died in infancy, others would grow to support their parents in old age. Today, at least in the city, expectations are changing. Husbands want to return home from work to their small apartment to find a calm and quiet household, their wife supervising no more than three children in their studies. Men emphasize that large families both drain the father's pocketbook and his patience; smart wives who wish to keep their husbands hesitate to have large families, fearing that the confusion and frustration will drive him away."

Amiry, in bringing up the second point, repeats an argument made by al-Ghazālī in *Ihyā' 'Ulūm al-Dīn (Revivification of the Religious Sciences).* Childbirth drains a woman's physical resources and repeated childbirth, without sufficient time for her body to regain strength, adversely affects the mother's health. Al-Ghazālī demonstrated concern for the woman's beauty as well and declared that it was legal to use contraceptive measures to preserve a woman's beauty. Although in al-Ghazālī's analysis it was the husband's decision to avoid procreation or not for this purpose, Amiry extended the argument. As a woman wishes to be beautiful for her husband, he said, she is justified in using family planning for this purpose.

ISLAM'S APPROACH TO FAMILY AND SOCIAL ISSUES

All four men stressed the compatibility of Islam with new ways of thinking, new practices, new medical advances—with one important caveat. In their discussions they repeatedly emphasized the welfare of Muslims and the importance both of understanding revelation and utilizing it to live a good life. Alaoui addressed this point explicitly and underlined the openness of Islam to programs that facilitate Muslims' lives. It is, he says, a tenet of Islamic philosophy to make things easier, not to oppress. He expanded his argument into social terms, stating that Islam inherently values the individual. Accordingly, each should live in security, both in terms of health and finances.

CONCLUSIONS

These discussions on family planning illustrate the possibility of applying Islamic principles to contemporary realities. The points brought up by Alaoui, Amiry, el-Fartakh and Kamlishi document their belief that Islam must be responsive to social needs. They concurred that Islam is both implicitly and explicitly committed to development in the sense of bettering living conditions for both men and women. They noted that contraception is seen as analogous to *'azl* and is judged permissible. Moroccan 'ulamā' generally agree with this interpretation.[7] This permissibility hinges on a form of *ijtihād,* an application of reason to legal sources (Qur'ān, hadith). The analogies by which they attempted to make their convictions more accessible to lesser-educated audiences also demonstrated the employment of reasonable thought stemming from generally agreed-upon religious principles.

Overall, the focus of the discussions was on separating religious teaching from traditional practice. Although custom can have the force of law in Islam, customary beliefs and practices can at times confound Islamic principles and the use of family planning is a good case in point. Traditionally, Muslims have encouraged large family size and this custom has taken on normative value. In order to sanction smaller families, activists have had the task of proving that this is compatible with Islamic law.

Education has been a crucial variable in explaining the positions which Moroccan religious leaders take on family size and composition. Well-educated religious leaders tend to advocate flexibility for the parents in determining family size. On a personal level, education is the single most significant variable which signals smaller family size in the Third World. The better educated the mother and the father, the greater chance their family will be small.[8] Education—both in the sense of schooling and in the sense of upbringing *(tarbīya)*—is also the means of communicating different ways of understanding family planning and different ways of presenting religious attitudes towards family planning to both local level religious leaders and the parents themselves. Moroccans also understand education to be a crucial component of social mobility. As Moroccan parents speak of their desires for their children, all focus on their children's future education, to enable them both to be worthwhile individuals and to gain respectable occupations. As Amiry and el-Fartakh defined good Muslims and a worthwhile upbringing, they focused repeatedly upon the importance of education.

None of the four men featured above graduated from a university or graduate school of Islamic religious studies (although Dr. Kamlishi's specialization in Moroccan private law required him gain expertise in aspects of Islamic law). The Moroccan debate on family planning included lectures by 'ulamā' on the religious legality of contraceptive usage. The professional work of Drs. Alaoui and Amiry and Mr. el-Fartakh's work for the Moroccan Association for Family Planning led each to specialized study of Islamic strictures on family planning. All four have done their homework on this subject and el-Fartakh in particular had employment incentives to master the subject. The information on classical Islamic jurisprudence and its contemporary applications benefits them in their work. It is important today when Muslim "fundamentalism" dominates the news, to recognize that approaches to Islam exist which seek religiously-sympathetic avenues to working constructively and progressively with contemporary issues. All four men emphasized the importance of Islamic input into social programs; none assumed that Islam should be downplayed or ignored. Each was unreserved in his conviction that no social program can be implemented unless it is in accord with the principles and practices of Islam. Attempts to ignore the vital place of Islam in the Moroccan community would doom a program to lack of popular support and, when it concerned areas traditionally associated with family questions, to failure.

NOTES

1. Population Reference Bureau, "World Population Data Sheet 1995," Washington D.C.

2. Sources which speak of Islam and family planning include Olivia Shiefflien, compiler and editor, *Muslim Attitudes Toward Family Planning* (New York: The Population Council, 1967); The International Planned Parenthood Federation, *Islam and Family Planning,* 2 vol. (Beirut: The International Planned Parenthood Federation, 1974); Basim F. Musallam, *Sex and Society in Islam* (Cambridge: Cambridge University Press, 1983); Abdel Rahim Omran, *Family Planning in the Legacy of Islam* (Cairo, 1988; London & New York: Routledge, 1992); Donna Lee Bowen, *Islam and Family Planning* (Washington, D.C.: World Bank; Europe, Middle East and North Africa Technical Department, Vol. 1 #1, 1991).

3. Although not all 'ulamā' have agreed upon the permissibility of contraception or family planning, the majority of classical jurists and the majority of contemporary jurists believe it permissible. For dissenting opinions see *Islam and Family Planning*. I note that, however, over time, many 'ulamā' originally opposed have changed their stances and do not object to family planning.

4. CERED, Direction de la Statistique, Royaume du Maroc, *Population l'an 2062* (Rabat, Morocco: Centre d'Études et de Recherches Demographiques, 1991), p. 264.

5. Kingdom of Morocco, Ministry of Public Health, "Population et santé de la mère et de l'enfant au Maroc: Résultats préliminaires de l'enquète nationale sur la population et la santé, Panel 1995. June 1995.

6. The terms used for family planning are *tanzīm al-'usra* or *takhtīt al-'ā'ila* which give the sense of planning or organization. The term, *tahdīd al-nasl,* or preventing birth (progeny), is avoided.

7. Donna Lee Bowen, "Islam and Family Planning in Morocco," *Maghreb Review* 3/10(1980): 20–29.

8. Susan H. Cochrane, *Fertility and Education: What Do We Really Know?* (Baltimore: The Johns Hopkins University Press, 1970).

PART IV.
SUFISM AND POETRY

Chapter 8

HEART-SECRET, INTIMACY AND AWE IN FORMATIVE SUFISM[1]

Michael A. Sells

It is not difficult to read in translation the masterworks of later Sufism. The works of Jalal al-Din Rumi, Farid al-Din 'Attar, and Ibn al-'Arabi are widely known and cherished, not only within Islam and among Islamicists, but within the world community generally.

Formative Sufism is another matter. Until very recently, the majority of the classic texts had not been critical editions. In general, the figures of formative Sufism can be divided into two categories. The first category consists of the "founders" of the tradition, such as Hasan al-Basri, Bistami, Junayd, Tustari, Dhu'al-Nun, Shibli, al-Hallaj, Muhasibi, Saqati, and Niffari—to name only a few examples. Many of these figures wrote little, and what they did write themselves has come down in rough condition, sometimes in the form of only one or two manuscripts. Much of what we know of them comes through the oral tradition as it was collected, codified, and analyzed by those in the second category: the expounders of Sufi thought, such as al-Sarraj, al-Sulami, Abu Talib al-Makki, Sahlaji, and al-Qushayri.[2] In many cases the picture of a given figure in one source will differ from the picture of the same figure in another source. Thus there are as many Bistami's as there are sources, and Sulami's Bistami differs from the Bistami of Qushayri or a later author like 'Attar.

In the Islamicist scholarly world, we are beginning to touch upon the brilliance and depth of this vast repertoire of literature. The story of formative Sufism, in both Islamicist Western and Islamic scholarship, has been characterized with simplifications and generalities: the division between "sober" Sufis such as Junayd, and allegedly "intoxicated" Sufis such as Bistami;[3] the scholarly dogma that Abu Hamid al-Ghazali was the first to create an intellectual synthesis between ritual Islam and Sufism;[4] the tendency to focus upon sensational incidents, such as the execution of al-Hallaj, without contextualizing such incidents through a close study of the writings of the Sufis themselves.[5]

With major new advances in our understanding of early Sufism,[6] a re-evaluation of the intricate terrain of formative Sufi literature and thought is an exciting one, but one that is not without its difficulties. Among the major difficulties is translation. I will be exploring the "translation" of early Sufi language on a number of levels, from the translator's task of rendering powerful and complex concepts into English with some of the grace of the original, to the larger issue of translation as a mode of interpretation.[7]

In the following pages, I have attempted to render into modern, poetic English the combination of dread and intimacy, constriction and expansion, dynamism and fixity that is at the heart of some of the more profound early Sufi sayings and writings. My critical comments will be limited to short discussions of each selection. The goal of this essay is to allow the poetic sections and the more discursive sections to explain and play off one another.

THE POETICS AND DIALECTICS OF AL-QUSHAYRI

In refinement of style, the ability to combine a searching discussion of the most difficult concepts with a lucid and readable exposition, and to successfully combine precise analysis and theatrical anecdote, there are few works in early Sufism that can rival the famous Treatise of Qushayri.[8]

Presented here are selections from Section Three of the Treatise on key Sufi terms and concepts.[9] Immediately apparent in this section is its intricate discursive texture. The analysis of each major concept is woven around the sayings of earlier Sufis, and we encounter the living oral tradition as it is preserved by a literary master who creates within his treatise, a subtle and powerful conversation among the early Sufis. Qushayri is particularly fond of the unattributed proverb, often introduced by the phrase "they say," "some say" or "someone said."[10] When Qushayri does cite named shaykhs (Sufi masters), his citations tend to cluster around a few figures; most frequently cited are Qushayri's teacher al-Daqqaq and al-Daqqaq's teacher, Sulami. The various proverbs and poetic verses are woven into a highly sophisticated analysis. A single term, such as *waqt* (moment) will be defined from various points of view, non-Sufi, and Sufi, and as each short essay progresses, deeper understandings of the term gradually unfold. In many cases, a term will undergo a progression through various meanings in one essay, only to be viewed in the following essay from the opposite point of view. Multiple reversals can and do occur within a single essay as a term is viewed positively, then negatively, and then in a manner that transcends both or takes both aspects up into a new term. This perspectivalism keeps the essay in a continual state of dynamic tension; no single static definition stands on its own.

Stylistic and emotive variation provides another element of surprise. The endings of individual sections can range from Junayd's unforgettable and searing account of the mystical states of *qabd* (constriction) and *bast* (expansion), to the comic episode of two Sufis who, carried away by the experience of ecstatic existentiality (*wujūd*), rip trees out by the roots and wrestle one another into submission in *wajd* combat. The closing episodes, often relating stories of strange behavior and miracles, condense and dramatize the previous, highly nuanced and sophisticated discussion in a story indelibly fixed in the reader's imagination.

There is far more involved here than the title "explanation of expressions" (*tafsīr alfāz*) might suggest. The discussion of each term does include an acknowledgement of the common meaning of the term and its basic semantic field, and a discussion of the various ways it is defined and employed by different groups of Sufis. Also included, however, is a probing analysis of the emotive and psychological ramifications of the concept, along with its moral and experiential dimensions; an analysis of the theological implications of the concept, with special attention to the classic tension between human free-agency and divine all-powerfulness; and a careful relation of the term and concept to the dimensions of the lyric (through poetry citations) and the dramatic (through extended anecdotes).

In addition to the multi-dimensional character of each essay in itself, the various essays are interconnected by both foreshadowing and retrospection. Frequently an essay will explain one term in terms of another not yet introduced;

or a later discussion of a new term will cause the reader to re-evaluate the understanding of a term previously introduced. Of course, any "dictionary" must explain one term through others, but Qushayri's treatise intensifies the sense that the key Sufi terms and concepts create an interdependent web of meaning in which each key work or nexus is made up of and dependent upon all the others. In this way, the treatise is not only a brilliant examination of Sufi concepts, but also an illustration of the dynamic and multi-perspectival character of Sufi discourse. The following selections focus upon the concepts of the moment, the concept of the "condition", and the conditions of constriction, expansion, intimacy, and awe.

SELECTIONS FROM QUSHAYRI'S *RISĀLA*

FROM THE INTERPRETATION OF SUFI EXPRESSIONS *(TAFSĪR ALFĀZ)*

THE MOMENT (*Waqt*)

Qushayri's exposition of the term waqt (moment, instant) is an explosive opening to this section of the treatise, with a searching discussion of the relationships among time, experience, and identity. In Sufism, the waqt is the period of the *hāl* (state, condition). There is constant progression through stages of intensity in both moments and states, aiming at a complete giving over of the self to each moment, as if that moment were the totality of one's existence.[11] A further element of the Sufi moment is the lack of self-will or choice (*ikhtiyār*). A moment comes upon the Sufi independent of any intention or deliberate effort, spontaneously. However, in this section, as throughout the *Treatise*, Qushayri is especially careful to stress that such radical spontaneity is never seen as an excuse to evade ritual obligations, such as the five prescribed prayers, and is never seen in contradiction with them. It is not by accident that Qushayri begins his essay on the twenty-seven central Sufi concepts with the "moment." The moment, a time-out-of-time within time, bringing of eschatological afterworld into the present, is the basis on which the Sufi psychology of the "states" (*ahwāl*) will be constructed.

Realized masters[12] employ the term "moment" (*waqt*) to refer to the relation between the anticipation of an event and the event's actual occurrence. Conversely, the actual occurrence can be considered the "moment" of the anticipated occurrence. You say, for example: "I'll meet you at the beginning of the month." The meeting is an anticipation. The beginning of the month is its actual occurrence. Thus, the beginning of the month is the moment of the meeting.

I heard the teacher Abu 'Ali al-Daqqaq, God's mercy upon him, say: "The moment is what you are in. If you are in the world, your moment is the world. If you are in the afterworld, your moment is the afterworld. If you are in happiness, your moment is happiness. If you are in sorrow, your moment is sorrow." By that he means that the moment is that which dominates a person.[13]

Some people mean by the moment the time in which a person happens to be. Some of the folk say that the moment is between two times, between the past and the present.

They call the Sufi "a son of his moment" (*ibn waqtihi*), meaning that he is completely occupied with the religious obligation of his present state, carrying out what is demanded of him at the time. It is said that the renunciate[14] has concern neither for the moment past nor for the moment to come. He is concerned only with the present moment in which he finds himself. They also say: "to be preoccupied with a past moment is to lose a second moment."[15]

By "moment" they can also mean that which happens to them through the dispositions of the real[16] that come upon them without any choice on their part. They say: "So and so is in the power of his moment" that is, he surrenders to whatever comes over him, without his own will, from the unknown (*ghayb*). This meaning applies only for those things that are not under God's prophetically—given command or injunction. To neglect or to consign to providence what has been commanded or to neglect the complete carrying out of the command is to be outside the faith.

They say: "The moment is a sword, that is, just as the sword is cutting, so the moment prevails in what the real brings to pass and completes." It is said: "The sword is gentle to the touch, but its edge cuts. Whoever handles it gently is unharmed. Whoever treats it roughly is cut." Similarly for the moment, whoever submits to its decree is saved, and whoever opposes it is thrown over and destroyed. In this regard they composed the following verse:

> Like a sword—if you handle it gently its touch is gentle, but its
> edges, if you treat it roughly are rough.

When the moment favors someone, the moment for him is just a moment. When the moment opposes someone, the moment for him is loathing.

I heard my teacher Abu 'Ali al-Daqqaq say: "The moment is a file. It files you down without effacing you." He means that were it to efface you and make you pass away, you would be—in your passing away—liberated. However the moment takes from you without entirely annihilating you. He recited in this regard:

> Every day that passes takes part of me, leaves my heart a portion of loss, and passes away.

He also recited:

> Just as the people of fire when their skin is well roasted have prepared for their wretchedness new skin.

And with similar meaning:

> No one truly dies who finds rest in dying. To truly die is to live your death.

Astute is one who remains in the rule of his moment. If his moment is waking consciousness (*sahw*), his performance is of the *sharī'a*, and if his moment is effacement, the rule of reality prevails upon him.

THE STATE (*Hāl*)

In the essay on the state (*hāl*), Qushayri begins with the common emphasis upon the ephemerality of the states, as opposed to the relative stability of the stations. He then offers another perspective, according to which some states are not ephemeral, and those that are ephemeral are viewed as inferior. The example given is the state of *ridā* (contentedness, acceptance) which is relatively stable. Much depends upon the particularities of classification.[17] Qushayri, in a dialectical move, accepts the non-ephemeral state, but as taste or portion (*shirb*) of something that can then grow. Ephemeral experiences are not inferior states, but beacons of a yet higher consciousness that will gradually be realized as more continuous. The discussion deepens to an examination of the continual progressivity and movement within the consciousness of the seeker as he moves ever deeper along the infinite road to the real.[18] Of special importance is Qushayri's use of the word *ma'nā* here. The word can mean "meaning," "essence," or "feeling." Qushayri uses it to refer to the "content" of the individual state (delight, constriction, longing, anxiety, terror). The word indicates more than a "feeling" and yet something more specific that "consciousness." I have used the term "mode of consciousness."

> Among the folk, the state is a mode of consciousness that comes upon the heart without a person's intending it, attracting it, or trying to gain it—a feeling of delight or sorrow, constriction, longing, anxiety, terror, or want. States are bestowed; stations are gained. States come without *wujūd* (ecstatic existentiality)[19] while stations are gained with *majhūd* (the expending of efforts). The possessor of a station is secure in his station, while the possessor of a state can be taken up out of his state.
>
> Dhu'al-Nun al-Misri was asked about the knower. He said: "He was here but left!" Some shaykhs say: "States are like lightning flashes. If it continues, it is a talking-to-oneself." They also say: "States reflect their name," that is, just as they alight upon the heart, they pass on with the moment.[20]
>
> They recite:
>
> If it did not change it would not be named a state Everything that changes, passes.
>
> Look at the shadow as it comes to its end,
> It moves toward its decline when it grows long.
>
> On the other hand, some of the folk have maintained the stability and perdurance of the states. They claim that if the experiences do not last or continue, they are shimmerings (*lawā'ih*) and flashes of intuition (*bawādih*), and their possessor has not yet attained true states. Insofar as the attribute lasts, then they are properly called states. Abu 'Uthman al-Hiri said: "For forty years Allah did not place me in a state that I disliked." He was referring to the continuation of contentedness which is numbered among the states. What must be said of all this is that they are correct who claim that the state is continuous. The particular mode of consciousness (*ma'nā*) is a taste or portion (*shirb*) in a person that can

> later grow into something more. But the possessor of such a continuous state has other states beyond those that have become a taste for him. These other states are ephemeral. When these ephemeral happenings become continuous for him like those previous states, then he rises up to another, higher and subtler state.[21] He never ceases to rise higher. The prophet, God's peace and blessings upon him, said: "My heart becomes shrouded, so that I ask God Most High for pardon seventy times a day."[22] In regard to this hadith, I heard Abu 'Ali al-Daqqaq, God's mercy upon him, say: "The prophet (God's mercy and blessings upon him) was continually rising in his states. When he rose from one condition (*hāla*) to a higher one, he might glance at the condition he has risen beyond, and he would count it as a covering or shroud in relationship to what he had attained. His states were continually being intensified.
>
> The providential graces of the real Most Glorious are infinite. For if the real Most High is deserving of majesty, and a truly realized attainment of it is impossible, then the servant will be perpetually rising from state to state.[23]
>
> He can attain no mode of consciousness which does not have yet a higher mode within the decree of the All-praised, which it is destined to attain. This is how the following saying is to be taken: "The good deeds of the pious are the bad deeds of the intimates of God."
>
> When Junayd was asked about this, he recited:
>
> Sudden gleams of light when they appear, apparitions, revealing
> a secret, telling of union.

CONSTRICTION (*Qabd*) AND EXPANSION (*Bast*)

In his essay on the conditions of constriction (*qabd*) and expansion (*bast*), Qushayri plunges into the heart of Sufi psychology with a crucial distinction between states involving future expectations (such as hope and fear) and states involving immediate experience (such as constriction and expansion)." Constriction is a gripping of the heart, an experience analogous to fear, but far more intense in that it is an experience of the immediate and in the present. Expansion is a dilation, an expansive feeling of peace or well-being, again intensified down into the immediate present. Although expansion is originally viewed as the more desirable state, the essay turns—in a typically Qushayrian twist—to a sudden reversal of perspective in which the comfort of expansion is seen as a trap.

The essay ends with Junayd's comments on qabd and bast. The comments of Junayd come as a shock. His writing is rough, stacatto, and searing. The voice speaks from the point of "I am there." Coming at the end of Qushayri's brilliant "set up" of the concepts, Junayd's comments resonate down through centuries of Sufi thought and experience.[24]

In order to bring across the literary quality of Junayd's sayings, I have changed vocabulary. The terms "contriction" and "expansion," while reasonably accurate as translations of their Arabic equivalents on the conceptual level, are unworkable within the short semantic bursts of Junayd. I have therefore switched to shorter, less Latinate terms: "Fear grips me...." However we interpret a passage such as that of Junayd (and like all foundational passages, it is open to continual interpretation and reinterpretation), it is unlikely that we can ascribe to it the characteristic so often attributed to him: "sobriety."

Qushayri then goes on to discuss intimacy and awe as intensified conditions of contriction and expansion (as if, after his essay and Junayd's words, we could imagine anything more intense). I present only the first part of the essay on intimacy and awe. The second part is a preparation for Qushayri's exploration of the concept of *wujūd* (ecstatic existentiality) and *wajd* (finding, ecstasy)—a complex semantic field beyond the bounds of this essay. Qushayri's words on constriction, expansion, intimacy, and awe, prepare us for the next selections in this article, two of Niffari's that embody in literary terms, those four categories.

Beyond constriction and expansion, Qushayri leads us to awe and intimacy. Rudolf Otto, in his influential definition of holy as the *mysterium tremendum* (dread-inspiring mystery), attributed to the human experience of the holy the simultaneous modes of intense desire and intense fear.[25] For the early Sufis, the mysterium tremendum is based upon a somewhat different pair of modes of consciousness: the experience of intense intimacy and intense dread or awe. Intimacy (*uns*) and dread (*hayba*) are two of the fundamental modes of Qur'ānic discourse and in classical poetry, and Sufis have taken these modes into a highly sophisticated experiential psychology. Qushayri quite naturally turns to the classical poetic tradition for proof texts on the experience of intimacy.[26]

CONSTRICTION (*Qabd*) AND EXPANSION (*Bast*)

These two states arise after the servant has risen beyond the condition of fear *(khawf)* and hope *(rajā')*. Constriction is to the master as fear is to the beginner. Expansion is to the master as hope is to the beginner. What is the precise distinction between constriction and fear, and between expansion and hope? Fear concerns something in future only. One might fear, for example, the loss of something desired, or the onslaught of something unwanted. The same holds true for hope, whether the hope arises in contemplating something desired for the future or in awaiting the anticipated cessation of something unwanted or detested.

As for constriction and expansion, their mode of consciousness occurs in the present moment. The heart of the possessor of fear or hope is related to these two conditions through a deferring *(bi ājilihi)* of the expected. But the possessor of constriction and expansion is a captive of his moment in the "oncomings"[27] that prevail upon him in the immediate now *(fī 'ājilihi)*. [28]A person's attributes in constriction and expansion are ranked in accordance with his rankings in the states. There are oncomings that cause constriction, even while there remains place for other things in the person gripped by constriction, because the constriction has not filled him completely. And there are people so constricted that they have no room for the oncoming of anything else, because all such room has been snatched away entirely in a single oncoming. That leaves no room for any other oncoming because the first oncoming has taken over the person completely. Thus the expression used by some: "I am full," i.e. there is no more room left in me.

The same is true for a person experiencing expansion. He might have an expansion that contains all creatures, so that the most spectacular things do not move him. He experiences an expansion so great that no state can affect him. I heard the master Abu 'Ali al-Daqqaq, God's mercy upon him, say:

> Some people came to visit 'Ali Abu Bakr al-Qahti.[29] He had a son who was occupying himself as boys will do. The visitors crossed the path of the boy, but he and his companions were so occupied they did not notice. His heart was moved to pity and commiseration for al-Qahti, and he said: "Poor Shaykh, how he must be tried by the misbehavior of such a son!" Then he approached al-Qahti and found him completely unaware of these amusements and goings-on. He marvelled at him and said: "May I be ransom for one whom the rock-rooted mountains cannot

> move!" Al-Qahti replied: "We have been liberated in eternity from the bondage of things."

Among the more common occasions of constriction is an oncoming that overwhelms the heart as an intimation of fault or a sign that blame is deserved. Inevitably, constriction comes upon the heart. Another occasion of oncoming might be a sign of nearness or approach to favor and acceptance. Then expansion comes upon the heart.

In general, each person undergoes constriction in proportion to his expansion and expansion in proportion to his constriction. One can undergo constriction while its cause remains uncertain; he finds constriction in his heart without knowing its occasion or cause. The proper path for one undergoing such constriction is to submit to it until the moment passes. If he goes to the trouble of expelling it or tries to anticipate the [new] moment through his own choice before it comes upon him, his constriction will only increase. Or his action may be accounted as poor behavior. However, if he submits to the provision of the moment, then the constriction should shortly pass. The All-praised said (2:245): God constricts [the heart] and expands it.

Expansion can also occur all of a sudden, happening upon a person unexpectedly, without any recognizable cause. It shakes him up and disconcerts him. The proper path for anyone undergoing it is to stay still and to tend his behavior. In such a moment there is a great danger. Let the one undergoing it be on guard against a hidden snare. In this regard, one of them [the Sufis] said: "The door of expansion was opened before me and I slipped and became veiled from my station." For this reason they say: "stay on the prayer carpet (*bisāt*), beware of expansion (*inbisāt*)." The realized masters have numbered the states of constriction and expansion among those from which one should ask refuge; in relation to what is above them—perishing of the godservant and advancement in reality—they are poverty and harm.

I heard the Shaykh Abu 'Abdallah al-Sulami say: I heard al-Husayn ibn Yahya say: I heard Ja'far ibn Muhammad say: I heard al-Junayd say:

> Fear grips me. Hope unfolds me. Reality draws me together. The real sets me apart. When he grips me with fear, he makes me pass away from myself. When he expands me with hope, he returns me to myself. When he brings me together in reality, he makes me present. When he separates me through the real, he makes my witness the other-than-me and veils me from him. He is exalted beyond all of that, moving me rather than holding me

secure, deserting me rather than keeping intimate company with me. Through my being-present I taste the flavor of my *wujūd* (ecstatic existentiality). Would that he had annihilated me from myself and gratified me or absented me from myself and revived me.

AWE (*Hayba*) AND INTIMACY (*Uns*)

These two states [awe and intimacy] are above constriction and expansion, just as constriction is above the rank of fear and expansion is above the level of hope. For awe is higher than constriction and intimacy is more perfect than expansion. The reality of *hayba* (awe) is *ghayba* (absence); every *hā'ib* (person in a state of awe) is *ghā'ib* (absent, disappeared). The awe-struck are ranked in awe according to their distinction in absence; some are higher than others. Intimacy on the other hand requires a proper wakefulness (*sahw*). Every intimate is awake. Each is distinguished according to his distinction in the initial taste (*shirb*). Therefore they say: "The lowest way-station of intimacy is this: that if a person were thrown into a blazing fire, his intimacy would not be troubled."

FROM THE STANDINGS (*MAWAQIF*) OF NIFFARI

Some of the more remarkable works of early Sufi literature (and of mystical literature of any place or period) are attributed to a Sufi who does not appear in any of the major Sufi biographical sources: Muhammad ibn 'Abd al-Jabbar ibn al-Hasan al-Niffari (d. 354/965). Niffari's most famous work is the *Book of Standings* (*Kitāb al-Mawāqif*), but according to its commentator Tilimnsani, the book was actually put together in book form by Niffari's son.[30]

The work's title and central term, *mawāqif* (standings), is part of complex Sufi semantic field. As with Junayd's use of the word *wajd*, Niffari's use of the term *mawāqif* involves a sophisticated play upon the etymological and morphological possibilities of the term. Like Junayd, Niffari refashions and reconfigures those possibilities into unusual, often striking new forms. A brief look at the semantic field of *mawāqif* will provide an entrance into Niffari's distinctive, often striking, sometimes shocking conception of "standings".

The basic radical, w/q/f, yields the primary verb form *waqafa* (to stand, stop, halt). However, Niffari uses the less common causative form of the verb, *awqafa*, meaning "to make someone stand." He then employs the standard verbal noun *waqfa*, not in its normal sense as the act of standing, but in a causal sense, from the point of view of the one standing, as the "act of being stood" somewhere. The prefix "m" yields *mawqif (*plural *mawāqif)* as the place were the standing or being stood occurs. Though the term can be translated as "station," such a translation loses the causal force peculiar to Niffari's writing,[31] in addition to losing the power and force of the distinctive manner in which Niffari configures its various connotations. What is at stake here is the sense of being stood in place, riveted, by some overwhelming power or experience. A waqf ("standing" or "staying") is Niffari's term for the state of being riveted, as it were, in a particular place in the divine presence. The term resonates with the Qur'ānic "standing" of each person before the revelation of her destiny during the apocalyptic moment of truth. It also echoes the poet-lover's standing before his fate of separation from the beloved at the *ghadāt al-bayn* (morning of her departure). In a single "standing" Niffari condenses a full range of language worlds and a complexity of referential and antecedental play.

Much of the literary effect of Niffari's sayings resides in their placement of the visionary moment in a bipolar world that can be interpreted as the mystical event in the present, or the apocalyptic event of the final moment of truth. Of course, almost any Sufi representation of visionary experience can be read through eschatological lenses, but Niffari's staccato series of stayings, sayings, and visions engages the interface between the mystical and the eschatological in a particularly persistent manner. The experiences oscillate between the Sufi states of *qabd* (constriction) and *bast* (expansion). Standing (or being stood) before an overwhelming power and at the edge of the dissolution of ego yields expressions of terror and awe that can suddenly change into expressions of profound inner peace beneath and beyond the turmoil, which can then turn back just as suddenly to expressions of terror.

Previous scholars have attempted to place Niffari's revelations within a theological framework. Some consistent ideas come through the highly elusive texts. There is a clear progression suggested, for example, from *'ilm* (traditional knowledge) through *ma'rifa* (intuitive knowledge or recollection) to *mushāhada* (witnessing). At times the notion of *waqfa* seems to represent the highest of these stations; at other times it seems to be used more generically for the act of being stood, stayed, or riveted in any particular station or state.

The two "standings" translated here demonstrate the manner in which Niffari's discourse oscillates between referential poles and between emotional poles or modes of consciousness. The dialogue between human and deity is stark, and, as in the Qur'ān, it is sometimes a challenge to know who is speaking and where one party's speech ends and the other party's begins. In some "standings" in fact, the deity and the human seem to change voices (the "I" becoming the "he" and the "he" the "I") suddenly, at the moment of mystical union, as if the two parties had become one—yet there remains two voices, and then, after the union, the two parties have traded places. [32]

The "conditions," are similarly unstable. In the first selection below, there is a movement toward peace and reconciliation, as the deity at the moment of judgement, judges the fire itself and sends it away never to return. In the second selection, there is a moment of unequivocal dread and drowning. These selections illustrate the manner in which Niffari allows the eschatological to become "present" in the moment. Indeed, the subtle Sufi psychology of the moment, of the condition, and of intimacy and awe, that Qushayri had so brilliantly analyzed is embodied here in these rough-hewn, searing statements.

THE STANDING NO. 5: *"MY TIME HAS COME"*

He stood me, saying:
If you cannot see me, you are not with me
If you see an-other-than-me, you do not see me
Intimations of me in anything
    efface the meaning of meaning within it,
    and affirm it from, not through [33]

In you is something
    that cannot be relinquished
    that cannot be turned away

When you are silent of yourself
the proclaimer (*nāṭiq*) must speak

In everything is a trace of me
If you speak of it, you change it

Put remembrance of me behind you,
Or you'll revert to the other-than-me,
between you and it, nothing

My moment has come
The time has come for me to unveil my face and
manifest my splendor
My light will reach the courtyards
and what is beyond
Eyes will gaze upon me, hearts will gaze
You will see my enemy loving me,
my intimate companions judging

I will raise up thrones for them
They will send away the fire
never to return
I will inhabit once more
my ruined abodes
adorning them with the real
You will see how a measure of me
expels otherness

I will gather all people into well-being
Never again will they be divided or abased
Take out my hidden treasure
Realize my tidings
my readiness,
my imminent rising
I will rise and the stars will gather around me
I will bring sun and moon together
I will enter every dwelling
"Peace to you," they will greet me
"And to you, peace," I will reply

At my beckon, the hour will rise
I am the almighty, the compassionate

THE STANDING NO. 6: *OF THE SEA*

He stood me in the sea
I saw the ships sinking and the planks floating
I saw the planks sinking
He said to me
    No one on board will be saved.

Peril for one who throws himself in and does not come
    on board
Destruction for those who come on board and do not
    accept danger

He said: In peril is a portion of salvation.
    Then the wave came
        and lifted what was beneath it
            and ran along the shore.

He said to me:
    The surface of the sea is an unattainable brilliance
    Its depth is an unfathomable darkness.
    Between them are sea-creatures that offer no refuge

    Do not sail on the sea, or the vessel will veil you
    Do not throw yourself in, or the sea itself will veil you.

In the sea are brinks. Which will support you?

When you grant yourself to the sea and drown,
    you become like one of its creatures

I deceive you if I guide you to an other-than-me

If you perish in an other-than-me, you belong to that in
    which you perish

This world belongs to the person I have turned away from it, and from whom I have turned away the world

The afterworld belongs to whomever I turn it,
to whomever turn to me.

THE HEART-SECRET (*SIRR*) IN QUSHAYRI AND HALLAJ

One of the most elusive terms of Sufism is the *sirr*, a word that I translate as "heart-secret." Sometimes, of course, the term simply means "secret" or "mystery." Sometimes it refers to a secret thought. And for early Sufis the sirr is also that inner being of the human, the most authentic personhood, the locus of the ineffability of the human's existence, the human relationship to the deity, and the mystical union in the deity. The term also resonates with the classical, love-poetry, tradition, the "secret" between the lover and beloved that must never be betrayed; although in some sense the poem is in fact an act of both divulging and veiling the secret.

Qushayri had begun his mini-treatise on the 27 terms with waqt and a meditation of Sufi notions of time, identity, and experience. He ends his essay with sirr which is both the "locus" of time, experience, and the timeless, as well as that which transcends all "location," and ultimately all expression.

After presenting my translation of Qushayri's remarks on "heart-secret," I return to the poem with which this essay began. There the term sirr is used several times. The poem appears to draw on the famous Qur'ānic statements about Allah blinding humans with lightning, allowing them to grope forward in its light, and then stop and wait in utter darkness until the next flash. It contains in its poetic register the vital dynamic between intimacy and awe, constriction and expansion that we saw analyzed with such precision and subtlety by Qushayri. It explores the ancient poetic roots of the "secret" between the lover and beloved, the "signs" (in poetry, the traces or *atlāl*) that the poet reads sometimes in the abandoned campsite, sometimes, as Imru al-Qays, sleepless in remembrance of the beloved, in the movement of the stars, and in the Qur'ān with the shrouding of the lote tree. It engages that paradox of absence and presence, nearness and separation, that is at the heart of Sufi discourse.[34] It brings across, in as intensely lyrical a fashion as I have found in early Sufi verse, the meditation of the "conditions", and, without mentioning them explicitly, on *fanā'* and *baqā'*.

QUSHAYRI ON THE HEART-SECRET/SECRET (*Sirr*)

The heart-secret is considered a subtle essence in the bodily mold, similar to the spirit.[35] They base this definition upon its being the locus (*mahall*) of witness, just as the spirits are the locus of love, and the heart is the locus of recognitions. They say: the heart-secret is what you cannot look upon, and the secret of the secret is known only to the real.

Following their particular usage and their basic premise, the folk hold that the heart-secret is more subtle than the spirit, and the spirit is more subtle than the heart.

They say: the heart-secrets have been formed from the bondage of the others, from traces and ruins.[36]

The term "secret" is employed for what is protected and concealed between the servant and the real in the states. In reference to this, someone said our secrets are virgin, undeflowered by anyone's guess.

They say: "The breasts of the free are the graves of secrets."

They say: "If the button of my cloak recognized my secret, I would throw it away."

From the *Diwan* of poetry attributed to al-Hallaj

The most secret of secret thoughts
    enveloped and fixed
along the horizon
in folds of light.

    How? The 'how' is known
along the outside,
    while the interior of beyond
to and for the heart of being.

    Creatures perish
        in the darkened blind

of quest, knowing
only intimations.

Guessing and dreaming
they pursue the real,
faces turned toward the sky
whispering secrets to the heavens.

While the lord remains among them
in every turn of time
abiding in their every condition
in every instant.

They are never without him,
not for the blink of an eye
if only they knew!
nor he for a moment without them.

NOTES

1. Fazlur Rahman was not known as a specialist on Sufism or an enthusiast about Sufi thought. When people ask where I developed an interested in Sufi literature they are sometimes puzzled to hear that the interest developed through the courses of Fazlur Rahman. Indeed, however, a number of his students were inspired by his course in Islamic mysticism and went on to devote their further work to studies in Sufism.

Each course Fazlur Rahman taught had a very different tenor and feeling. The course on Islamic mysticism was the most intellectually far-ranging, and would lead to discussions of everything from poetic allusions to the history of reinterpretation of key ideas of Ibn 'Arabi. His style was simply to plunge into the text, with students reading a passage aloud in the Arabic, and whenever necessary, Fazlur Rahman would give extemporaneous mini-lectures on particular issues. He was steeped in the Sufi tradition, and taught with a combination of philosophical rigor and an exquisite lyrical taste (*dhawq*) that allowed the most subtle resonances of the text to come forth.

Fazlur Rahman also appreciated Sufism's intellectually unruly side, and some of the more outrageous puns and false etymologies would bring about an explosion of laughter. My most vivid memory is of him taking off his two sets of glasses (rather than use bifocals, he would put reading glasses on over his regular glasses, particularly when using the *Mu'jam al-Mufahris* which was ever present in his readings), and his eyes becoming watery as he laughed over Ibn 'Arabi's strange statement about Thamudians or some other Sufi statement that managed to be self-satirizing yet make an important and subtle point.

2. See for example, al-Sarrāj, *Kitāb al-Luma' fi al-Tasawwuf* (Book of the Flashes on Sufism), ed. R. A. Nicholson (London and Leiden: Gibb Memorial Series, no. 22, 1914), pp. 43–54.

3. John Esposito, *Islam: The Straight Path* (Oxford: Oxford University Press, 1990), pp. 104–5, offers an example of the standard generalizations: "Mystics like al-Muhasibi of Baghdad (d. 857), Dhu al-Nun of Egypt (d. 859), Junayd of Baghdad (d. 910) and the Persians Abu Yazid al-Bistami (d. 874) and Mansur al-Hallaj (d. 922) made major contributions to the formation of the Sufi way....They represented a range of mystical doctrines from the 'sober' to the 'intoxicated', from the doctrinal safe followers of the law and a path of selfless love and service of God to ecstatic rebels like Abu Yazid and al-Hallaj, whose experience of God as indwelling in their souls moved them to actions and statements that scandalized many and drew the ire of the *'ulamā'*. Abu Yazid's consciousness of the transience of the material world and the inner presence of God led him to declare, 'Glory to me. How great is my majesty!' Equally offensive and blasphemous to orthodox ears was al-Hallaj's claim, 'I am the Truth,' for which he was crucified."

4. For example, John Esposito, *ibid.*, pp. 102: "Amid the turmoil, al-Ghazali emerged...to save the day by providing the needed religious synthesis."

5. Still useful for the study of Hallaj is the work of Louis Massignon. Despite Massignon's well-known, apologetic Christian perspective, his meticulous scholarship makes his work essential to any further study of Hallaj. See *The Passion of al-Hallaj: Mystic and Martyr of Islam,* translated from the French by Herbert Mason (Princeton, NJ: Princeton University Press, 1982), other works by Massignon, and the more recent work by Paul Nwyia.

6. Most recently and notably, the extraordinary work of Richard Gramlich. Two of his recent contributions are Richard Gramlich, *Schlaglichter Über Das Sufitum: Abū Nasr as-Sarrāj's Kitāb al-luma'* (Stuttgart: Steiner, 1990) and R. Gramlich, *Das Sendschreiben al-Qushayrīs* (Wiesbaden: Steiner, 1989), pp. 146 ff.

7. This present article includes short excerpts from longer translations that have now appeared in Michael Sells, *Early Islamic Mysticism* (New York: Paulist Press Classics of Western Spirituality, 1996). *Early Islamic Mysticism* focuses upon pre-Sufi material Qur'ān, Mi'rāj texts, and classical poetry); texts of the foundation period (from works attributed to Ja'far al-Sadiq, Tustari, Rabi'a, Junayd, Bistami, Hallaj, and Niffari); and the early synoptic works of Sarraj,

Sulami, and Qushayri.

8. 'Abd al-Karim b. Hawazin al-Qushayri was born near Nishapur in Khurasan during the period of the Ghaznavids. He received the full Islamic education of the time, memorizing the Qur'ān, studying Islamic law (*fiqh*) and 'Asharite theology, and becoming a disciple to the Sufi master Abu 'Ali ad-Daqqaq (41/1021). His *Risāla* continued the movement toward an analytic understanding Sufi thought and practice and an integration of Sufism with ritual Islam that had already been begun by figures such as Sarrāj (d. 378/988), Sulami (d. 1021), Kalabadhi (d. 380/990), and Abu Talib al-Makki (d. 966). Qushayri's treatise was followed in turn by the *Hilyat al-awliya'* of Abu Nu'aym al-Isfahani (d. 428/1037) and the *Kashf al-Mahjūb* of Hujwiri (d. 466/1074).

9. Abū-l Qāsim 'Abd al-Karīm al-Qushayrī, *Al-Riāla al-Qushayriyya fī 'ilm al-Tasawwuf* (The Qushayrian Treatise on Sufism). Qushayri's treatise contains: (1) a synoptic introductory discussion; (2) a section consisting of the hagiographies of 83 early Sufis; (3) the brilliant short treatise itself, the "interpretation of expressions" (*Tafsīr Alfāz*), giving interpretations of 27 key Sufi terms and expressions; (4) and a section of 57 longer essays on Sufi states, stations, beliefs, and practices. Section Three has never been translated into English. Section Four has recently been translated by B.R. Von Schlegell, *Principles of Sufism*, trans. B.R. Von Schlegell (Berkeley: Mizan Press, 1990).

The Gramlich annotated German translation of Section Three can be found in *Das Sendschreiben al-Qushayrīs. Übersetzt, eingeleitet und kommentiert von Richard Gramlich* (Freiburger Islamstudien, Band 12: Wiesbaden: Steiner, 1989), pp. 106–145. I have based my translation on pp. 87–101. Cf. the brilliant essay on the stations and conditions by al-Qushayri (d. 1072 c.e.): Abūl-Qāsim 'abd al-Karīm al-Qushayrī, *Al-Risāla al-Qushayriyya fī 'ilm al-Tasawwuf* (The Qushayrian Treatise on Sufism) (Cairo: Dār al-Kutub al-Jadīd, 1988), vol. 1, 191–96.

10. Like other Sufi writers, Qushayri uses the term "folk" (*qawm*) to designate those we might call Sufis. The term is an important indication of the effort by Sufi thinkers to avoid isolating and selecting Sufis out as a distinct and possibly elite element; for them, they were simply qawm. Throughout this chapter, wherever the term "folk" occurs, it translates qawm used in this particular sense. Sometimes Qushayri will refer simply to "them" without specifying "them" as Sufis. Although it can sound strange in English at first to use this unspecified "they," I have used it rather than interpolating in words like "Sufis," to avoid setting up the kind of separate category Qushayri deliberately avoided.

11. Indeed, in the later theosophical philosophy of the moment found in Ibn 'Arabi, the moment becomes an "eternal moment" in which it is, indeed, such a

totality.

12. "Realized masters": *ahl al-tahqīq*.

13. "The teacher": *al-ustādh*, "The afterworld": *al-uqbā*.

14. The renunciate: *al-faqīr*.

15. As will be the case throughout this section from Qushayri's treatise, the antecedent of "they" is often unclear in itself, and in its relationship (the same as or different from) to previous unspecified speakers.

16. "Dispositions of the real": *tasrīf al-haqq*.

17. Sarrāj places contentedness among the stations, rather than the states.

18. At times, Qushayri refers to *hāla*, (with the added "a" at the end) which I translate as "condition." The term is closely related to the *hāl* and seems to be used almost interchangeably.

19. The real: *al-haqq*, used, of course, to signify the deity, but with a significantly different semantic field from the more personal term Allah.

20. There is an etymological play upon the two terms, *hāla* (to change, be transformed) and *halla* (to alight at). Though the radicals of the two words are different (h/w/l vs. h/l/l) in some cases the weak verbs such as h/w/l are in fact related to verbs with a doubled consonant (like h/l/l). Whatever the etymological justifications for the play, the association of the state of the lover (or beloved) and the "alightings" (usually of the beloved in a journey away from the poet) were well established in pre-Islamic poetry.

21. At times, Qushayri's analysis comes close to collapsing the distinction between the station (as more permanent and product of individual endeavor) and state (as ephemeral and bestowed), especially in his insistence that even the station is ultimately bestowed and in his discussion of states that are at least relatively stable. As with most of the key Sufi concepts, the analysis begins by clarifying them, and then pushes them to the point of dissolution, as if the final answer to their meaning could only be understood through the reader's own experience.

22. See Wensinck, *Concordance et Indices de la Tradition Musulmane* (Leiden: Brill, 1982) 5, 38 b; 4, 537b, and Gramlich, *Das Sendschreiben al-Qushayris,* p. 111. Qushayri offers another use of this hadith in his essay on *sitr* later on in section 3 of *The Treatise*.

23. "Truly realized attainment": *al-wusūl ilayhi bi al-tahqīq*. Here Qushayri undermines the very phrase he uses so frequently: "realized masters" (*ahl al-tahqīq*). In the dynamic world of Sufi psychology, no complete master can ever be attained, since the path is infinite, and the modes of consciousness can be infinitely deepened and expanded. In this particular notion, we might be reminded of Gregory of Nyssa's *epektasis*, the ever-continuing movement toward reality in which each experience of presence leads to an absence and to a more profound presence. See Bernard McGinn, *Foundations of Mysticism* (New York: Crossroad, 1991), pp. 139–142.

24. These same comments appear in the treatises (*al-rasā'il*) of Junayd, in a series of analyses of the concept of *tawhīd* (affirmation of unity). The analyses are both lucid and powerful, but they occur in a third person, discursive context. Each of the eight analyses is labeled "another point *(mas'ala ukhrā)*." Thus the rather emotionless title: "another point." The reader plunges with shock into Junayd's first person discourse: "Fear grips me. Hope unfolds me. Reality draws me together. The real sets me apart...."

The text from the *rasā'il* contains a number of subtle differences, and some sentences in the end that are absent from Qushayri. Those ending sentences are: "My annihilation is my endurance *(fanā'ī baqā'ī)*. From the reality of my annihilation, he annihilated me from my enduring and from my annihilation. I was, upon the reality of annihilation, without *baqā'* and without *fanā'*, through my *baqā'* and my *fanā'* for the finding/existence (*wujūd*) of the *fanā'* and *baqā'*, for the *wujūd* of my other, in my annihilation." See Abdel Kader, *The Life, Personality and Writings of Al-Junayd* (London: Luzac, 1962), Arabic text, pp. 51–58, with the "fear grips me" section on p. 53.

25. Rudolf Otto, *Das Heilege*, 1917; *Rudolf Otto, The Idea of the Holy*, translated by John W. Harvey (Oxford: Oxford University Press, 1950).

26. The section ends with several occurrences of the term *wujūd*, one of the more definitively untranslatable terms in Sufism, combining as it does the senses of ecstasy, discovery, and existence. For the moment I use the phrase "ecstatic existentiality" as a gloss for the term. In the very next essay, Qushayri provides an extended analysis of the subtle semantic field of this central Sufi concept.

27. The *wārid*, for which I have coined the term "oncoming," is the "coming down upon" a person of a particular state or mode of consciousness. It is more active and invasive that an "occurrence" or "happening" though it shares with the man independence from the will and intention of the person upon whom the state alights. Qushayri introduces the term in this essay, and later explains it in a separate essay.

28. A common play upon the near homonyms for that which is expected or deferred to the future (*ājil*) and that which is immediate (*'ājil*), a play that derives from Qur'ānic meditation on the day of resurrection and judgment (*yawm al-qiyāma, yawm ad-dīn*) and its deferral.

29. Or al-Qahtabī.

30. "And this is one of the indications in favor of the assertion that the man who composed the *Mawāqif* was the son of Shaykh al-Niffari, and not the Skaykh himself. Indeed, the Skaykh never composed any book; but he used to write down these revelations on scraps of paper, which were handed down after him. He was a wanderer in deserts, and dwelt in no land, nor did he make himself known to any man. It is mentioned that he died in one of the villages of Egypt. God knows best the truth of the matter." Translated by A.J. Arberry (with some slight revisions by the present author). The commentator, 'Afif al-Din al-Tilimnsani (d. 690AH) says in another place that it was actually the son of the Shaykh's daughter who put the sayings into their present order. See *The Mawāqif and Mukhātabāt of Muhammad ibn 'Abdi l-Jabbār al-Niffarī, with other fragments*, edited, with translations, commentary, and indices, by Arthur John Arberry (London: Luzac, for the "E.J.W. Gibb Memorial", 1935), p. 1. My translations are based upon Arberry's edition of the Arabic text, hereafter referred to simply as *The Mawāqif*. For a brief biography of Niffari, see A.J. Arberry's entry, "Niffari," in the *Encyclopedia of Islam*, first edition (Leiden: Brill, 1936), p. 910.

31. Another disadvantage to "station" is that it the same term used to translate other, more common Sufi terms such as *maqām* and *manzil* as noted above.

32. For further discussion of this reference to fusion and inversion, see Michael A. Sells, "Bewildered Tongue: The Semantics of Mystical Union in Islam" in Moshe Idel and Bernard McGinn, eds., *Mystical Union and Monotheistic Faith* (New York: MacMillan, 1989), pp. 87-124.

33. The pronominal antecedents are ambiguous. All the pronouns are *hu* (it/he). Arberry, p. 31, introduces a distinction among the antecedents: "My indications in a thing annihilate in it the real reality, and establish it as belonging to God, not as existing through itself."

34. Qushayri devotes entire essays to these concepts in his 27-term mini-treatise.

35. Subtle essence: *latīfa*; bodily mold: *qālib*.

36. *Al-asrār mu'taqatun min raqqi al-aghyāri min al-āthāri wa al-atlāl*. Qushayri is drawing clearly upon the *atlāl* motif of the *nasīb* here.

Chapter 9

CITING THE SIGHTS OF THE HOLY SITES: VISIONARY PILGRIMAGE NARRATIVES OF PRE-MODERN SOUTH ASIAN SUFIS

Marcia K. Hermansen

This paper explores the theme of citing/sighting/siting[1] the Holy through studying a genre of pilgrimage narratives written by pre-modern Sufis from South Asia. These accounts were written by persons affiliated with the Naqshbandi tariqa in the late seventeenth and early eighteenth centuries. In them a succession of individuals recounted their visionary experiences which were inspired by the specific circumstances of performing the pilgrimage to the Holy Cities.[2]

This genre is only biographical in the broadest sense, for as Barbara Metcalf notes, "In the Indian sub-continent, even travellers to the holy places of Mecca and Madina did not write about their travels before the late eighteenth century, except in so far as they recorded visions or wrote treatises while there." She dates the earliest of the more personal South Asian pilgrimage accounts to 1787.[3]

The texts of an earlier period which I will be considering are thus neither personal travel reminiscences nor pilgrimage itineraries in anything like the modern sense of these genres. I rather characterize them as visionary pilgrimage narratives. Through the discussion of a number of the visionary sightings cited in these texts I wish to demonstrate how a process of recounting symbolic elements of visionary experiences allowed the compilers of these texts to represent and in some cases to reorder the hierarchical categories which with they thought.[4] The visionary elements in these texts are thus deployed to serve a polemic as well as a descriptive purpose.

In presenting my argument here I will consider two examples of this genre: *Hasanāt al-Haramain* of Khwāja Muhammad Ma'sūm (1599–1688)[5] who made the pilgrimage in 1068/1657–58 and *Fuyūd al-Haramain* of Shah Wali Allah (1703–1762) who made the pilgrimage in 1143–44/1730–31.

There are other examples of this type of visionary pilgrimage account still in manuscript such as "Latā'if al-Madaniyya" of Shaikh 'Abd al-Ahad Wahdat Sirhindī[6] and "Natā'ij al-Haramain" of Muhammad Āmīn Badakhshī[7] (completed in 1682) which could be incorporated in a future expanded study. All of these accounts were written within a century of each other and there seems to have been a direct influence of each person and text on the subsequent ones. The connection of Shah Wali Allah to the Naqshbandiyya-Mujaddidiyya Sufi order is explicit since he lists in his chain of initiation into the order, first his father, Shāh 'Abd al-Rahīm (d. 1131/1719),[8] then al-Sayyid 'Abd Allāh,[9] then Shaikh Ādam Banurī (d. 1643),[10] then Ahmad Sirhindī (d. 1625).[11] The *Natā 'ij al-Haramain* is a biography and collection of visions and miracles of Shaikh Ādam Banuri;[12] thus, the connection of these pilgrimage narratives through this branch of the Naqshbandiyya-Mujaddidiyya is clear and direct.[13]

HASANĀT AL-HARAMAIN

Khwāja Muhammad Ma'sūm was the son of Shaikh Ahmad Sirhindī, the Indian mystic known as the "Renewer (*Mujaddid*) of the Second Millenium."[14] Ma'sūm continued his father's work as a spiritual guide. Ma'sūm performed the pilgrimage in 1068/1657 accompanied by some of his relatives and disciples. Some of his disciples, however, were already living in the Holy Cities.

The period between 1642–1661 seems to have been quite significant in terms of the spreading of the Naqshbandiyya Sufi order to the Holy Cities of the Hijaz. It was first introduced there by Shaikh Tājuddin Sambhalī, a pupil of Khwāja Bāqī b'illāh and "fellow student and fierce enemy of Ahmad Sirhindī."[15] Therefore, Ma'sum and his followers encountered both support and opposition from the Hijazi Naqshbandis.

The *Hasanāt al-Haramain* was first compiled by his son Muhammad `Ubaid Allah (1038/1629–1083/1673)[16] in Arabic with the title *Yawāqīt al-Haramain* (Rubies of the Two Holy Cities).[17] Its Persian translation was made in 1661 by Muhammad Shākir Allāh, son of Badr al-Dīn Sirhindī, a khalīfa of Ahmad Sirhindī.[18] That the work had a fairly wide currency is evidenced by the fact that a number of subsequent of Naqshbandi biographical works cite heavily from it.[19]

The text of *Hasanāt al-Haramain* is presented in three sections based on the spatio-temporal arrangement of the pilgrimage. The first section comprises seven citings/sightings dealing with the preparations for the journey and the trip itself, the second section describes twenty visions which take place in Mecca, the third section features twenty-three visions occurring in Madina and on the return home. Let us begin by recounting the first vision of the first section of the work which occurs as Ma'sūm is seated in an assembly of Sufis reciting pious phrases and the names of God.

> One day after completing the morning prayer before sunrise I was sitting in a dhikr circle when I saw a vision (*mushāhada*) that many groups of angels from the World of Malakut[20] had surrounded me and were prostrating to me in prayer.
>
> I was struck by astonishment so I reflected on this visionary disclosure (*kashf*). After much contemplation I realized that the "Beautiful Ka'ba" had come to meet me and had surrounded me and thus in the World of Images it seemed to me that those groups who were prostrating to the Ka'ba were actually making me their object of prostration.[21]

The compiler of the work then notes the similarity of this vision to one which had occurred to Shaikh Ahmad Sirhindī. The vision of Sirhindī is only briefly alluded to in the *Hasanāt* but a full description may be found in the *Hadarāt al-Quds* of Badr al Dīn Sirhindī.[22]

> It was the practice of Hadrat [Ahmad Sirhindī] that after the prayer he would sit concentrating on the requests for spiritual assistance of the assembly and after a petitionary invocation he would occupy himself with meditation.
>
> On one occasion he was seated doing the practices of assistance after the farewell salutation of the dawn prayer in the usual way with his face turned to

> the qibla and thus he remained until the sun rose. After that he raised his head from the posture of meditation and said, "Today I longed (to see) the Ka'ba and the sacred mosque. Suddenly I saw that the Noble Ka'ba had come and was circumambulating me. It is amazing that my companions who possess spiritual insight remained unaware of this for if they had been aware, they should have surrounded me at that time and performed the circumambulation."[23]

The motif of the Ka'ba coming to visit a saint or a saint substituting for the Ka'ba is not unusual in Sufi literature. For example, the hagiographies of Rabī'a and Abū Yazīd al-Bistāmī feature such accounts.[24] I would therefore characterize this first visionary citation of the *Hasanāt al-Haramain* as one which constitutes a clear case of a vision which establishes the rank of the person having the vision. A further vision of the Ka'ba is cited as the seventh visionary episode which occurred on the 23rd of Sha'bān 1068 (1657/8). According to the compiler, the travellers had been seeing visions of the lights of the Ka'ba since boarding the ship but these had begun to increase.

On this day while riding in a howdah, Ma'sūm saw a vision that the Ka'ba was approaching him in the form of a tall, fair woman[25] dressed in red[26] garments, radiating lights, smiling, and cheerful. The same sort of lights appeared at the sunset prayer and remained until he started to speak.[27] The compiler of the text then comments on a similar vision which had occurred to Ibn al-'Arabi.[28] It is instructive to review both the compiler's version and the text of the vision as cited by Ibn 'Arabi in *al-Futūhāt al-Makkiyya.*

COMPARISON OF THE VISIONS

The compiler of *Hasanāt* cites a (supposed) vision that Ibn 'Arabi had while making the pilgrimage in Mecca. It seems that as Ibn 'Arabi was about to commence the circumambulations of the Ka'ba he thought to himself, "I am better than the Ka'ba because the reality of the human being is higher than the reality of a stone." Suddenly he saw a beautiful woman who attacked him with a weapon she was holding in her hand saying, "I won't let you perform the circumambulation of me." He then relented and acknowledged the error of his opinion.[29]

It seems, however, that our Naqshbandi compiler had actually recast the imagery of Ibn 'Arabi's vision to make precisely the opposite point to that of the original vision. Let us now cite the original text of Ibn 'Arabi's vision as recounted in *al-Futūhāt al-Makkiyya:*

> On one occasion when I was circumambulating His ancient House, and while I was engaged in this praising and glorifying God....I came to the Black Stone and met the eagle stone of the youth steadfast in devotion who is both speaker and silent, neither alive nor dead, both complex and simple, encompassing and encompassed. When I saw him circumambulating the House, the living circumambulating the dead,[30] I grasped what he was and his significance and realized that the circumambulation of the House is like the prayer over the dead....Then God showed me the spiritual degree of that youth, that he was far beyond all considerations of space and time. When I realized this...I kissed his right hand...and said to him, "O bearer of tidings, look how I seek your company and desire your friendship." Then he indicated to me by hint and sign that he was created to speak only by signs....I begged him to reveal his secrets to me.[31]

Why would the Naqshbandi account seem to reverse the hierarchy intimated by the symbolism to exalt the Ka'ba over the living person? I contend that this is an example of the use of visionary elements to represent and argue specific points of Sufi doctrine.

CONTROVERSY CONCERNING THE "REALITY OF THE KA'BA" (HAQĪQAT-I-KA'BA)

We note that many of Khwaja Muhammad Ma'sūm's visions in *Hasanāt* al-Haramain are tied to the issue of the "Reality of the Ka'ba." This can be understood against the controversial background of this concept in the Naqshbandi theory of an aspirant's itinerary (*sulūk*) of spiritual progress and a "model of" the metaphysical hierarchy attending the relationship of the divine power to the world.[32]

The founder of the Naqshbandiyya-Mujaddidiyya, Shaikh Ahmad Sirhindī, is said to have written a treatise on "The True Reality of the Ka'ba" and had certainly referred to this concept in some of his other writings.[33] A fairly succinct statement of his controversial position on the rank of the Ka'ba is taken from Ahmad Sirhindī's *Mabda' va Ma'ād:* (Origin and Return):[34]

> The Reality of the Qur'ān and the Reality of the Lord's Ka'ba are higher than the Reality of Muhammad. Therefore the Reality of the Qur'ān has precedence over the Muhammadan Reality and the Reality of the Lord's Ka'ba became the locus of prostration for the Muhammadan Reality. Despite this the Reality of the Ka'ba is above the Qur'ānic Reality. At that level everything is without attribute or color and there is no scope for modalities and expressions.
>
> Transcendence and sanctification are beyond that presence.
> There, everything is ineffable.
>
> This is a gnostic realization which not one of the people of God has articulated before nor has any one spoken of it. This dervish has been ennobled by this knowledge and exalted above his fellows. All of this is through the truthfulness of the beloved of God and the blessings of the Messenger of God, may peace be upon him.
>
> You should know that since the form of the Ka'ba is the locus of prostration for the forms of all things, (then) the Reality of the Ka'ba is also the locus of prostration for the true essences of these things.[35]

This Naqshbandi understanding of the Ka'ba seems to have been found objectionable by a number of the 'ulamā', especially in the Hijaz, and they in return launched a series of counter polemic treatises and eventually a fatwa of heresy against Sirhindi.[36]

According to Muhammad Iqbāl Mujaddidī,

> On the arrival of Hadrat (Muhammad Ma'sūm) in the Noble Holy Cities the discussion of the Reality of the Ka'ba became increasingly frequent among the religious scholars. The concept of the Naqshbandis was that "the Ka'ba is not the name for stone and clay but rather the 'Reality of the Ka'ba' is better than that of all other realities, even that of the noble prophets."
>
> This subject became the object of heated discussion. From the time when the Khalifa of Mujaddid, Shaikh Ādam Banurī (1052/1643),[37] emigrated to settle in the Holy Cities until the arrival of the Sirhindī's sons on pilgrimage in 1068/(1657/58), a number of treatises supporting and refuting this had already been composed.[38] Sirhindī himself had written treatises on this subject and sent them to the scholars of the Holy Cities, in which he cited copious proofs for his previously stated opinions.

In short, the Naqshbandis who followed Sirhindī considered the Ka'ba to be much more than a stone structure. Its spiritual reality seems to have been accorded the highest status, even above that of the Prophet. More evidence of the controversial nature of this doctrine is found in the writings of Badr al-Dīn Sirhindī, a khalīfa of Ahmad Sirhindī and the father of the translator of *Hasanāt al-Haramain* into Persian. In his *Hadarat al-Quds*, Hadarat 7, Badr al-Dīn writes to dispel five criticisms or aspersions (*shubhāt*) cast on Mujaddid's teachings.

The third of these aspersions concerns his Sirhindī's statement in the *Mabda' va Ma'ād* is that "since the form of the Ka'ba is the locus of prostration for the form of Muhammad, then the Reality of the Ka'ba is the locus of prostration of the 'Muhammadan Reality.'" The author of the *Hadarat al-Quds* writes,

> From this the preeminence of the "Reality of the Ka'ba" over the "Reality of Muhammad" is entailed, although it is established that he, may the peace and blessings of God be upon him, was the goal of the creation of this world and the universes, and that Adam and all human beings are his dependents. "If not for him God would not have created the spheres and lordship would not have been manifest."[39]

The reply: In the course of defending against this aspersion Hadrat (Ahmad Sirhindī) wrote,

> The form of the Ka'ba is not an expression for stone and mud since even if stone and mud were not involved the Ka'ba would still be the Ka'ba and the place of prostration for created things. Rather, the form of the Ka'ba, in that it is from the World of Creation (*'alam al-khalq*), is something concealed in terms of the color of the essences of things which is beyond the ken of perception and imagination of the sensible world. No tangible thing faces it and it faces nothing. It is a being which wears the garment of non-being and a non-being which shows itself in the attire (*kiswa*)[40] of its own being. It is in the direction without directionality and the path without path.
>
> In summary, this form is a reality created of wonder, which the mind falls short of identifying and is perplexed in defining. It is as if it is the model of the divine world and a trace of the unique is expressed in it. For if it were not, prostration to it would not be allowed and the best of existent things, may the peace and blessings of God be upon him, would not have chosen it as his qibla with the ardent hope of God.

> O brother! Now that you know a portion of the form of the Ka'ba, listen to a discourse about the reality of the noble Ka'ba. The "Reality of the Ka'ba" is an expression of the unqualified essence of the Necessary Being, may His power be exalted, which emerges from the appearance of tenebrous existence. Thus, there is no access to Him other than through prostration and servantship.
>
> If they call this Reality "the place of prostration of the Reality of Muhammad", what danger is entailed and what shortcoming occurs with respect to his superiority? Indeed the "Reality of Muhammad" is nobler than the rest of the realities of the world, but the "Reality of the Ka'ba" is not of this world so that it should have this relationship to him and stop short at his superiority. It is the confusion of the forms of these two things which has entailed perplexity.

We also have evidence of the course of this dispute during the intervening years in the *Ma'ārij al-Wilāyat* of 'Abd Allāh Khweishgī Qasūrī (1043–1106/1633–1694).[41] This important work is still in manuscript. According to Muhammad Iqbāl Mujaddidī, this manuscript recounts an important debate which occurred in the Hijaz between Shaikh Ādam Banurī (1053/1643), who had emigrated there, and Shaikh Ahmad Qashāshī (1071/1661),[42] concerning the "Reality of the Ka'ba." While Banurī initially claimed its precedence over all of the Prophets, Qashāshī, through proofs and textual indicants was able to finally get him to acknowledge the superiority of Muhammad, although not that of the other Prophets, to the Ka'ba.

> Qashāshī demanded, "What is your proof for the superiority of the Ka'ba?" He (Banurī) replied, "The proof of the superiority of the Ka'ba over Muhammad Mustafa, may the peace and blessings of God be upon him, is his prostrating to it and its being the locus of his prostration. The form of the Ka'ba is not this stone and clay, not this roof and walls but rather it is a manifestation (*zuhūr*) without a form which reason falls short of comprehending."
>
> Qashāshī disputed this on the basis of the firm consensus of the community that the master of all beings (Muhammad) was the best of created things and that even his grave was superior to the Ka'ba.[43]
>
> Further, a denial of the importance of the form of the Ka'ba amounted to a clear rejection of the clear injunction of the Qur'ān contained in several verses and innumerable authentic traditions. As the 'ulamā' regarded those who did not recognize the Ka'ba as infidels, one who denied his significance was even a more reprehensible infidel. Finally, to call the Ka'ba a stone was an

insult to the House of Allah and one who treated it so contemptuously was an infidel.[44]

Qashashi wrote a treatise on this subject which was copied by Qasūrī in his *Ma'ārij al-Walāyat*. Mujaddidī notes that, given Qasūrī's opposition to Ahmad Sirhindī and other evidence, his statement regarding Banurī's retraction of his belief in the superiority of the Ka'ba did not in fact seem to have been accurate.[45]

It may be further observed that the hierarchical tension between the Ka'ba and the human is paralleled in both Sirhindī and Ibn 'Arabi by a tension between the respective ranks of the Prophet and the Saint. Citing from the same provocative passage in Sirhindī's *Mabda' va Ma'ād:*

"And I utter an amazing saying which no one has ever heard nor has any informer ever told of it by the announcement of God, may he be praised...that after one thousand and some years since the time of the passing of that master, may peace and blessings be upon him and his family, a time has come that the Reality of Muhammad has ascended from its station and united with the station of the reality of the Ka'ba."[46]

It is well known that Sirhindī further formulated that the union of these two stages on the eve of the second millenium was to create a new station, the "Reality of Ahmad," which seemed to be a reference to his own enhanced stature as the Renewer (Mujaddid) of that second millenium.[47]

Let us briefly note that the Ka'ba had also been the site for Ibn 'Arabi's vision on a similar theme:

I saw a vision of this kind concerning myself which I took as good tidings to me from God, since it had a similarity to the tradition of the Prophet in which he indicated to us his position in respect to the other Prophets. He says, "As regards my position among the other Prophets, it is as if a man built a wall leaving out one brick. I am that brick and no apostle or Prophet will come after me." Here he likens the prophethood to the wall and the prophets to the bricks which make it up...I was in Mecca in the year 599 when I saw, as in a dream, the Ka'ba built of gold and silver bricks; but when I looked at a spot on the face between the Yemeni and Syrian corners I noticed that there were two bricks missing, one of gold, the other of silver, one on the top row and the other on

> the row below it. Then I saw myself being put into the place of the missing bricks...I woke up and thanked God and said to myself, "I am to the followers of my kind (the saints) as the Apostle of God is to the other prophets."[48]

Comparing these visions of Ibn 'Arabi to those of Sirhindī and his followers one finds elements representing both change and continuity. Both are preoccupied with issues of ranking and hierarchy—is the saint higher than the Prophet—is the human better than the Ka'ba and their implications for charismatic authority—is a living teacher higher than a religious symbol?

Thus the following binary oppositions apply in both of the visions: inanimate/alive; prophet/saint; Ka'ba/human. Although the outcome is more nuanced than the following conclusion will imply, Ibn 'Arabi's vision apparently resolves the tension in favor of the living human saint, while Sirhindī's favors the inanimate, the Ka'ba, and the Prophet. Echoes of this tension persist in the broader Islamic community, and especially among South Asian Muslims, in the ongoing debate as to whether the Prophet is a dead historical personage[49] or a living spiritual presence.[50]

Pursuing the symbolic codes further is suggestive. We may tentatively conclude that by identifying the union of the "Reality of the Ka'ba" and the "Reality of the Prophet Muhammad" with himself, Sirhindī, by linking himself to the idea of the living representative which he at times articulated as being "heir and follower to the prophet," resolves the oppositions laid out previously.[51] This conceptualization is also congruent with his controversial formulation that there were, in fact, two levels of Muhammad's individual instantiation of the perfections of prophecy; the spiritual level and the human level. According to Sirhindī, as time passed from the era of the Prophet Muhammad, his spiritual role supplanted the human side to such an extent that the situation of his community in the world had deteriorated.[52] Sirhindī as the "Renewer of the Second Millenium" was to have the role of ushering in the restoration of this human reformist side and opening the way for further heirs and successors of the Prophet to continue and fulfill this aspect of his mission.

From the standpoint of the sociology of religion, this necessary mediating role is clearly one of the continuity in a living figure of the charismatic authority of the founder.

Let us now briefly summarize some of the remaining visions of the *Hasanāt*. The second section recalls twenty visions which take place in Mecca. These seem to be organized according to location rather than chronology since some visions which are cited occurred before he visited al-Madina and some took place during his return journey.[53]

A summary of some of the visions of this section of the *Hasanāt* follows: (1) He sees the angels and their performing circumambulation (*tawāf*) of the Ka'ba. (2) He goes to Mount 'Arafāt and has a vision of the Prophet at the Khaif mosque. (3) During the *Tashrīq*[54] days when he goes to Mecca from Mina to perform the circumambulation he sees a vision informing him that his Hajj has been accepted by God. (4) While staying in Mecca he often performed circumambulations of the Ka'ba. On one of these occasions he sees the Ka'ba hugging him and kissing him passionately. He feels overwhelmed by lights which efface everything else and on reflection he realizes that he has become empty of himself and that he subsists through the Ka'ba.[55] (5) On the 3rd of Muharram while visiting the Ma'āla cemetery he encounters Khadīja, 'Abd al-Rahmān ibn Abī Bakr, and others buried there. In this and the following section he makes particular reference to visiting the graves of followers of Ahmad Sirhindi who are buried there. Due to the shortcomings of some of these followers in devotion to Sirhindi, Muhammad Ma'sūm is not able to spiritually connect with them in a proper way. Vision 7 is worthy of more attention because it goes into a detailed discussion of the "Reality of the Ka'ba" and issue of rank. The compiler of the text describes it as follows.

> Because the writings of Mujaddid contain various expressions about "The Reality of the Ka'ba", Hadrat Khwāja (Ma'sūm) attempted to collate them and bring them into correspondence with one another. He asked for help from the World of the Unseen in revealing its true nature and those seekers of certainty who were attached to him waited hopefully for the results of those gnostic revelations. Finally, one day while in Mecca he said with great happiness and exultation to his sons, who had been experiencing the benefits of retreat with him, "Once I had deeply reflected on this matter then I got to the very basis of this truth, I saw the Ka'ba having priority over all realities and felt that all things were prostrating to it and that it was from this highest pinnacle that all things connected with servitude (*'ubūdiyya*), even the ranks of prophecy and

> apostleship, had descended. Anything touched by contingency or tainted by servitude stops at this point, and beyond it lies the `Reality of Being Worshipped' (*ma'būdiyya*)."
>
> "Once I had again considered and gone more deeply into reflecting, then an extremely delicate secret was disclosed and this is that I became aware that the Reality of the Ka'ba despite all of the previously explained stages of drawing nearer and descending nearness and explained ranks.... In fact, progress and ascent are the particularities of human beings, nothing else can share this with them. Therefore, the reality which belongs to the Ka'ba, has no share of what lies beyond itself, and I also sensed that those human individuals who were the most perfected especially, Muhammad, Abraham, and Moses may peace and blessings be upon them, although their natures as living beings are below the Reality of the Ka'ba, due to progress and ascent they were able to pass beyond it. Thus, despite the Ka'ba's priority over all things, some humans are able to achieve the level beyond it."[56]

On the basis of this passage one may assert that Muhammad Ma'sūm's position of the Reality of the Ka'ba had already moderated. This compromise which averts asserting the absolute superiority of either the Ka'ba or the Prophet is evident from later Naqshbandi diagrams of the spiritual itinerary which place the two stations in a parallel, rather than a hierarchical relationship.[57] (9.) He briefly recounts another vision of the Ka'ba embracing him. (13) He enters the second level of the Ka'ba and is presented with a green robe of honor. (14.) He sees spirits performing the circumambulation and refers to the Prophet's vision of Moses praying in his grave. (15.) He speaks of the Ka'ba coming to him physically as he performs the dhikr. It leaves its place and approaches, embracing him, kissing him every time he repeats the profession of faith.

THIRD SECTION (23 VISIONS) IN MADINA AND ON THE RETURN HOME

The visions in this section are connected with sites of Madina and the return such as those connected with the martyrs of Badr, the graves of Fātima and 'Ā'isha, and the Baqī' cemetery. Overall, the main factors in the arrangement of the visions of the *Hasanāt* seem to be time and place. The dominant themes of the visions are receiving tokens of spiritual rank and blessings, and meeting with the spirits of departed great and saintly persons.

SHAH WALI ALLAH AND THE FUYŪD AL-HARAMAIN

Shah Wali Allah (d. 1762) was a more prolific writer and a better-known intellectual than Muhammad Ma'sūm. In his Sufi practice he could be characterized as being more eclectic, although his early training was in the same Naqshbandi tradition.[58] He made the pilgrimage in 1730–31 as a relatively young man. He had been initiating disciples since his father's death when he was about 16, but during his stay in the two Holy Cities he seems to have generally had the role of student in the religious sciences, especially hadith studies, and in Sufism.[59]

His visionary account is, in contrast to the sightings of the *Hasanāt*, his own composition, not that of a compiler. It is less structured, less focused on specific times, places, and sites and the text only occasionally mentions specific visionary images and symbols. Although some of the visions are dated, it is not overtly chronologically or thematically organized. For example, in many sections it seems that the context is one in which he, while in a visionary state, is asking the Prophet questions and receiving answers.

Shah Wali Allah, in a fashion which was typical of his style, uses his visions to work out issues which he found problematic, especially contemporary debates over spiritual and religious ranking and the accommodation of divergent opinions.[60] Shah Wali Allah seems to have used the vehicle of visionary pilgrimage accounts to explore many of the controversial issues which would preoccupy him in future works written after his return to India.

Among these conflicting perspectives were the respective rankings of 'Ali and the first two caliphs,[61] of the Hanafis vs. the other legal schools,[62] of saints vs. 'ulamā',[63] and of the adherents of *wahdat al-wujūd* vs. *wahdat al-shuhūd*.[64] The work is introduced by the following passage:

> By the great grace of God I was able to make the pilgrimage to the house of God and visit the Messenger of God in 1143/1730. An even greater blessing than this is that my Hajj was accompanied by divine visions and gneiss, and neither being veiled nor ignorance stood in my way. And the greatest blessing according to me is that my visit was one of insight (*ziyāra mubsira*) not one of ignorance (*ziyāra 'amīya'*).[65]

His first visionary experience, which occurred in a dream, does not mention time or place. It concerned the philosophy of *wahdat al-wujūd*. One of his most concrete and often cited visions is 6, that of 10 Safar 1144 (Tuesday, 14 August 1731) in which he speaks of having a dream in Mecca in which the grandsons of the Prophet, Hasan and Husain, come to his house. Hasan is holding in his hand a pen with a broken tip, which he holds out to Wali Allah saying, "This is the pen of my grandfather, the Prophet."[66] He then has Husain repair it and gives it to him. Wali Allah is happy at this. Hasan and Husain then present him with their grandfather's mantle. This is a clearly visionary experience which is initiatory and establishes rank and a sense of Wali Allah's mission as extending that of the Prophet.

The majority of his dreams/visions, however, are discursive, rather than symbolic or concrete, although Wali Allah does on occasion speak of a concrete vision of the Prophet. An example is his ninth vision, "At the time I arrived in Madina Munawwara and arrived at the Rauda [the Prophet's tomb] I saw his holy spirit externally, with my eyes."[67] In the many visions which mention the Prophet, his role is primarily that of a guide or interlocutor rather than that of a symbol or image. The following passage is typical of the tone and subject matter of the visionary citings of the *Fuyūd al-Haramain*.

> I asked the Prophet for advice about certain things which bothered me and which went against my natural inclination. Then proofs concerning these matters came from God.
>
> One thing which had concerned me was the counsel to practice taqlid of one of the four legal schools and not to go beyond this school and to agree with it as much as possible. I had by nature inherently rejected *taqlīd* and totally despised it. I felt that something had been sought of me with regard to worship with which I felt myself to be in conflict.
>
> Thank God I was given an inspiration regarding the nature of this situation.

These two visionary pilgrimage texts are comparable in some features but not in others. Ma'sūm's follows the built-in spatial and temporal structure of before, during, and after the pilgrimage or departure, arrival and return. The visions of Muhammad Ma'sūm are recounted in a much more visual and concrete way. Shah Wali Allah's account is less visual and spatial in arrangement and in his visions a range of recurrent themes seem to be atomistically treated.

The themes of Muhammad Ma'sūm's visions of the Ka'ba emphasize rank, hierarchy, the distinctive identity of the Naqshbandi tariqa, and its understanding of the cosmology underlying its particular spiritual itinerary. The fact that Shah Wali Allah does not choose to continue the discussion of the Reality of the Ka'ba indicates that it had been resolved in his thought and also indicates that its significance for pro and counter Sirhindī polemic has receded. One may already see evidence of a moderation of the Naqshbandi-Mujaddidi position in Ma'sūm's visions. By Shah Wali Allah's time the millennium itself had passed over a hundred years before. Rather than invoking *tajdīd* in the same radical mode as Sirhindī,[68] Shah Wali Allah primarily claimed for himself the less controversial positions of *mufahhim*[69] and *muhaddath*[70] and worked both of these roles into his cosmological depiction of the spiritual itinerary.

A further observation is that in Wali Allah's text the themes of rank and hierarchy are continued but the specific identity and superiority of a particular Sufi path is less an issue, as I have argued elsewhere.[71]

CONCLUSIONS

The play upon sighting/siting, it seems to me, evokes the interaction between the visual and the physical experience of space. This is rendered more complex through the fact that these experiences must be further translated into the medium of narrative, i.e., they must be *cited* through the written word. The problem is thus raised of recounting in language what has been seen, or in the case of our Naqshbandi Sufis, what has been seen by the inner eye. In many cases the thought or epiphany generated by the vision/sight seems to take precedence over the form of what is seen. The actual site of pilgrimage, the Ka'ba, is not a geographical or physical space but rather primarily a spiritual presence.

All of this is interwoven with the experience of the great pilgrimage. For our Indian voyagers, this was indeed a great journey which could last for several years. Why did this inspire visionary reflection? Was it a sense of the spiritual presence of the Prophet?

Some clues to this may be found in contemporary studies by anthropologists on initiatory dreams in South Asian Sufism.[72] The initiatory dream in Sufism establishes one's relationship with the pir or spiritual master. Since the Prophet is the master of all masters, the visit to Madina would naturally occasion this type of visionary initiation, whether in a dream of hypnagogic state.[73]

In terms of the local elements of the seventeenth and eighteenth century pilgrims' experiences, one may imagine that they did encounter diversity and dislocation in the new environment of the Holy Cities. The disciples of Sirhindī seem to have been subjected to some opposition, described as "jealousy,"[74] and their teacher was condemned as heretical by at least some scholars of the two Holy Cities. A few references in the *Fuyūd al-Haramin* suggest the necessity for some cultural adjustments on the part of the South Asian pilgrims, for example, a reference to having to adjust to the troublesome habits of the people of Mecca.[75]

What then could have been the purpose behind the visionary pilgrimage narratives composed in the seventeenth and eighteenth centuries? One element is that common to much of Sufi literature, including contemporary works, i.e., confirming the stature of the visionary because he is the one having these spiritual experiences such as visions and initiatory experiences with the Prophet.

Another appears to be ideological. Each one of these narratives argues one or more points of theological controversy. As I have postulated elsewhere,[76] visions are "good to think" and the fact that these occurred and were recorded in conjunction with the great pilgrimage is consistent with an experience of liminality, shifting hierarchies, and induction techniques of retreats and hardship. In this case the specific sights or visions seem to recede in the face of their interpretations or the thoughts which they occasion.

Historical shifts in Sufi orientation are reflected in our comparison of the two texts. Thematically, Shah Wali Allah's visions deal most prominently with the Prophet and occur at his tomb or in some kind of spiritual encounter with him.[77] Although there are several which occur at the Ka'ba, the Ka'ba is no longer personified or figures prominently in the visionary imagination. Perhaps this thematic shift could be co-related with the emergence of "Neo-Sufi" tendencies which some scholars feel is typical of eighteenth century Islam. John Voll enumerates as a feature of Neo-Sufism less focus on the aspiration to unite with the ultimate "One" which characterized the earlier school of wahdat al-wujūd, and instead a more personal devotion to the figure of the Prophet combined with the study of his sayings. One may suggest that as a consequence of this development Shah Wali Allah and the nineteenth century Naqshbandis ceased to assert the priority of the Ka'ba to the Prophet. For example, they iconographically resolved this tension in their cosmological diagrams by placing the stations of the "Reality of Muhammad" and the "Reality of the Ka'ba" in a parallel rather than a hierarchical relationship.[78]

Historically, we may also suggest that this particular use of visionary pilgrimage narratives to pursue problematic issues of theology, was typical of the late pre-modern period of Sufism in South Asia. One topic for further study would be earlier South Asian writings on the pilgrimage, for example, Shāh 'Abd al-Haqq Muhaddith Dihlavī's (1551–1642), *Jadhb al-Qulūb,* a text of the previous century (he made the pilgrimage in (996/1587). The text is more formal and less visionary, but this may simply reflect 'Abd al-Haqq's more sober mystical attitude or the conventions of another genre, *fadā'il* literature.[79] The argumentative mode is used by 'Abd al-Haqq when he discusses the permissibility of visiting graves and whether the saints are alive in their tombs,[80] but rhetorically this discussion is presented more explicitly rather than being couched in visionary symbols.

Subsequent pilgrimage accounts seem to become, as Metcalf has noted, more personal and individual, reflecting changes in cultural and intellectual life.[81] The journey to the holy sites continues to provoke reflection and transformation, but in more recent accounts this is encountered and interpreted in a more personal way rather than through visionary symbols which represent and trigger rearrangements of hierarchical categories of thought.

NOTES

1. The juxtaposition of citing, siting and sighting is made in part to indicate the intriguing relationship among these aspects of pre-modern visionary pilgrimage narratives. Elements of this genre play on the difficulty of moving between visionary experiences and narration. At the same time certain beliefs or ideologies cognitively mapped shape the nature of the visionary event as experienced, or at least as told.

2. The inspiration for this genre seems to have been Ibn al-'Arabī's (d. 1240) *al-Futūhāt al-Makkiyya* (Meccan Revelations), a wide-ranging stream of consciousness excursion through discursive and spiritual insights. This text, however, runs to many volumes and is less specifically focussed on actual sites and sights of pilgrimage. A recent partial French/English translation is *Les*

Illuminations de la Mecque, trans. W. Chittick, C. Chodkiewicz, D. Gril, J. Morris (Paris: Sindbad, 1988).

3. Barbara Metcalf, "The Pilgrimage Remembered" in *Muslim Travellers*, Dale Eickleman & James Piscatori, eds. (Berkeley: University of California Press, 1990), p. 86.

4. For more on the process of using visionary elements as tools for thought see Marcia K. Hermansen "Mystical Visions as 'Good to Think': A Cognitive Approach to Visionary Experience," *Religion* 27 (1, 1977): 25-43.

5. A biography of Muhammad Ma'sūm in Urdu is *Anvār-i-Ma'sūmiyya*, by S. Zawwār Husain Shāh (Karachi: Idāra Mujaddidiyya, 1980). This also features an Urdu translation of much of the *Hasanāt al-Haramain*. The second volume of the Naqshbandi work *Rauda Qayyūmiyya* by Muhammad Ihsān Mujaddidī, Urdu translation by Iqbāl Ahmad Fārūqī (Lahore: Maktaba Nabawiyya, 1989) also concerns his life and activities. His letters were published in three volumes as *Maktūbāt* (Kanpur: Nizami Press, 1304 A.H.) and his prayers in *Adhkar-e-Ma'sūmiyya* (Lahore: Maktaba Hakim Saifi, 1384 A.H.). An Urdu abridgement of his letters is *Maktūbāt-i-Hadrat Muhammad Ma'sūm*, by Maulānā Nasīm Ahmad Farīdī Amrohī (Mūsā Zā'ī: Maktaba Sirājiyya, 1981), p. 30.

6. Written about the pilgrimage of his father Khwaja Muhammad Sa'id in 1068/1658. Cited in *Hasanāt al-Haramain*, ed Persian text and Urdu translation by Muhammad Iqbāl Mujaddidī (Mūsā Zā'ī: Maktaba Sirajiyya, 1981), p. 30.

7. His treatise "Al-Mufādila baina al-insān wal-Ka'ba" (Competition for Superiority between the Human Being and the Ka'ba), which is still in manuscript as part of the *Natā'ij al-Haramain*, would also be relevant to the theme of this paper. The only legible manuscript seems to be in Peshawar, Pakistan. The India Office manuscript, although cited by Mujaddidī, is not the copy he used since it is badly scrambled.

8. Shāh 'Abd al-Rahīm lists the same line of transmission in his, *Irshād-i Rahimiyya dar Tarīqa Hazarat Naqshbandiyya* (Delhi?: Matba Ahmadī, n.d.), p. 3.

9. See also Shāh Walī Allāh, *Anfas al-'Ārifīn*, Urdu trans. by Muhammad Fārūq al-Qādirī (Lahore: Ma'ārif, 1974), pp. 40–56.

10. Banurī's grave in the Baqi' cemetery was visited by Muhammad Ma'sūm. *Hasanāt*, pp. 196–197, 245. Some sources refer to strained relations between Banurī and Muhammad Ma'sūm based on the notice in *Rauda Qayyūmiyya*, Vol. II by Muhammad Ihsān Mujaddidī, Urdu translation by Iqbāl Ahmad Fārūqī

(Lahore: Maktaba Nabawiyya, 1989), pp. 136–141. M. Iqbāl Mujaddidī strongly disputes this, on the basis of more primary sources. *Hasanāt*, pp. 35–42.

11. Walī Allāh, *al-Tafhimāt al-Ilāhiyya*, I, pp. 11–12 and *al-Intibāh fi Salāsil Auliyā' Allāh* (Karachi: 'Abbas Kutub Khānah, 1976 [reprint of 1344]).

12. By his disciple, Muhammad Āmin.

13. It appears that some members of the Indian Mahdavi movement also composed visionary pilgrimage narratives. Personal communication, Darryl MacLean.

14. For studies of Sirhindī and his thought see Yohanan Friedmann, *Shaikh Ahmad Sirhindi* (Montreal: McGill University Press, 1971): J.G. ter Haar, *Follower and Heir of the Prophet: Shaikh Ahmad Sirhindi (1534–1624) as Mystic* (Leiden: Het Oosters Instituut, 1992); Fazlur Rahman, *Selected Letters of Shaikh Ahmad Sirhindi* (Karachi: Iqbal Academy, 1968).

15. Werner Kraus, "Some Notes on the Introduction of the Naqshbandiyya-Khālidiyya into Indonesia" in *Naqshbandis*, ed. Marc Gaborieau, Alexandre Popovic, and Theirry Zarcone (Paris/Istanbul: Editions Isis, 1990), p. 692.

16. Mujaddidī, *Hasanāt*, p. 53.

17. *Ibid.*, p. 19.

18. More on the teachings and history of the Naqshbandiyya-Mujaddiyya in the Indian sub-continent may be found in two unpublished Ph.D. dissertations: Warren Fusfeld, "The Shaping of Sufi Leadership in Delhi," University of Pennsylvania, 1982 and Arthur Buehler, "Charisma and Exemplar: Naqshbandi Spiritual Authority in the Panjab, 1857–1947," Committee on the Study of Religion, Harvard, 1993. A useful article on this topic is "The Naqshbandiyya Order" by Khaliq Ahmad Nizami in *Islamic Spirituality II: Manifestations*, ed. Sayyid Hossein Nasr (New York: Crossroads, 1991), pp. 162–193.

19. Mujaddidī, *Hasanāt*, pp. 64–65.

20. The World of Malakūt, according to Sufi cosmology, is the plane of the angels or the "World of Images" where the ideal forms of events and objects take on similitudinary form before becoming instantiated in the physical world.

21. Mujaddidī, *Hasanāt*, p. 216.

22. The *Hadarāt al-Quds* (Lahore: Mahkama-e-Auqāf-e-Panjāb, 1971) is a biography of Shaikh Ahmad Sirhindī by his khalīfa, Badr al-Dīn (b. 971/1563–4),

which features chapters on previous Naqshbandi Shaikhs, Ahmad Sirhindī's life, spiritual experiences, miracles, and daily habits as well as refuting the views of his critics. Badr al-Dīn includes his own autobiography on pages 386–412. This edition features only the latter half of the work which deals with Sirhindī and his followers.

23. Badr al-Dīn Sirhindī, *Hadarāt al-Quds*, p. 106.

24. For example, in 'Attar, *Tazkira al-'Auliyā'*, as cited in Javad Nurbakhsh *Sufi Women* (London: Khaniqahi Nimatullahi Publications, 1990), pp. 24–26. The motif of a person substituting for the Ka'ba may be found in A.J. Arberry's translation of 'Attār, *Muslim Saints and Mystics* (Chicago: University of Chicago, 1966), p. 114.

25. This, as well as a number of Ma'sūm's other visions, personify the Ka'ba as a female who may even embrace or kiss the Sufi. For examples, see visions 4, and 9, Pt. 2 cited below. The gendered nature of Ka'ba imagery seems to be carried through in a number of Islamic ritual activities such as its being garbed in the special kiswa covering (for the Ka'ba see below n. 40). For a discussion of this female imagery and its significance see William C. Young, "The Ka'ba, Gender, and the Rites of Pilgrimage" in *International Journal of Middle East Studies*, 25 (1993):285–300.

26. In South Asia, brides generally wear red. William C. Young notes that the interior part of the kiswa was "made of red satin decorated with silver thread" and that the combination of black and red was reminiscent of women's garments in Arabia and nearby regions. *Ibid*, 292–93.

27. *Hasanāt*, Persian text p. 171, Urdu translation pp. 221ff.

28. For a discussion of Ibn 'Arabi and the Naqshbandis see Hamid Algar, "Reflections of Ibn 'Arabi in Early Naqshbandi Tradition," *Journal of the Muhyiuddin ibn Arabi Society*, 10 (1991):45–66.

29. *Hasanāt*, pp. 171, 221, paraphrased in *Rauda Qayyūmiyya* II, p. 179.

30. A further statement of Ibn 'Arabi's position is his poem XI of the *Tarjumān al-Ashwāq*, "What is the rank of the House (Ka'ba) compared to that of the human?" In a famous verse later in the same poem, the poet remarks that his heart can take on the form of the Ka'ba for the circling pilgrim. Ibn al-'Arabī, *Tajumān al-Ashwāq*, trans. R. A. Nicholson (London: Royal Asiatic Society, 1911). I am indebted to Michael Sells' paper on Ibn 'Arabi's poem presented at the Middle East Studies Association Conference, 1992, for drawing my attention to the role of the Ka'ba in this poem.

31. Ralph Austin, trans., *Sufis of Andulusia*, p. 37, *al-Futūhāt al-Makkiyya I*, ed. 'Uthmān Yahyā (Cairo: Maktaba al-'Arabiyya, 1972), pp. 216–217. See M. Chodkiewicz, *An Ocean Without Shore: Ibn Arabi, The Book, and the Law* (Albany: New York, 1993), pp. 27–29 for a discussion of this vision. An earlier study by Fritz Meier, "The Mystery of the Ka'ba", included a discussion of this vision. This may be found in *The Mysteries* (Papers from the Eranos Year Books, Bollingen Series XXX, 1955), pp. 149–68.

32. The formulation of religious symbols as both "models of" and "models for" reality is derived from Clifford Geertz, "Religion as a Cultural System" in *The Interpretation of Cultures* (New York: Basic Books, 1973) pp. 93–95. On Naqshbandi suluk see my "Shah Wali Allah's Theory of the Subtle Spiritual Centers: A Sufi Theory of Personhood and Self-Transformation" in *Journal of Near Eastern Studies* (January, 1988), 1–25 and "Mystical Paths and Authorative Knowledge: A Semiotic Analysis of Sufi Cosmological Diagrams" in *Journal of Religious Studies and Theology* 12 (1, 1992):52–77. A recent detailed review of the Naqshbandi spiritual itinerary is Arthur F. Buehler, "Charisma and Exemplar: Naqshbandi Spiritual Authority in the Punjab, 1857–1947," Unpublished Ph.D. thesis, Harvard, 1993, Chapter 3.

33. For example, the passage cited shortly in the text of this paper and Sirhindī's letter in the *Maktūbāt* 3, p. 164 (Lahore: reprint of the Nur Ahmad edition, 1964–1971). The separate treatise may not be extant. Muhammad Sa'id's letter 68 in *Maktūbāt Sa'idiyya* (Lahore: Maktaba Saifi, 1965), pp. 127–129, addressed to the 'ulama' of the Holy Cities, deals with Sirhindi's theory of the *Haqiqat-i Ka'ba*. He directly associates the *Haqiqat-i Ahmadiyya* with the *Haqiqat-i Ka'ba* (p. 128) confirming the association of these two ideas and the notion of hierarchy. *Hadrāt al-Quds* 1:126 Urdu trans., 2:99 contains Badr al-Dīn Sirhindī's defense of the Mujaddidī position. Mention is also made in Ghulām 'Ali, *Sab'a Sā'ira* (Delhi: Maktaba 'Alavi, n.d.), p. 50. See the discussion of opposition to this doctrine in Friedmann, *Shaykh Ahmad Sirhindi*, pp. 94–101.

34. *Madba'va Ma'ād* is one of the author's esoteric works. Ter Haar briefly situates it, p. 6. I used the edition in Persian with the accompanying Urdu translation of Zawwār Husain Shāh (Karachi: Idāra Mujaddiya, 1968).

35. *Mabda'va Ma'ād*, pp. 72–73. Some of these phrases are written in Arabic, rather than Persian.

36. Mujaddidī, *Hasanāt*, p. 32. Yohanan Friedmann, *Shaykh Ahmad Sirhindī*, pp. 94–101.

37. See footnote 9.

38. *Hasanāt al-Haramain*, pp. 32–33. Mujaddidī mentions the separate treatise on this subject, *Al-mufādila baina al-insān wa al-ka'ba* composed by Badahkshī and included as part of the *Natā'ij al-Haramain*.

39. Referring to a hadith Qudsi, "If not for you I would not have created the spheres," which conveys the idea that Muhammad pre-exists the entire creation or, in the form of "the Muhammadan Light," is the source of all creation. See Annemarie Schimmel, *Mystical Dimensions of Islam* (Chapel Hill: University of North Carolina, 1975), pp. 215f.

40. The "kiswa" is the name of the black velvet cloth which traditionally covers the Ka'ba. An article concerning the kiswa is Richard T. Mourtel, "The Kiswa: Its Origins and Development from Pre-Islamic Times Until the End of the Mamluk Period" in *Ages: A Semi-Annual Journal of Historical, Archaeological, and Civilizational Studies* (Riyadh) 3/2 (July 1988):38–43.

41. Mujaddidī, *Ahwāl va Athār 'Abdullāh Khweshgi Qāsuri* (Lahore: Dār al-Mu'arrikhin, 1972), p. 144. See also Friedmann, pp. 95–96.

42. He, along with Ibrahīm al-Kurānī who also opposed this doctrine of Sirhindī, were in the line of the teachers of Shāh Wali Allāh. His biographical notice composed by Shāh Wali-Allāh may be found in *Anfas al-'Ārifin,* Urdu trans. by Muhammad Fārūq al-Qādiri (Lahore: Ma'arif, 1974), pp. 376–380. See also A.H. Johns "al-Kushāshī" in *Encyclopedia of Islam* (Leiden: E.J. Brill, 2nd ed.), V: 525-6.

43. Mujaddidī, *Ahwāl*, p. 153.

44. Translation by S. A. A. Rizvi, *A History of Sufism in India*, II (New Delhi: Munshiram Manoharlal, 1983), p. 339.

45. Mujaddidī, *Ahwāl*, p. 153.

46. *Mabda'va Ma'ād*, p. 72–73.

47. Friedmann, pp. 15ff, Ter Haar, pp. 145–153.

48. Translation from Ralph Austin, *Sufis of Andalusia,* p. 38. *Futūhāt*, V:68–69.

49. The position held by groups such as the Wahhabis and the Ahl al-Hadith.

50. The position generally held by the Sufis and groups such as the Ahl-e Sunnat (Barelvis) of South Asia. For a discussion of these positions see Barbara Daly Metcalf, *Islamic Revival in British India: Deoband, 1860-1900* (Princeton: Princeton University Press, 1982). On the Ahl-e Sunnat specifically see Usha

Sanya, *Devotional Islam and Politics in British India: Ahmad Riza Khan and His Movement 1870–1921* (Deli: Oxford University Press, 1996).

51. Friedmann, p. 18, characterizes his position: "The perfection (*kamālāt*) of Prophecy which have gradually disappeared since the death of Muhammad will reappear in persons who deserve this blessing because they are the Prophet's heirs and followers."

52. These two levels of the Prophet's role were symbolized by the two mims in the name of Muhammad. See Y. Friedmann, *Shaykh Ahmad Sirhindi*, p. 15.

53. *Hasanāt*, p. 254.

54. The three days immediately following the sacrifice during the Hajj when meat was traditionally hung up to dry.

55. *Ibid.*, p. 226.

56. This passage is cited and partly translated in K.A. Nizami, "The Naqshbandiyya Order" in *Islamic Spirituality II: Manifestations*, ed. S.H. Nasr (New York: Crossroads, 1989), pp. 180–181. In the *Hasanāt* it is found on pp. 177–8 (Persian) and pp. 226–7 (Urdu).

57. This aspect is discussed in my paper "Shāh Wali Allāh's Concept," pp. 14, 23.

58. In *al-Tafhimāt al-Ilāhiyya* I (Hyderabad, Pakistan: Shah Wali Allah Academy, 1967), 4, he mentions receiving the Qadiri, Chishti, and Naqshbandi paths from his father, Shāh 'Abd al-Rahīm. His chain of Naqshbandi initiation was mentioned earlier in this paper, as cited in *al-Tafhiāt al-Ilāhiyya*, I:11–12.

59. His biography, *al-Qaul al-Jali,* Urdu translation by Maulānā Hāfiz Taqi Anwār 'Alavi Kakorvi (Kakorvi: Maktaba Anwāri, 1988), pp. 52–81, recounts many of the visions reported in *Fuyūd al-Haramain.*

60. Among his more well-known accommodations are that of *wahdat al-wujūd* and *shuhūd*. On his fiqh see Mazhār Baqā', *Usūl-i Fiqh Shāh Wali Allāh* (Islamabad. Idāra Tahqīqat Islāmi, 1979). His comparative approach to Sufism is best articulated in *Hama'āt* (Hyderabad, Sindh: Shah Wali Allah Academy, 1964), pp. 84ff. In the later part of his career he became increasingly concerned with Sunni/Shi'i rival claims about the early caliphs and wrote two books on this topic, *Izālat al-Khafā' 'an Khilāfat al-Khulafā'* [Persian] (Lahore: Suhail Academy, 1976) and *Qurrat al-'Aynain fi-Tafdīl al-Shaikhain* [Persian] (Lahore: Maktaba al-Salafiyya, 1976).

61. *Fuyūd al-Haramain*, 22, p. 144:33, p. 184.

62. *Ibid.*, 19, pp. 136–137.

63. *Ibid.*, 21, pp. 139–143.

64. *Ibid.*, 1, pp. 21–25.

65. *Ibid.*, p. 20.

66. *Ibid.*, pp. 21–22.

67. *Ibid.*, p. 81.

68. This is not to say that among his various roles Shāh Wali Allāh did not number the role of mujaddid. On a number of occasions including vision 15 of *Fuyūd*, he laid claim to this role for the 12th century A.H.

69. A person who is guided to inner interpretation, as was the Prophet Muhammad or Joseph.

70. A role associated in the hadith with 'Umar. The muhaddathūn are those pupils of the Prophets who follow in their footsteps and are likewise inspired by higher forces. In the text *Altāf al-Quds*, Shāh Wali Allāh describes the muhaddath as one who synthesizes the paths of saintship and prophecy. This again resolves the hierarchical tension between the role of the prophet and saint through conceiving of them as parallel tracks which can be integrated by a single individual. *Altāf al-Quds* [Original Persian with Urdu trans. by 'Abd al-Hamid Swāti] (Gujranwala: Madrasa Nusrat al-'Ulūm, 1964). English translation, *The Sacred Knowledge*. G.H. Jalbani and D. Pendelberry (London: Octagon Press, 1984). See also my "Shah Wali Allah's Theory of the Subtle Spiritual Centers: A Sufi Theory of Personhood and Self-Transformation" in *Journal of Near Eastern Studies* (January, 1988):23 for a discussion of how Shah Wali Allah resolves the issue of hierarchy in the roles of saintship and prophecy.

71. In my paper "Mystical Paths and Authoritative Knowledge: A Semiotic Analysis of Sufi Cosmological Diagrams" in *Journal of Religious Studies and Theology*, pp. 66–67.

72. Katherine P. Ewing, "The Dream of Spiritual Initiation and the Organization of Self-Representations among Pakistani Sufis" in *American Ethnologist*, 17/1 (1990):56–74.

73. On the hypnagogic state see Andreas Mavromatis, *Hypnagogia: The Unique State of Consciousness between Wakefulness and Sleep* (London and New York:

Routledge, 1987); Daniel Merkur, *Gnosis: An Esoteric Tradition of Mystical Visions and Unions* (Albany: SUNY Press, 1993.

74. Mujaddidī describing material from an unpublished *Risāla Manāqib Ahmadiyya wa Maqāmāt Ma'sūmiyya* by Muhammad Amin Badadkshi, *Hasanāt al-Haramain*, p. 32.

75. *Fuyūd al-Haramain*, p. 93.

76. Marcia K. Hermansen, "Visions as 'Good to Think': A Cognitive Approach to Visionary Experience."

77. The increasing prominence of the Prophet in Wali Allāh's visions may be somehow related to what John O. Voll finds to be one of the characteristics of "Neo-Sufism," see "Hadith Scholars and Tariqahs: An 'Ulema' Group" in *Journal of Asian and African Studies*, Vol. 15, July-October, 1980, 262–267. A recent review of this debate may be found in R.S. O'Fahey, *Enigmatic Saint: Ahmad ibn Idris and the Idrisi Tradition* (Evanston: Northwestern, 1990, pp. 1–9 and his article "Neo-Sufism Reconsidered" in *Islam: Zeitschrift fur Geschichte und Kultur des Orients*, LXX/1 (1993):52–87.

78. This aspect is discussed in more detail in my paper, "Shah Wali Allah's Theory of the Subtle Spiritual Centers. A Sufi Theory of Personhood and Self-Transformation" in *Journal of Near Eastern Studies* 47, 1 (January, 1988):1–25.

79. Fadā'il literature enumerates the virtues of a particular person or place. It is a sub-topic of the hadith collections as well as a separate genre. See article "Fadila" by R. Sellhein, *Encyclopedia of Islam* (Leiden: E.J. Brill, 1965), II:728–729.

80. 'Abd al-Haqq Muhaddith Dihlavi, *Jadhb al-Qulūb ilā Diyār al-Mahbūb* (Hyderabad: Matba-i-Quddūsi 1273/1856) Urdu translation, *Tarikh-e-Madina* by Muhammad Sādiq (Lahore: Sang-i-Mil, 1959).

81. Metcalf briefly evokes Shāh Wali Allāh's attitude towards his dream and visionary experiences in comparison with that of a contemporary Pakistani intellectual, in "What Happened in Mecca: Mumtaz Mufti's 'Labbaik'" in *The Culture of Autobiography: Constructions of Self-Representation*, ed. Robert Folkenflik (Stanford: Stanford University Press, 1993): 149–167. See pp. 152–53.

Chapter 10

IN THE GARDENS OF AL-ZAHRĀ': LOVE ECHOES IN A POEM BY IBN ZAYDŪN[1]

Th. Emil Homerin

Fazlur Rahman loved poetry. Often in class he would recite from memory verse by a host of poets, from Shelly and Goethe to Iqbāl, Rūmi, and Labid. Fazlur Rahman impressed upon his students the necessity of studying Arabic poetry for a firm grasp of the Qur'ānic text and context. But his appreciation of verse went well beyond philological or historical interests. Most of all, he stressed poetry's special power to elicit emotion and evoke action, and this aspect of verse is reflected in Fazlur Rahman's own writings. On several occasions he quoted verse to drive home charges against scholasticism, secularism, and popular religious beliefs which, he believed, had compromised the original Qur'ānic message.[1] Elsewhere, he cited verse to highlight more personal dimensions of Islam, particularly those involving Islamic mysticism, he noted that poetry can stretch language beyond its normally descriptive and discursive functions in order to intimate deeper spiritual concerns.[2]

---

[1] I read an earlier version of this paper for The Gest Program, Haverford College. I want to thank Michael Sells, who organized the program, my co-participants Hanna Kassis and Raymond Scheindlin, and the students and other faculty in the audience; I greatly appreciate their kind and insightful comments on my reading of the poems.

For Fazlur Rahman, then, poetry was far more than rhymed words, or witty anecdotes; it was an essential form of human discourse. This is certainly true for Islamic civilization where early on there was a confluence of the Arabic poetic tradition with vital currents of Islamic belief and practice, particularly those flowing from philosophy and mysticism. In fact, poetry was such an integral element of classical Islamic culture that our current, largely dialectical categories of "secular" and "sacred" poetry are not only inadequate but often misleading when speaking of Arabic verse composed prior to the twentieth century. This is especially the case for poems on love.

Classical Arabic love poetry stems from the moods and themes of the pre-Islamic *qasīdah* and, in this case, specifically from the *nasīb*, the elegiac prelude. There, the poet recollects his departed beloved, and often describes his mistress or his encounters with her and her companions who chide him for being immoderate and reckless.[3] The early love poems or *ghazals* of the 7th–8th centuries developed these and other elements of the nasib, especially the dialogue between the poet and his beloved, and so significantly enhanced the nasib's lyrical qualities. As a result, these *ghazals* are sentimental, not heroic like the early *qasīdahs*, and this probably reflects increasingly individual and less tribal perceptions of existence refined by the courtly life of the cities. The influence of folk poetry and singing girls is also apparent in the simple charm of this uninhibited sexual poetry, best illustrated by the *ghazals* of 'Umar Ibn Abī Rabī'ah (d. ca. 102/720) with their playful seductions of noble ladies:[4]

> Then she said to her friend,
> "Don't keep staring at him!"
> "Slyly, sister, coyly."
> —and I listened in—
> "Sister, he'll cut us off
> if he gets what he wants!"
> I said, "You've got real class;
> there's no danger from me,"
> "So take a lover,
> one ready to die,"
> "Then let God shame
> whoever's ungrateful!"

In contrast to the mock seriousness of such verse are the 'Udhrī ghazals, which retain the deep sentiments of the early nasib. Verse by Jamil (d. ca. 82/701) and other 'Udhrī poets sadly relate tales of an undying love which is rarely consummated as fate and society scheme to prevent a happy union between the lover and his beloved. A sense of loss and despair pervades these poems as the martyrdom of love becomes a substitute for the heroic quest. Unable to attain the object of his desire, the 'Udhrī poet wastes away or is driven insane. This chaste 'Udhrī love became an Arab-Muslim ideal sanctified by the prophetic tradition: "One who loves, remains chaste, never reveals his secret, and dies, dies the death of a martyr."[5] This saying supposedly reflects the fate of many lovers who became emaciated, fell ill, and died from love. The spiritual nature of 'Udhrī love is further underscored by its religious vocabulary and frequent references to God, the Qur'ān, and Islamic beliefs and rituals. Nevertheless, it is the beloved's will, or the law of love, that must be obeyed at all costs, even if this will lead to the violation of social and religious norms:[6]

How lovely the work of Satan
    if from his work
        is my love for her!

Unlike 'Umar ibn Abi Rabī'ah's compliant lady, the beloved of 'Udhrī poetry is a sacred ideal aspired to but never won. Thus the lover must renounce his physical existence and self-will and passively accept the cruelties of unrequited love. Remaining chaste, mortifying the flesh, the lover longs for a reunion between spirits destined for each other since pre-eternity:[7]

My spirit clung to hers
    before our creation
        and after we were sperm drops,
            and then in the cradle.

Yet due to the impurities of the physical body, this true union may never be consummated before death and, so, the lover burns with the fires of passion, consumed in an exaltation of emotion. The unattainable beloved remains his despair and, like the pre-Islamic poet mourning in the abandoned campsite, the 'Udhrī poet laments his lost garden of paradise:[8]

> Oh my two friends, Laylā is my garden,
> her staying away, my hell,
> and she my ascetic devotion
> when I desire to pray.

The concept of 'Udhrī love was shaped by classical Greek and later Hellenistic love theories which asserted love's power to ennoble and spiritually transform the individual, and so overcome physical mortality. Nevertheless, 'Udhrī poetry is rooted in the early nasib whose elegiac tone and mood are pervasive as the lover grieves for his departed lover, his fading youth, and the tragedy of a permanent separation. Again we hear humanity's lament before relentless time. Likewise, the sensual poetry of illicit love and sexual gratification gives expression to individual and collective yearnings, particularly the desire to be free from the ambivalent and confining strictures of conscience and society, restraints tightened by Islam and the repressive centralization of various regimes throughout Muslim lands.[9]

In the ensuing centuries, 'Udhrī love blended with ideas of decorum and refinement producing a spirit of courtliness, which permeated many later ghazals, like this one by the tenth century Andalusian poet Ahmad Ibn Faraj (d. 366/976):[10]

> Although she was ready to give
> herself to me, I abstained
> and did not accept
> the temptation Satan offered
>
> She came unveiled in the night.
> Illuminated by her face,
> night put aside its shadowy
> veil as well.
>
> Each one of her glances
> could cause hearts to turn over.

But I clung to the divine precept
that condemns lust and reined in
the capricious horses of my passion
so that my instinct
would not rebel against chastity.

And so I passed the night with her
like a thirsty little camel
whose muzzle keeps it from nursing.

She was a field of fruit and flowers
offering one like me no other enjoyment
than sight and scent.

Know then that I am not
one of those beasts gone wild
who takes gardens for pastures.

Naturally, human love continued to be a powerful spiritual force, and the bliss of union and the pains of separation remained central concerns. But as is apparent from this and other poems, the 'Udhrī ideals were gradually altered by romantic courtly love, while more erotic love interests tempered the self-effacing and masochistic aspects of the 'Udhrī spirit. Still, the 'Udhrī passion for an ideal beloved and union with her were preserved—if somewhat transfigured—in Arabic Sufi poetry.

By the ninth century, verse had begun to be ascribed to Muslim mystics. The early Sufis were known for their life of material poverty and sincere piety based on trust in God, and these preoccupations color their verse, which is often moralizing and didactic.[11]

He who seeks refuge in God is rescued by God,
    and sweet to him is God's bitter decree.

If my soul is not in the hand of God,
    then how can I obey God's judgment?

To God are the souls who rush to God;
I have no strength among them without God.

Such ascetic poetry relied heavily on images found in the elegy with its somber mood, but most early mystical verse borrowed directly from love poetry, especially the 'Udhrī ghazal. This reflected an increasing emphasis among Sufis on the reciprocal love between God and His believing servants, which is at the heart of Islamic mysticism. Central to this mystical love is the human's divine spirit (*rūh*), which has an affinity (*munāsabah*) to God, thus permitting a loving relationship between the two. For many Sufi's this relationship began in pre-eternity when the progeny of Adam bore witness to God's lordship and, thereby, took a covenant (*mīthāq*) with Him. Once in creation, humanity undergoes a period of trial (*ibtilā'*) during which individuals either follow the prophets in obedience to God, or go astray. Then, on the day of resurrection, humanity will again be brought before their Lord for judgement.[12]

However, for the mystic, life on earth is not only a moral trial; it is also an excruciating exile from the divine beloved. Thus, the devotee waits for death and the last day, desiring a reunion with God and the beatific vision. But until that time, the mystic must willingly accept the divine will and constantly recollect (*dhikr*) the day of the covenant and God's loving presence within the human heart (*qalb/sirr*). By so doing, the mystic lover may cope with his exile, tasting rare moments of spiritual communion in which God annihilates mortal self-consciousness and assumes its place. According to one tradition, God says:[13]

...and My servant continues to draw near to Me through voluntary acts of worship until I love him, and when I love him, I become his ear through which he hears and his eye through which he sees and his hand with which he grasps and his foot with which he walks.

It is the quest for such a mystical experience of loving union that dominates Arabic Sufi poetry, and given the centrality of love within the Islamic mystical tradition, it was only natural that Sufis appropriated and allegorized Arabic love poetry to speak of mystical concerns. In fact, their reinterpretation of this poetry was so thorough that the 'Udhrī poet Majnūn became the archetypal mystic obsessed with God to the point of apparent insanity.[14] Even 'Umar ibn Abī Rabī'ah's risqué conversational style found a place in Sufi verse:[15]

And when I claimed love, she countered:
"You lied to me!
Why are your limbs
still clothed in flesh?"

"There's no love
until skin clings to bone
and you, so parched,
can't answer the caller,"

"And you dry up,
shrivelled by passion,
left with an eye
to weep and confide!"

In these verses, the famous Sufi Sarī al-Saqatī (d. 253/867) transforms the traditional theme of the blaming woman who chides her presumptuous suitor, into a harangue on the importance of the *via negativa* for the mystical life. Read in terms of al-Saqatī's mystical ideas, this poem demands the eradication of the seeker's selfish desires and volition *vis à vis* his beloved as prerequisites for pure spiritual love. But this mystical reading is plausible only if these verses are embedded in a clear mystical context, for al-Saqatī's poem, as well as the majority of Arabic Sufi verse, both draws from and contributes to a larger poetic tradition. Indeed, court poets also employed Sufi styles, themes, and terms to rarify their verse such that, by the eleventh century, mystical love was an intimate part of numerous ghazals, whether composed by court poets or Sufi masters. Many verses ascribed to Sufis could have easily been attributed to poets of mortal love.

Yet here, too, the matter is not so simple. Muslim and medieval European notions of love are permeated with Hellenistic, often Neoplatonic elements as is readily apparent in medieval Arab treatises on love, especially those by the Ikhwān al-Safā' (fl. 4th/10th) and Ibn Dāwūd (d. 279/909), by Ibn Sīnā (d. 428/1037) and his contemporary in Spain, Ibn Hazm (d. 456/1064) of Cordoba.

For instance, grounding Ibn Hazm's famous treatise on love, the *Tawq al-hamāmah* ("The Ring of the Dove"), is the familiar Platonic distinction between bestial sensuality and pure and ennobling spiritual love, and Ibn Hazm goes so far as to suggest that the human beloved may, in fact, embody and manifest celestial realities.[16]

Further, we should remember that what is termed "love theory" by scholars today was often considered scientific fact by the medieval world. This is vividly illustrated by a 4th 10th century epistle that describes how the vital spirit or five force (*nasīm rūh al-hayāh*) of the lover merges in union with the life force of his beloved:[17]

> When each of two lovers breathes in his partner's face, portions of each vital spirit emerge and mingle with the air particles. When the lovers inhale some of that air, spirit particles enter their nostrils along with the inhaled air, and some reach the forepart of the brain, passing into it as does light through a crystal object. Both lovers are enraptured by breathing this spirit-laden air! Some particles of that air also reach the lungs via the throat, and from the lungs travel to the heart, where the throbbing of the arteries takes them to all parts of the body. There, the spirit particles mingle with the blood, flesh, and other bodily substances, and the vital spirit that was released from one lover's body becomes firmly enmeshed in the body of the other.

Given the power and pervasiveness of such beliefs, it was only natural that many love poets—mystical or otherwise—would draw from philosophical, mystical, and related sources with similar metaphysical groundings, and a good example of this common heritage is the love verse of the Andalusian master poet Ibn Zaydūn (d. 463/1071).

Born into an aristocratic Arab family in Muslim Spain in 394/1003, Ibn Zaydūn received a fine education and, in time, served as a courtier, a personal secretary, and a vizier in various courts. Ibn Zaydūn was an ambitious participant in the political conflicts of his day, and several times he was imprisoned or exiled from the capital at Cordoba. This apparently strained his relationship with his lover, the poetess Wallādah (d. 473/1080), daughter of the caliph al-Mustakfi (r. 415–423/1024–1032), and she became the mistress of one of Ibn Zaydūn's political rivals. Ibn Zaydūn responded by composing a biting satire against

Wallādah's new companion, together with verse chiding Wallādah's infidelity and mourning his lost love.[18] According to tradition, many of these beautiful love poems represent Ibn Zaydūn's unsuccessful attempts to persuade Wallādah to return to him. But instead of a reunion, the poet was left alone to grieve for his physical separation from his beloved who, he believed, would remain spiritually united to him forever. Invoking the physiological blending of vital spirits mentioned above, Ibn Zaydūn wrote:[19]

> When you were united to me
> like the heart
> to its membrane,
>
> Then you were mixed with me
> like the spirit
> in its body.

Not surprisingly, Ibn Zaydūn's beloved takes on heavenly proportions as he cries out for her: "Oh Garden of Paradise,"[20] and this 'Udhrī-like devotional spirit arises in many other verses, as well:[21]

> After you,
> we have adhered to no view
> save being faithful to you,
>
> And other than that,
> we are bound
> by no other faith.

Conjuring the tone and mood of the classical nasib, Ibn Zaydūn remembers his lost beloved and their embracing love in the gardens of al-Zahrā':[22]

> Full of passion,
> I remembered you in al-Zahrā'—
> The horizon was clear; the earth's face shining.

The breeze grew faint at dusk;
it seemed to pity me and lingered
full of tenderness.

The meadow was smiling, revealing a stream
silverylike necklaces
unclasped from the breast.

We were distracted by a flower
catching the eye,
dripping with dew, bending it over,

As if its eyes,
when they saw my sleeplessness,
wept for me with iridescent tears.

A rose glowed in its sun-drenched bed
making forenoon brighter still
to the eyes.

Beginning to entangle the rose
was a white water lily, fragrant,
drowsy, sleepy-eyed, roused by dawn.

Everything stirs up our memory
of passion for you,
but my chest can't bear it.

May God not calm a heart that remembered you
but failed to fly
on passion's beating wings.

Had a passing breeze wished to carry me along,
it would have brought you a warrior true
worn out by his encounter.

Or had a day, like our delicious days gone by—
as time slept, we passed the nights,
thieves of pleasure—

Had it fulfilled our desire
for union with you,
that would have been the noblest day.

Oh, my most precious gem, the most sublime,
beloved of my soul—
as if lovers dealt in jewels—

For a time, we traded pure love
on the track of intimacy
where we ran with abandon.

How sacred the covenant we kept with you.
Though you have found comfort with another now,
we still remain as lovers.

Like a pre-Islamic qasīdah, Ibn Zaydūn's ode opens in remembrance of the beloved and her former dwelling place. However, this is not an abandoned campsite in Arabia; it is the verdant Andalusian gardens at the palace of al-Zahrā' where Ibn Zaydūn and Wallādah passed heavenly love-nights. Still, in both cases, the beloved is gone. But, whereas the pre-Islamic poet flees his memories and the desert encampment seeking solace in battle, Ibn Zaydūn recalls lingering amid the idyllic gardens. There, in the sparkling waters and refulgent flowers, he sees his own emotional turmoil. The tragic humanism of the pre-Islamic ode has been polished to mirror sentiments of a refined and rarified passion.[23]

In the opening verses, Ibn Zaydūn personifies the scene; sky and earth are a clear and shining face, the breeze pities him, the meadow smiles, encircled with silver necklaces. Reversing the ancient pre-Islamic metaphor of the beloved as a garden or virgin meadow, Ibn Zaydūn finds traces of his lover in a garden at sunset (vv. 1–3). References to eyes and tears are to be seen in the following four verses (vv. 4–7), which introduce elaborate floral images. A flower filled and bent over by dew parallels the sleepless poet, head bent in tearful sorrow. The rose nearly overwhelms in its brightness; the sleepy-eyed water-lily is equally beautiful and redolent.

In these verses, Ibn Zaydūn uses the word *'ayn* (vv. 4, 6) and related terms (v. 5 *a'yun, 'āyana*) to underscore the psychological and emotional nature of his love and suffering, for 'ayn may mean not only "eye," but also a "spring," or "source of water,"—hence a "tearing eye"—as well as "one's inner most self."[24] It is this very being of the poet which is aroused and gripped by his passionate memory of the beloved; his heart still beats in excited desire for her. However, the poet's separation from his love has left him sleepless and exhausted, like the brave pre-Islamic poet who crossed the forbidding desert to be with those whom he loved (vv. 8–10).

The spiritual nature of the poet's abiding love is further revealed by the mystical references contained in several verses. In v. 9 the poet calls upon God to deny peace to a heart not impassioned by memory of the beloved.

> May God not calm a heart that remembered you
> but failed to fly
> on passion's beating wings!

In this context, the word dhikr ("memory," "remembrance") brings to mind not only the bedouin poets' recollections of their beloveds and a paradise lost, but, too, the many Qur'ānic exhortations to "remember" God, as well as the Sufi ritual practice of invoking God's many names. In addition, Ibn Zaydūn's word choice for "heart"—*qalb*—has a mystical connotation since it is a word often used by Sufis to refer to the site of personal religious enlightenment. A similar situation arises in vv. 11–12:[25]

> Or had a day, like our delicious days gone by—
> as time slept, we passed the nights,
> thieves of pleasure—
>
> Had it fulfilled our desire
> for union with you,
> that would have been the noblest day.

In the pre-Islamic ode, *ayām*, or "days," refers to times of raids and battles with enemy tribes. However, Ibn Zaydūn applies the term to love, not war, as he and his beloved "stole" blissful moments from the hands of time. Further, he alludes to the near mystical quality of his love experience with the term *jam'*, "union," which in the Sufi lexicon invariably designates mystical union. Another possible mystical allusion occurs in v. 14 and the term *uns*, "intimacy," which for the Muslim mystics means "intimacy" with God. Ibn Zaydūn uses this term within an elaborate commercial metaphor:

> Oh, my most precious gem, the most sublime,
> beloved of my soul—
> as if lovers dealt in jewels—
>
> For a time, payment we trailed pure love
> on the track of intimacy
> where we ran with abandon.

Ibn Zaydūn likens his beloved to a precious, guarded object, while noting that lovers are not concerned with "acquisition" but rather with giving. Indeed, for a time, he and his beloved gave to one another love that was true or "pure." In this context, the Arabic term for "pure," *mahd*, means "unalloyed" when referring to metal or coinage. But the term can refer to liquids in the sense of "unmixed," and, perhaps, Ibn Zaydūn is implying that he and his lover drank the pure wine of love. Whatever the case, the two lovers ran wild like horses unchecked.

Yet, as in the classical nasīb, *dahr* or "fate" (v. 11) has conspired to separate the poet from his beloved. While Ibn Zaydūn declares his unfailing devotion to her, she has broken her covenant with him (v. 16). The tension between Ibn Zaydūn's spiritual love and its earthly object is pronounced in this final verse.

> How sacred the covenant we kept with you.
> Though you have found comfort with another now,
> we still remain as lovers.

Translated more prosaically, the line begins: "But now—most praiseworthy was what we were to your covenant...," that is to say, "We kept our covenant with you." The sacred nature of this love-pact is alluded to with the phrase *ahmada*, "how praiseworthy," which echoes the oft-repeated declaration, *al-hamdu-l-lillāh*, "Praise be to God." Further, the common poetic term for a covenant or love-pact,

ʿahd, is also found throughout the Qur'ān in reference to God's promise to guide humanity provided they worship Him alone. This provides a clue as to the human nature of the beloved. For while God adheres steadfast to the divine covenant, ungrateful humans break it, just as Ibn Zaydūn's fickle lover has severed their pact and found consolation in someone new.

Despite the beloved's infidelity, Ibn Zaydūn has remained true to her and, at the poem's end, we again encounter allusions to the Qur'ān and Sufism. The final passage reads: *baqīnā ʿushshāqā* "we remained/abided as lovers." The Qur'ān states that the transient things of this world will pass away while God's countenance "abides" forever (LV:26–27). In addition, baqā' or "abiding" is a key Sufi technical term designating the ultimate mystical state in which the seeker passes away from all self-will to "abide" in God. As for *ʿushshāq*, or "lovers," this word is related to *ʿishq*, or "eros." Hence, while eros draws out creation, true lovers are drawn back through pure love to their first source where Ibn Zaydūn claims he stays still. Ibn Zaydūn's use of "we" in this verse and throughout the poem is indicative of his smooth blending of elements from poetic, philosophical, and religious traditions. In the early and classical qasidah, the poet is often accompanied at the ruins by several companions, hence the use of the first-person plural. While this seems applicable to the beginning of Ibn Zaydūn's ode amidst the gardens of al-Zahrā' (vv. 1–4), later in the poem the "we" seems to refer more to the poet in union with his beloved (vv. 11–12). In the final verse, too, "we still remain as lovers," could refer to Ibn Zaydūn and his love/Love, and/or to Ibn Zaydūn and others enraptured by the beloved/ Beloved. Of course, the plural "we" could mean "I" which is often the case in Arabic poetry and, we should note, in the Qur'ān, where God repeatedly speaks with the royal "We." Clearly, Ibn Zaydūn's play with the first-person plural intimates deeper meanings within his verse, as it elicits a sympathetic identification from his reader.[26]

This poem by Ibn Zaydūn, then, may be more than a sad lament for a personal tragedy; it may also mourn a dying way of life in Arab Andalusia. Madinat al-Zahrā' was sacked and burned early in Ibn Zaydūn's lifetime as the Umayyad dynasty of Andalusia was shattered into fragmented warring factions leading to a century of intrigue and instability. Later, several Berber dynasties actively pursued reform to shore up Muslim rule and stave off a growing threat from united Christian opponents. But, in 1492, all was lost, and the Muslims abandoned Andalusia. Madinat al-Zahrā' fell further into ruin; forgotten, the language of its inscriptions, worn traces "broken letters scarce remembered." The massive complex became a quarry and piece by piece was dismembered.[27] Yet as a quarry, the Muslim palace provided the building blocks for new construction, just as seven centuries of Arab Muslim culture in Andalusia paved the way for later works: the songs of the troubadours, our notions of romantic love, and the mystical poems of John of the Cross. Perhaps, too, we hear echoes of Ibn Zaydūn, catch a fleeting glimpse of the ancient gardens of al-Zahrā' in a poem by Federico Garcia Lorca entitled "Casida VII De La Rosa:"[28]

La rosa
no buscaba la aurora:
casi eterna en su ramo,
buscaba otra cosa.

La rosa
no buscaba ni ciencia ni sombra:
confín de carna y sueño,
buscaba otra cosa.

La rosa
no buscaba la rosa:
inmóvil por el cielo,
buscaba otra cosa.

The rose
was not looking for the dawn:
almost eternal on its stem,
it looked for something else.

The rose
was not looking for science or shadow:
confine of flesh and dream,
it looked for something else.

The rose
was not looking for the rose.
Through the sky, immobile,
it looked for something else.

NOTES

1. See Fazlur Rahman, *Islam and Modernity* (Chicago: University of Chicago Press, 1982), pp. 49, 56–58, and his *Islam* (Anchor Books, 1968), pp. 187–88, 277.

2. Fazlur Rahman, *Islam*, pp. 156, 175.

3. For more on the classical *qasīdah*, see Jaroslav Stetkevych, *The Zephyrs of Najd* (Chicago: University of Chicago Press, 1993), esp. pp. 1-49, and Michael Sells, *Desert Tracings* (1989).

4. 'Umar ibn Abi Rabi'ah, *Diwān*, 2nd ed. (Beirut: Dār al-Andalus, 1983), pp. 162–163. For more on early Arabic love poetry see Stetkevych, *Zephyrs*, pp. 55-57; J.C. Bürgel, "Love, Lust, and Longing: Eroticism in Early Islam as Reflected in Literary Sources" in *Society and the Sexes in Medieval Islam*, edited by Afaf Lutfi al-Sayyid Marsot (Malibu, CA: University of California Press, 1979), pp. 83–85, 94–97; Salma K. Jayyusi, "Umayyad Poetry" in A.F.L. Beeston, et al, eds., *The Cambridge History of Arabic Literature* (Cambridge: Cambridge University Press, 1983), 1:419–427, and the *Encyclopedia of Islam*, 2nd ed., II:1028–1036.

5. For this and related matters on love see Joseph N. Bell, *Love Theory in Later Hanbalite Islam* (Albany: State University of New York Press, 1979), and James T. Monroe, "Hispano-Arabic Poetry During the Caliphate of Cordova: Theory and Practice" in *Arabic Poetry: Theory and Development*, edited by G.E. Von Grunebaum (Wiesbaden: O. Harrassowitz, 1973), pp. 125–154. Regarding the themes of love, loss, and longing in classical Arabic poetry, see the penetrating mediations by Stetkevtch in *Zephyrs*.

6. Ascribed to Majnūn by Ibn Qutaybah, *al-Shi'r wa-al-shu'arā'*, ed. M.J. De Goeje (Leiden: E.J. Brill, 1904), p. 362. For more on the Majnūn, see J.-C. Vadet, *L'esprit courtois en orient* (Paris: G.-P. Maisonneuve et Larose, 1968), pp. 362–378, and Muhammad Ghunaymi Hilal, *Laylā wa-al-Majnūn* (Beirut: Dār al-'Awdah, 1980). Insightful interpretations of the larger 'Udhrī tradition, including Majnūn, may be found in Stetkevych, *Zephyrs*, pp. 115-117, 143-45, 265 n. 58; Tahar Labib Djedidi, *La Poesie amoureuse des Arabes: le cas des*

'Udhrites (Algiers, 197–), esp. pp. 90–157; Andras Hamori, *The Art of Medieval Arabic Literature* (Princeton: Princeton University Press, 1974), pp. 38–47, who also quotes this verse; As'ad E. Khairallah, *Love, Madness, and Poetry* (Beirut: In kommssion Franz Steiner Verlag, Wiesbaden, 1980), who quotes this verse, pp. 75–96, and Ibrāhīm al-Sinjilāwī, *al-Hubb wa-al-mawt fī shi'r al-shu'arā' fī 'asr al-Ummawī* (Amman: Maktabat `Ammān, 1985), pp. 17–25.

7. Jamīl, *Diwān* (Beirut: Dār Sādir, 1966), 42/10; also quoted by Hamouri, *Art*, pp. 43–44, and see Khairallah, *Madness*, pp. 82-96; Djedidi, *'Udhrites*, pp. 90–92, and EI2, 2:1030–1033.

8. Majnūn, *Diwān*, ed. 'Abd al-Sattār Ahmad Farrāj (Cairo: Maktabat Misr, 1963), 96; also quoted in Khairallah, *Madness*, pp. 76-77. Also see Stetkevych, *Zephyrs*, pp. 168-201, and Vadet, *L'esprit*, pp. 249–263.

9. Jayyusi, "Umayyad Poetry," 1:387–432.

10. Cola Franzen trans., *Poems of Arab Andalusia* (San Francisco: City Lights, 1989), pp. 3-4. Also see James T. Monroe, *Hispano-Arabic Poetry: A Student Anthology* (Berkeley: University of California Press, 1974), pp. 16–17.

11. Dhū al-Nūn quoted in Abū Nasr al-Sarrāj, *al-Luma'*, edited by 'Abd al-Halīm Mahmūd and 'Abd al-Bāqī Surūr (Cairo: Dār al-Kutub al-Hadīthah, 1960), p. 318. Also see A. Schimmel, *As Through a Veil: Mystical Poetry in Islam* (New York: Columbia University Press, 1982), pp. 24–25.

12. For an detailed introduction to Sufism see A. Schimmel, *Mystical Dimensions of Islam* (Chapel Hill: University of North Carolina Press, 1975).

13. Ibid., 43.

14. See the work above (note 4) by Khairallah.

15. For this poem and an analysis of early Sufi verse see Th. Emil Homerin, "Tangled Words: Toward a Stylistics of Arabic Verse" in *Reorientation: Essays on Arabic and Persian Poetry* edited by Suzanne P. Stetkevych (Bloomington, IN: University of Indiana Press, 1994), pp. 190-198.

16. See Monroe, "Cordova," pp. 125–154.

17. *Rasā'il Ikhwān al-Safā'* (Beirut: Dār al-Sādir, n.d.), 3:274–275; my translation. Also see Monroe's translation in "Cordova," p. 150.

18. For Ibn Zaydūn, see the *Encyclopedia of Islam*, second edition (Leiden: Brill) III:973–974.

19. Ibn Zaydūn, *Dīwān* (Cairo: Dār al-Nahdat Misr li'-Tab' wa-al-Nashr, 1957), edited by 'Ali 'Abd al-'Azm, p. 167. My translation following Monroe, "Cordova," 150.

20. See Monroe, "Cordova," 150; Ibn Zaydūn *Dīwān*, p. 146, from v. 35 of the *Nūnīyah.*

21. Ibn Zaydūn *Dīwān*, 142; my translation of v. 9 of the *Nūnīyah*, following Monroe, "Cordova," p. 151.

22. Ibn Zaydūn, *Diwān,* pp. 139–140. For another translation and analysis of several love themes in this poem see Fedwa Malti Douglas, "Ibn Zaydūn: Towards a Thematic Analysis" in *Arabica* 29 (1976):63–76. However, my translation and reading of the poem are significantly different. Also see the translation by A.J. Arberry in his *Arabic Poetry* (Cambridge: Cambridge University Press, 1965), pp. 114–117.

23. See Stetkevych, *Zephyrs*, 192-210. To accommodate his expanding court and mercenary army, Caliph 'Abd al-Rahmān III (r. 912–961) began the construction of a new royal city in 936. Completed forty-years later by his successor al-Hakam II, Madinat al-Zahrā' was a magnificent collection of offices and reception halls, palaces and formal gardens.

24. Concerning this elegaic *'ayn*, see Th. Emil Homerin, "A Bird Ascends the Night: Elegy and Immortality in Islam" in *Journal of the American Academy of Religion* 59/2:262–263.

25. Regarding these and other Sufi technical terms referred to below see Schimmel, *Dimensions*.

26. See Stetkevych, *Zephyrs*, pp. 194-99, regarding Qur'ānic allusions in Ibn Zaydūn's verse on al-Zahrā' and Cordova; for more on the poet's use of the first person plural see Monroe, *Hispano-Arabic Poetry*, pp. 20–21, 178–187, which also contains the text and translation of the poet's *al-Nūnīyah.*

27. See Stetkevych, *Zephyrs*, pp. 192-210, esp. pp. 192-193.

28. Federico Garcia Lorca, *Divan del Tamarit* (1936), in *Collected Poems*, ed. Christopher Maurer (New York: Farrar Straus Giroux, 1989), pp. 676–677; poem translated by Catherine Brown.

PART V.
COMMUNITY IN CHANGE

Chapter 11

CHURCH/SECT THEORY AND EMERGING NORTH AMERICAN MUSLIM COMMUNITIES: ISSUES AND TRENDS

Frederick M. Denny

There are now more than four million Muslims in the United States and perhaps half a million in Canada. At the current rate of growth in the community, Muslims will likely outnumber Jews in the United States (they probably do so already in Canada) early in the next decade. Most North American Muslims are immigrants or children of immigrants. Recent waves of immigration have come especially from war-torn regions such as Iran, Lebanon, and Afghanistan (there are estimated to be some 400,000 Iranians living in Southern California alone).[1] But there is also a significant Muslim population comprised of longer established North Americans, primarily African-Americans, but also from other ethnic groups.

The great variety of national, ethnic, and cultural backgrounds of North American Muslims, all living in the same pluralistic and secular societies under democratic political systems, is unprecedented in Islamic history. Although Muslim unity is so deeply ingrained as to have a doctrinal status, the fact is that the diverse Muslim population sub-groups here are forming their own separate communities for worship, education, mutual support, economic activities, political activism and other things. The Christian-style "parish" model of community religious life has never been native to Muslim religious sociology, but "parishes," so to speak, are forming and prospering here, increasingly with well-qualified "pastor-imams" leading them, along with local, "congregational" boards of directors.[2] The reason for the adaptation to the dominant forms of North American religio-communal polities and orderings is that they work best for Muslims trying to sustain their religious life as minorities in a religious "free-market," where there are no higher—such as governmental—bodies regulating religious affairs. Muslim legists are having to demonstrate, to themselves and their co-religionists, that such developments are Islamically acceptable. The jury is still out on many North American innovations by Muslims (the legal term for "heresy" is *bid'a*, lit. "innovation"), but change and novelty and degrees of assimilation of dominant religio-social patterns are inevitable. (There is a category of innovations that some 'ulamā' recognize as *bid'a hasana*, "salutary innovation.") Research on North American Islam has not yet been extensively conducted. It is a wide open field, growing daily. The valuable studies that do exist are useful in laying out major areas for further research. Examples are: dietary regulations, social regulations and relations with non-Muslims (mixing of sexes, especially), ritual obligations and the workplace, fears of Christian evangelistic and missionary aggressiveness, intermarriage with non-Muslims, managing and maintaining mosques and centers, health care, Muslim burials and cemeteries, education, Sunni-Shi'i relations (or lack thereof), defense against prejudice and bigotry from the dominant population, relations between often economically and educationally more advantaged immigrant Muslims and poor African-American Muslims, Muslims in American prisons, and others.

CHURCH-DENOMINATION-SECT THEORY AND ISLAM

Ever since Ernst Troeltsch set forth his church-sect hypothesis in his *Social Teaching of the Christian Churches* (1911), scholars have been generating ever more complex and sophisticated models and typologies of religious organization, such as church, ecclesia, denomination, sect, established sect, and cult.[3] Weber extended church-sect theory to other religions.[4] H. Richard Niebuhr's *Social Sources of Denominationism* viewed the denomination neither as all-encompassing church nor separate community of saints, but as an intermediary reality, a "compromise...between Christianity and the world."[5] Niebuhr's contribution was to show how the denomination sustains itself in complex and dynamic relations with the wider society in which it is located. As Roland Robertson has put it, Niebuhr "was concerned to explain how theological ideas are mediated by the character of the social structure to influence the course of religious organization."[6]

Troeltsch, Niebuhr and most other scholars have intended their typologies to refer to Christian, and most often Protestant cases, and they have gone to great lengths to explicate the close ties between doctrinal and theological factors and their social outcomes. Others, such as the sect specialist Bryan R. Wilson, have argued that the exclusive tying of sect-theory, at least, to doctrine is severely limiting:

> From the sociologist's point of view, there are three sorts of drawback to the theological or doctrinal classification of sects. First of all, such a classification limits the possibilities for the comparative study of sects within different religious traditions. In the second place, it prevents recognition of other significant aspects of the character of sects, for the doctrine may persist when the social organization and the orientation of the movement have changed. Thus, classification which grows from doctrinal description does not sufficiently take into account the organizational and dynamic aspects of sects. Thirdly, because it is theological, this kind of classification runs the risk of stigmatizing the sect and characterizing it in terms which are essentially normative.[7]

I obviously agree with Wilson's approach, for I am interested in applying church-sect theory to Islam, particularly in North American contexts, where I think there may be interesting results both for our understanding of Muslim communities here and for church-sect theory as applied to non-Christian cases. At this point of my research, I am reviewing church-sect theory quite extensively. But it is neither possible nor necessary to focus on this in the present essay beyond generalities. What I shall do instead is consider some data concerning actual Muslim communities and activities in North America, with special emphasis on a federation movement called "ISNA", i.e., "The Islamic Society of North America."

I noted above that Islam has not conformed to a parish model of community life in its long existence. What I meant was that in dominantly Muslim societies, especially where there is Islamic government, religion and state are ideally one. So the Islamic civilization of classical, pre-modern times in the Afro-Eurasian landmass (Spain, Sicily, the Balkans, North Africa, the Arabian Peninsula, Anatolia, the Nile-to-Oxus regions, and South and Central Asia) was an order in which mosques, cemeteries, religious schools and the like were as much a civic necessity as roads, bridges, waterworks and fortifications. The Muslim ummah or "community" within the Dar al-Islam, "the Abode of Submission" is, in some respects, analogous to Troeltsch's idea of the church (but obviously without the same kinds of embedded doctrinal factors): people are born into it, it is coextensive with society (Yinger), it is in close collaboration with the political authority in the interests of general order and stability, it seeks to extend itself universally and thereby establish a saving community for all people, and it reserves the right, through its enduring institutions, to interpret and apply God's commands for human life through the Shari'a. Certainly there are important differences between Troeltsch's church and Dar al-Islam, but following Wilson, if we focus on functional/dynamic aspects rather than doctrine, we will see important similarities that enable us to use the model for analytical as well as comparative purposes.

One major difference between the church and Dar al-Islam is the different relations between religious and secular authority structures. Since Islam generally views religion and state as unitary, a natural consequence is the relative political weakness of specifically religious leadership roles. There never developed the kind of ecclesiastical hierarchy in charge of a sacramental system in Islam. Instead of imposing order from above, Muslims have regulated and maintained their socio-religious practices and institutions from a broad popular base. From early times, Muslims have submitted to the Word of God in the Qur'ān and prophetic teaching and example as set forth in Muhammad's Sunna for their guidance. The remarkably uniform official cultus, centering in the five daily Salat-prayers, is not paralleled in Christianity with its many different clergy-led liturgies (albeit with a somewhat similar common core pattern traceable to early practice and the synagogue service).

And, although Muslims have not followed a parish model, with members or "souls" enrolled in specific local establishments, they have certainly congregated together regularly in their local mosques for daily Salats, and in Friday mosques for the required weekly congregational Salat with sermon. But there have not been doctrinal or polity differences from one mosque or community to another that would determine Muslims' choices. (Shi'i and Sunni mutual avoidance, although neither universal nor doctrinally required, is based on political and cultural differences, I think, when representatives of the two communities reside in the same region. Sunnis and Shi`is are increasingly staying with their own kind in North America.)

North American Muslims, desiring as full and authentic a communal and personal/individual religious life as possible, band together in various types of associations for mutual support, protection, worship, educational endeavors, Islamic (i.e., interest-free) financial activities, and other above mentioned requirements. They organize themselves into corporations, buy land or built property, and establish mosques and centers. Their activities have often been supported, in part, by gifts from Muslim constituencies abroad, such as in Saudi Arabia, the Gulf states, Libya, and Pakistan. But increasingly, immigrant Muslim groups, especially, are paying their own way by means of dues (sometimes called Zakat) and other fund-raising methods. (At an annual meeting of the Association of Muslim Social Scientists in Rochester, New York, one Muslim leader called on those present at the large banquet to stop expecting their financial debts and efforts at building new mosques and centers to be bankrolled by Muslims from the oil-rich Arab states. In his many travels seeking funds, he increasingly was asked why North American Muslims, who are among the wealthiest in the world, could not by now come of age and be responsible for their own building and missionary projects.[8] The speaker closed by admonishing the assembly, "They're getting tired of us, tired of us!" referring to Muslims in Arabia and the Gulf states.)

THE ISLAMIC SOCIETY OF NORTH AMERICA (ISNA)

There are more than 1,200 Islamic centers, Islamic schools, Islamic organizations, mosques and Muslim Student Association chapters in the United States and Canada, according to a recent directory published by the Islamic Society of North America, (ISNA). ISNA itself has more than 325 institutional members from among the categories just mentioned, representing "tens of thousands" of individual Muslims, according to recent annual report. In addition, ISNA accepts individual personal memberships and has at least 6,000 on its rolls.

The known Islamic organizations on this continent do not reflect the large population of Muslims here, by any means. One of the most urgent concerns of organizations like ISNA is to call Muslims to join up and strengthen the ranks. ISNA's *da'wa*, or "missionary" activities, are very much aimed at fellow Muslims as well as potential converts.

The 26th annual convention of ISNA, held in autumn 1989 in Dayton, Ohio, had as its theme "Reaching Out with Islam." There were about 5,000 present for the weekend convention. After about fifteen hours of attending plenary sessions, strolling through the extensive book and religious supplies exhibits, collecting literature from a wide range of special interest booths (for Somali relief, Afghani relief, South African Muslims' relief, Muslim youth camps, Islamic schools, and, significantly, many Islamic banking and credit enterprises), and seeing the participants observing their prayers in the huge mosque-space to the side of the assembly hall, I remarked to Dr. Ihsan Bagby, an African-American Muslim scholar and, then, a top executive of ISNA: "Ihsan, all this leads me to conjecture that ISNA is in the process of producing the first Islamic denomination." Dr. Bagby turned to me and said, "What!?" Then we talked about it for awhile and he smiled and said that he would share the news with his colleagues. He realized, after a few minutes, that I had meant "denomination" in the sociological and not in any Christian doctrinal sense. Since then, ISNA'a annual meeting attendance has grown much larger.

There are hazards in applying the denominational model to Islam, even in North America. There is less danger in applying sectarian models, especially in the quite ramified ways in which scholars like Wilson have suggested, in his attempts to generate universally valid categories for the sociology of religion. Muslim denominationalism, if there is such a thing (and I think there could be), is not doctrinally differentiated among Muslim communities, as has been the case with Protestantism. Rather, it is a ready-made model for federation of Muslim bodies in our pluralistic and highly secularized societies. Far from being, in Niebuhr's sense, an evidence of the sinfulness of divisions, it is rather a provisional means for their increasing union and strengthening in an environment where Dar al-Islam has yet to establish itself. ISNA, for example, as a quasi-denomination, is establishing a viable beachhead for Islamic activities as Muslims and Islam become domesticated in North America.

I prefer the classification "association" to "denomination" to "sect" in the case of ISNA because of its relative openness both or other Muslim organizations and styles, as well as its increasing readiness to take part in the wider contexts of North American life: social, cultural, and especially political. As one political adviser, a Christian Arab-American with long experience in Washington, advised the ISNA audience in Dayton, "Get involved in politics, especially at the local level, find non-Muslims with like-minded ideas about values, the environment, drug law enforcement, health care, etc., and work with them for the common good without feeling that you are compromising your Islamic ideals. But above all, be *both* Democrats and Republicans!" Internally, ISNA seeks to enable its members to strengthen and maintain their Islamic commitments, from Islamic education of youth to proper social and family life, to solidarity with Muslims worldwide, while at the same time serving, externally, as a liaison with other Muslim constituencies (a proper "denominational" thing to do) and the larger, non-Muslim context. There is an increasing awareness, expressed often at the annual convention, that Muslims in North America cannot—if they are from non-Western backgrounds—continue to carp about and condemn Western ways. As one respondent put it, "We should have the courage to assert our beliefs and values, of course. But we must also realize that we ourselves are part of the West now, too, and we most do our best to be both good Muslims and good citizens."

The prayer of Christ for the Church was that "All may be one" (Jn. 17:22). The Islamic doctrine of *tawhīd*, "divine unity," is also a powerful force for communal unity of Muslims. The separations and differences among Muslims are based on complex and varying factors, but the attempts of Islamic organizations like ISNA to bring Muslims together in North America are well worth the attention of sociologists of religion as well as students of religion and culture, for emerging Islamic collectivities may help us better understand the domestication process of Islam here as well as the models—old, like church sect theory—and yet to be developed, which enable us to understand our new religious neighbors as well as ourselves.

NOTES

1. By no means are they all Muslims: many are Jews, Bahais, Zoroastrians and secularized persons with Shi'ite roots.

2. See Earle H. Waugh, "The Imam in the New World: Models and Modifications," in *Transitions and Transformations in the History of Religions*, Frank E. Reynolds and Theodor M. Ludwig, eds. (Leiden: E.J. Brill, 1980), pp. 124–149). See also idem., "Muslim Leadership and the Shaping of the Umma: Classical Tradition and Religious Tension in the North American Setting," in *The Muslim Community in North America*, Earle H. Waugh, Baha Abu-Laban, and Regula B. Qureshi, eds. (Edmonton: University of Alberta Press, 1983), pp. 11-33. Another important study of Islam in North America that also treats mosques and leadership roles is Yvonne Y. Haddad and Adair T. Lummis, *Islamic Values in the United States* (New York: Oxford University Press, 1987).

3. The six types of religious organization listed were gathered by the American sociologist J. Milton Yinger in *Religion, Society and the Individual: An Introduction to the Sociology of Religion* (New York: Macmillan, 1957), pp. 144–155.

4. See, for example, Max Weber, *Economy and Society* (1922), Guenther Roth and Claus Wittich, eds. (Totowa, NJ: Bedminster Press, 1968), pp. 1164–66, 1207–10.

5. H. Richard Niebuhr, *The Social Sources of Denominationalism* (New York: Meridian Books, 1957; originally published in 1929), p. 6.

6. Roland Robertson, *The Sociological Interpretation of Religion* (New York: Schocken Books, 1970), p. 117.

7. Bryan R. Wilson, "A Typology of Sects," in *Sociology of Religion: Selected Readings*, Roland Robertson, ed. (Baltimore: Penguin, 1969), p. 363.

8. He was referring primarily to immigrant Muslims and their offspring, comparing them to their counterparts in communities in the Muslim world where, despite oil wealth, the per capita income is generally below that in North America.

Chapter 12

FAZLUR RAHMAN'S CONTRIBUTION TO RELIGIOUS STUDIES: A HISTORIAN OF RELIGION'S APPRAISAL

Richard C. Martin

REMEMBERING FAZLUR RAHMAN

I begin this critical assessment of Fazlur Rahman's contribution to the academic study of religion by recalling my relationship to him. Unlike the other contributors, I was never formally a student of Fazlur Rahman, at Chicago or any other institution. In fact, I only met him twice, in the 1980s at Giorgio Levi Della Vida conferences in Los Angeles. Nonetheless, by phone and by post, we communicated several times. In 1980, as I was preparing for publication the papers from a conference at Arizona State University on "Islam and the History of Religion," I decided to ask Prof. Rahman, who had not otherwise participated in the conference, to read the papers, and respond to them in a chapter to be published at the end of the volume.[1] He kindly accepted my request, and sent me a manuscript in his own hand, on time. More below about manuscripts in Fazlur Rahman's own hand.

In our conversations about the kind of response that he might make, I advised Prof. Rahman that the subtext of the conference itself—the tone if not the actual text of many of the papers and discussions—was the hermeneutical struggle between believers and non-believers for the right to say, within the academy, what religion means. I pointed out further that this had quickly devolved into a struggle over whether or not non-Muslims had the academic right to interpret Islam in particular—a position held by most of the Muslims present, as well as a few of the non-Muslims. I suggested to Fazlur Rahman that Robert K. Merton's essay, "The Perspectives of Insiders and Outsiders," might make a good theoretical talking point.[2] The conference had taken place in January of 1980, in the highly charged atmosphere occasioned by the Iranian Revolution and the taking of American hostages. Fazlur Rahman did read the Merton piece and commented on it briefly in his response, but he had other things on his mind after reading the conference papers.

The purpose of the conference and the subsequent volume was to link Islamic studies with history of religions scholarship. As I shall explain further below, the relationship between the discipline of history of religion and the field of Islamic studies has been tenuous at best. The idea was to try to cross-pollinate Islamic studies, which until then had been deeply embedded in Oriental studies and Middle Eastern area studies, with theories and ideas circulating in religious studies. Conference participants were asked to speak to a theoretical problem in the study of religion (for example, religious biography, conversion, the nature of scripture, literacy and text) and then to bring the discussion to bear on the data of Islam.

In his response, Fazlur Rahman demonstrated intellectual and thematic qualities that are now familiar in his work. His deeply irenic approach to Western scholarship on Islam is captured in the following confession:

> Indeed, there are many statements made about Islam by outsiders such as H.A.R. Gibb and Wilfred Smith which are rejected by many Muslims but which are regarded as highly meaningful by many other Muslims....The present writer must acknowledge that he has learned a great deal about Islam from the insights of several Western scholars just as he has learned much and gained fundamental insights from his Muslim teachers, particularly his father. And about some of their own statements concerning Islam, Muslims themselves are sharply divided. What does this mean?[3]

The profoundly intellectual nature of Fazlur Rahman's approach to Islamic studies was enriched by his grasp of the Western philosophical tradition. Perhaps this stemmed from his South Asian origins, with much stronger cultural linkages than many other non-Western Muslims to the English language and Western thought.

South Asian Muslims in particular have recently written very movingly, and often controversially, for Western non-Muslims about their own personal identities as Muslims, or as fallen Muslims, in a world dominated by Western thought and culture. Salman Rushdie is only the most notorious example.[4] The most recent example is Akbar S. Ahmed of Cambridge University. The cover of his book, *Postmodernism and Islam*, carries such provocative "hooks" for browsers as "Why is Madonna important for understanding Islamic fundamentalism?" and "Why have jeans failed to catch on in Islamic countries?"[5] The questions are answered between the two covers, in ways that address Muslims as well as "postmodern" Westerners. It is this quality of standing somewhere between the Islamic East and the non-Muslim West, and speaking critically to both on their own terms, that also sets Fazlur Rahman apart from many modern Muslim critics of the West. Fazlur Rahman, too, made a hijra out from his Muslim, South Asian homeland into the West, which for him as for other Muslims from the Subcontinent was primarily Great Britain (at least at first) in a struggle to establish his identity. With Rushdie and Ahmed, Fazlur Rahman's writing about this crisis of intellectual identity and affiliation with traditional religion was deeply personal.

Yet, also like the others, Fazlur Rahman used the medium of writing to work out the problem of religious identity in a non-religious world for a readership that went well beyond believing Muslims, but that was never really intended to exclude Muslims. At Oxford, he studied with the great historian of Islamic philosophy, Richard Walzer, *inter alia*. I later had the opportunity to take a seminar with Walzer during a semester visit he made to North America. In the course of that semester, we read some of the texts by Ibn Sina and other Muslim philosophers on the peripatetic tradition in prophecy—the same texts on which Fazlur Rahman had based his first major work on Islam for Western intellectuals, *Prophecy and Islam*.[6] While I was taking the seminar, I read Fazlur Rahman's work for the first time, and over coffee had the benefit of Walzer's sympathetic interpretation of Fazlur Rahman's youthful encounter at Oxford with the fallen Greek heritage of philosophy in medieval Islam.

I will conclude my recollections about Fazlur Rahman by recalling that the handwritten manuscript of the review essay he sent me was one of the most challenging interpretive tasks that I have ever undertaken. Line by line, word by word, often letter by letter, I spent hours deciphering his enigmatic script. I venture this comment about a person for whom I and other contributors have so much lingering admiration, affection and appreciation, because several others with whom I have shared this experience, and who knew the man, were amused because they had the same experience. His writing was so lucid and logical, yet his hand was minuscule and obscure. From then until his death in 1988, we had phone conversations from time to time. And I have read his work more deeply and extensively in the meantime. Indeed, I continue to ask my students to read and reflect on several of his texts.

I was greatly saddened to learn, upon my return from Egypt in the summer of 1988, that Fazlur Rahman had died. I would like to have gotten to know him better. Nonetheless, he still looms before us in the works he published as well as in the project he undertook: to interpret Islam to the modern world, to interpret Islam in light of the modern world, and to interpret the world in light of Islam. It is to the significance Fazlur Rahman's project has for Religious Studies that I now turn.

THE QUESTION AND ITS CONTEXT

I begin this section by confessing that I find Donald R. Berry's statement in this volume curious and unconvincing, that "[i]n Chicago, [Fazlur Rahman] found a haven where he could develop his understanding of the role of Islam in the context of modernity and bring Islamic Studies into the larger arena of Religious Studies."[7] The role of Islam in the context of modernity was the issue that Fazlur Rahman addressed so articulately and courageously. I am less sanguine about his influence on Religious Studies and history of religions scholarship, as I shall explain below. Only seldom did he interpret Islam in light of comparative data from other traditions, and usually this had to do with normative statements about Christianity and Judaism in comparison to Islam. The larger arena of Religious Studies is certainly enriched by such of his works as *Islam*, *Islam and Modernity*, and *Major Themes of the Qur'ān*. Nonetheless, Fazlur Rahman did not directly contribute to the integrity of that arena in the modern university. This rather stark appraisal of Fazlur Rahman's contribution to religious studies must be qualified by an important caveat. Virtually no other Orientalist, Muslim or non-Muslim, reflected as Fazlur Rahman did on the theoretical problems and hermeneutical issues involved in interpreting religious texts. By the term "text" I refer both to writing and to social performance, insofar as each kind of text is characterized by what Erich Auerbach called *Deutungsbedurftigkeit*; that is, it needs, indeed demands interpretation. Religious texts are often claimed by their adherents to be transparent in meaning and literally true, yet it is over the meaning of religious texts that some of the greatest human struggles have been waged and continue to be waged. Fazlur Rahman understood that and was willing and able to address the issue as few others in Islamic studies have. In his later books in particular, Fazlur Rahman opened with essays on a theory of interpretation that would support his thesis that underlying the Qur'ān as a whole is a deeper unity that evinces a definite *Weltanschauung*.

In her helpful essay (Chapter Six above) on "Fazlur Rahman and Islamic Feminism," Tamara Sonn unpacks the hermeneutical principles articulated by Fazlur Rahman, particularly in the introductory chapter to *Islam and Modernity*. Sonn rightly distances Fazlur Rahman from the postmodern approaches of scholars like Muhammad Arkun. Fazlur Rahman foresaw the non-referentiality of postmodern semiotics as anathema to the ultimate truths he believed could be derived from a holistic rereading of the Qur'ān. And while it is true, as Sonn tells us, that he "described his methodology in a purely Islamic idiom," the philosophical substance of his argument was based on the phenomenology of Edmund Husserl. Fazlur Rahman did allow for contextual determinants of meaning, the importance of the dialectic between the subject's horizon of understanding and the object of understanding. Nonetheless, his brief rebuttal to Gadamer makes it clear that, for him (as indeed for any religious claimant), when language is produced, meanings are intended and they are recoverable.[8]

There is room for argument with Fazlur Rahman's hermeneutical position, but the argument can take place on non-sacred intellectual grounds. That is where he chose to articulate his theoretical underpinnings. Argument with his position, therefore, is possible and, one might say, necessary.

RELIGION AND RELIGIONS

I began the preceding section by questioning whether Fazlur Rahman did much to bring Islamic studies into the larger arena of Religious Studies. I should now like to ask and attempt to answer: Why is the issue of Religious Studies in higher education so critically important at the turn of the century?

Since Fazlur Rahman's death in 1988, several departments of Religious Studies across North America have been targeted for elimination. These decisions are invariably the work of administrative middle managers (college deans) on behalf of central administrations, governing boards and, in the case of public universities, legislative bodies that garner public funds for such purposes. Deans, in turn, usually hand over the task of initially recommending which programs to be cut to "strategic planning" committees of faculty peers, who are asked to recommend ways to streamline academic programs more in keeping with current models of academic budgeting. This process of asking faculty to recommend solutions to the problems that are framed by deans and provosts is known as the principle of faculty "self-governance." Does it make any (managerial) sense, we often hear it asked, to have some departments with thirty or more faculty members and some with only five? Wouldn't the task of knowledge-dispensing be more susceptible to TQM (Total Quality Management) if administrative units were fewer and more equal in numerical personnel strength?

Let us be clear that the critical question thus far has not usually been whether religion is an important topic of research and instruction within the academy, as it was at mid-century. The problem, as Dean Rosemary A. Stevens put it in a letter explaining her decision to dismantle the Department of Religion at the University of Pennsylvania, is "how best to organize our [college] programs in Religious Studies." The solution, as the dean sees it, is to reorganize "our programs in religious studies on an inter-departmental basis [which] will allow us to draw on the strengths of our faculty across the School in this important field and, consequently, restore religious studies to its appropriate place in our curriculum."[9] The terms "restore" and "appropriate" are puzzling, if not chilling. Religious Studies, in this view, is an interdisciplinary field, not a discipline. Its subject matter belongs properly to other curricula (presumably history, anthropology, foreign languages, perhaps philosophy, and so on). The judgement of discipline for hiring, promotion and tenure belongs to those other disciplines.

Who is to blame for this view? There are many answers, but departments of Religious Studies and their professional societies should not cast the first stones.

Fin de siècle pessimism may seem like a strange mood in which to pursue an essay in honor of one of this century's most important modernist Sunni Muslim scholars. Fazlur Rahman's keen scholarship was almost entirely in the service of helping us better understand perhaps the most misunderstood religion by most Americans, namely, Islam.

Religion as such, however, was not an object of serious investigation in any of his writings with which I am familiar. Fazlur Rahman taught us more than most scholars have about a religion, Islam; about religion as such, however, and the discipline that studies it, he had little to say.

What concerns me about this focus is that many of the scholars contributing to Religious Studies during the latter half of the twentieth century have tended to be predominantly area or field specialists. To document this observation one needs only to read vacancy announcements in Religious Studies (wanted: Judaica scholar; Historian of the Reformation; specialist in Islamic law; etc.), or examine the way the American Academy of Religion is organized primarily around traditions and advocacy groups (Buddhism, North American Religions, African Religions, Black Theology, Feminist Studies, Eastern Orthodox Studies, Studies of Islam, etc.). This stands in noticeable contrast to scholars earlier in this century—such as Weber, Durkheim, Freud and even Marx—who recognized that religion as such was an object of scientific investigation, and that we have to find ways to explain and interpret religious phenomena that correlate them with other religious phenomena. Some may wish to object that Freud and Marx in particular had some harsh and negative things to say about the value of religion in human affairs. To this I would simply reply that a prior commitment to advocate, or even feel obliged in advance always to put a good face on, what one is studying is unacceptable in the academy—or at least it ought to be. It sometimes seems that the outright theological defense of Christianity in the "Bible Chair" departments of religion earlier this century has been replaced by a form of liberal humanism that seeks to disabuse the media, State Department, and general public of their patent misunderstandings and misrepresentations of "other" religions, especially Islam. While such outreach and service to the community is a recognized responsibility of the university, Dean Stevens is surely correct to conclude that maintaining a department and a discipline to perform this task is extravagant in the extreme. What, then, is the task of Religious Studies? And, as the case of Fazlur Rahman specifies, what is the relation of area studies to Religious Studies?

THE DISCIPLINE OF RELIGIOUS STUDIES

I take Religious Studies to be a discipline. At least, this is the function I think it ought to serve in the university. Religious studies ought to be that community of faculty and students in which theories and other claims made about religion and religions are expounded, tested, challenged, and extended to comparable data. That is what scientists say they are doing and what binds them together with other scientists under a common "discipline" or a related set of disciplines. In the humanities, philosophers, historians, and literary critics also maintain that published research must be disciplined.

One may wish to protest that in religious studies the data fields are too diverse—from ancient Israel to Japan, India, Africa, the Middle East, Native American societies, and more. Each of these "fields" has developed its own tradition of discourse and discipline. Those who take this line of argument, that Religious Studies is not a discipline but a concatenation of data fields and subdisciplines bound by a "common focus on religion" are making one of Dean Stevens's points for her. Instead of investing in a separate department, an informal, interdisciplinary program of Religious Studies could cheaply and effectively help students plan courses of study that have a common focus on religion. But is that the only justification for Religious Studies in the academy?

Let us take the example of ethnography. Anthropology departments (which have their own problems, to be sure) are more than units where students can go to learn about Yoruba or Zulu or Sioux or Pashtun peoples. One learns primarily how to theorize about social data and to interpret cultural systems. Only secondarily, after much training in theory and method, is one considered ready to go out and study "a" particular society or community. Common, comparative problems emerge, such as ethnicity, kinship patterns, and rites of passage. A specialist on the Pashtun may well move out of the "area" to study the Zulu later in his or her career. Non-specialists in Pashtun society have theoretical grounds to engage the interpretations of specialists.

Philosophy and literary criticism could also be taken as models, and once again the shared task is to construct and evaluate arguments and theories. That is what we mean by academic discipline. What about Religious Studies? In its short history in North America, religious studies at most colleges and universities has developed more as a field, or an aggregation of fields, and less as a discipline. In the post-World War II period, with the growth of area studies at select graduate institutions, a few scholars received training in non-Western (and non-biblical) languages and civilizations. Religion departments began to add specialists in "non-Western" religions, or to cross-list courses taught by area specialists in other departments (for example, history, anthropology, Middle Eastern studies). It was not uncommon for a department having a faculty of five to consist of a specialist in Old Testament, one in New Testament, a church historian, a theologian, and a person whose responsibility it was to cover the rest of the world (world religions).

More serious, however, has been the *ad hoc* manner in which departments of religion have grown since the 1960s. Theory and the study of religion as a discipline have been far less important than "plugging the holes" in the coverage of the world's religions. This explains, I think, the reason why job listings are still area specific (Islamicist, Buddhologist, church historian), often with no mention of theoretical or comparative skills.

Some readers may well wish to criticize my judgement that Fazlur Rahman did not contribute as much as we might have liked to Religious Studies as such. After all, there is evidence to the contrary in the number of books he wrote that are used in religious studies courses across North America (and elsewhere), including in courses taught by this author. It is also well known that some departments of religion tried to lure Fazlur Rahman away from Near Eastern studies at the University of Chicago, and numerous search committees seeking to make a junior appointment in Islamic religious studies sought his appraisal of available talent. I would simply reply that for courses on Islam, especially advanced undergraduate and graduate courses, Fazlur Rahman's studies on Islam and modernity, the Qur'ānic worldview, and Islamic law are among the best available in English. Nonetheless, to limit the religious studies curriculum to teaching traditions in isolation from each other is merely to concatenate area studies—to combine area studies in a single unit with respect to religion.

ISLAM AND THE HISTORY OF RELIGION

That Fazlur Rahman contributed much to the study of Islamic religion is clear from the depth and breadth of his writing on the topic. The number and diversity of his students also bears witness to his influence. Only one other Muslim scholar in North America in the twentieth century has drawn such large numbers of students (mostly Muslim) from as many parts of the Muslim world.[10] If some Muslims have been among Fazlur Rahman's most severe critics, others who have studied with him, or have read his work closely, have been stimulated by his critical acumen and intellectual courage.

His non-Muslim Western students are also numerous and distinguished, as this volume testifies. My concern is somewhat different, however. Appropriately, we are raising a question that was posed in 1967 in a volume by scholars in the history of religions from the University of Chicago, the university Fazlur Rahman served during the last two decades of his life.

In an essay titled "The History of Religions and the Study of Islam," which appeared in a volume dedicated to the memory of Joachim Wach, Charles J. Adams made the following now famous observation. After completing graduate study in the history of religions at the University of Chicago and then going on to immerse himself in Islamic studies in South Asia, Adams hoped and expected, based on the inspiration he received from "the illustrious Wach," as he put it, "that greater involvement in the study of Islam would bring me ever closer to the more universal interests of historians of religions. Or put the other way around, it was anticipated that the growing insights and developing methods of the history of religions would prove a major guide to an expanding and deepening grasp of Islamic religiousness." Despite his initial enthusiasm for this venture, Adams felt compelled to confess that "these expectations have not been realized. As time has gone by, it has proven increasingly difficult to see a direct and fructifying relationship between the activities of Islamicists and those of historians of religions."[11]

It is that difficulty of bringing about, or even being able to see, a "direct and fructifying relationship" between Islamic studies and the history of religions that occupies us in this essay. It is this problem of a "relationship" that poses the question we have wanted to ask about Chicago's greatest scholar of Islamic religion in the twentieth century, Fazlur Rahman.

Before we lay too much praise or blame on Professor Rahman in this matter, we might first ask how the academy, that complex of universities and professional associations of scholarly disciplines in North America, has construed the relationship between Islamic and Religious Studies. The answer is that with few exceptions the study of Islam has been remanded to Oriental studies and Middle Eastern studies departments, even at universities with strong graduate departments in religious studies.

This was and is true at University of Chicago, Fazlur Rahman's own institution and the very bastion of comparative religions, the scientific study of religion, and more recently, the history of religions. It has also been true at most of the few North American universities that have both graduate religion and Middle Eastern studies departments. Few religion departments at institutions with strong Middle Eastern studies programs have been able to hire scholar specialists on Islam.

In many cases, religion departments have left instruction about Islamic religion to colleagues in Middle Eastern studies. When searches have been conducted by religion faculties, key faculty in Middle Eastern studies have been asked to serve on the search committees, with the almost invariable result that religion departments have hired anthropologists, Arabists, or other specialists in area studies, not historians of religion. Reliance on area studies extends beyond departments of religion to such disciplines as history and literary criticism. Nonetheless, in the budget cuts of the late 1980s and early 1990s, it has been religion that most frequently found itself too small and too reliant on faculty in other departments to field the curriculum it claimed as its own.

This state of affairs suggests that the academic home of Islamic religious studies at major graduate institutions in North America is Middle Eastern (and to a lesser extent South Asian) area studies.[12] Thus, the study of Islamic religion often assumes the peripheral status of being "cross-listed." When it comes to Islam, students seeking courses and dissertation committee members must change venues. This peculiar academic doctrine that outsiders to Middle Eastern and Islamic studies are ill-prepared to understand Islam—its texts, languages, and religious phenomena—lends Islamic and Middle Eastern studies their aura of uniqueness. Only insiders—Muslims according to some, Middle East specialists according to others—are qualified to speak. It is a form of academic mysticism.

The claim of uniqueness implies incomparability of data, which in turn threatens comparative studies of religion—the very foundation of history of religions.[13] Why not send students seeking Islamic religious studies, as well as Chinese religions, Buddhism, etc., across campus to area studies departments within the university? The answer has to be that it is religion as such we want to understand, and want our students to understand. Once we have sent our students to Middle Eastern studies departments to learn Arabic, Islamic history and Islamic cultures and societies, who will teach them about Islam as religion? Jacob Neusner put it best when he said:

> Even though, through philology, we understand every word of a text, and, through history, we know just what happened in the event or time to which the text testifies, we still do not understand that text. A religious text serves not only the purposes of philology or history. It demands its proper place as a statement of religion. Read as anything but a statement of religion, it is misunderstood. Accordingly, despite the primitive condition of religious studies as presently practiced, the discipline in the making known as religious studies does promise for Jewish learning what has not yet been attained.[14]

Can we also claim that religious studies promises to help us understand Islam in ways that area studies has not? That is, is it sufficient to criticize Middle Eastern area studies for its simplistic understanding of religion (in historicist terms, as a form or aberration of politics, etc.) without making a case for Islam in religious studies? The answer to the first question, in my view, is yes, and to the second, no. The evidence I offer is necessarily circumstantial and negative in form. There is, for example, Mary Douglas's astonishment in 1982:

> Events have taken religious studies by surprise. This set of university institutions devoted to understanding religion without the constraints of the divinity school has generally included religious change in its subject matter. No one, however, foresaw the recent revivals of traditional religious forms.... Thus no one foretold the resurgence of Islam.[15]

Its well-known expansion in Africa was not expected to presage anything for its strength in modern Arabia—but why not? Douglas's astonishment was fueled by the Shi`i revolution that had occurred in Iran two years earlier. Political scientists and public policy experts were able neither to predict nor to account for the power of resurgent religion to bring down the modern, Westernized government of the Shah.

The 1991 Gulf War produced another realization about our public knowledge of "other" religions, or lack thereof, this time inside the D.C. Beltway. In 1991, a few months after the war, the United States Information Agency began initiatives to fund conferences and other venues for an exchange of ideas with Muslim religious leaders. Until the last decade of the twentieth century, conferences involving Muslims invariably overlooked Muslim religious figures, even on the topic of Islamic religion, in favor of more "rational," Westernized figures from the governments and the secular universities of Islamic countries. In part, this may be taken as an indication of the failure of area studies to train faculty and public policy area experts in the nature of religion in general, Islam in particular.

I do not wish to challenge the common sense claim that a profound understanding of any religion requires diligent study of its languages, texts and cultural phenomena. In 1976, Leonard Binder made the case well in his introduction to *The Study of the Middle East*. He went on to argue that in area studies the object of study is primary and requires methods of study derived from the subject matter itself.[16] The social sciences have accommodated this form of cultural relativism more readily than humanities disciplines, which tend to reject the notion that cultures are unique and thus essentially incomparable. The issue, as Binder makes clear, is area studies versus disciplines, for example, history, anthropology, sociology—to which I am arguing we should add religious studies. The problem for religious studies then becomes similar to that posed by Binder for history, anthropology and others: the area (Islam, Middle East) and not the discipline claims the prerogative to govern the academic study of the subject matter.

FINAL THOUGHTS

One is tempted to wonder what might have happened if Fazlur Rahman had come to North America in search of an academic appointment in the 1980s rather than the 1960s. Would he have ended up at Chicago, and if at Chicago, would it have been in area studies? By 1980, religion departments had discovered Islam. More precisely, religion departments in colleges and universities across North America discovered they had large Muslim student populations.

In the context of the 1980s, when some religion departments had acquired funds to find a Muslim scholar, Fazlur Rahman might well have ended up in Religious Studies, not in area studies. Campus Muslim groups were stimulated by the religious revolution in Iran and Islamic resurgence elsewhere. The Western misunderstanding of Islam was laid by Muslim intellectuals at the doorsteps of the academy where it belonged, at least in large part.

Some universities that previously had no curriculum in Islamic or Middle Eastern studies received large endowments from Middle Eastern governments and from American corporations with business interests in the Middle East. Others found enlightened and sympathetic deans who would support a budget line (and usually no more) for an Islam specialist. In many cases, these universities had no library holdings in Middle Eastern languages or appropriate reference and secondary materials. Arabic and other languages essential to Islamic studies were either not taught at all or on an *ad hoc* basis, relying on native speakers with little or no training in applied linguistics. The phrase heard most often from search committee chairs, as recently as the 1993 American Academy of Religion annual meeting, was that a position in Islamic religious studies was now becoming desirable because of the increasing number of Muslim students on campus. The campus ministerial function of Religious Studies lingers on.

I began this paper by acknowledging that Fazlur Rahman was not my mentor, though I would like to have studied with him. I have argued throughout the paper that I do not believe Fazlur Rahman contributed much to the discipline of Religious Studies. And further, I would argue that Religious Studies needed his clear and philosophical mind to help make the theoretical connections between religions and religion. That was a problematic Fazlur Rahman never recognized, and never would be challenged to recognize, so long as he labored in an intellectual environment shaped by the tenaciously held belief that subject matter, and not discipline, yields its own what, how, and why it should be studied.

Nonetheless, my reading of Fazlur Rahman's texts and my limited personal acquaintance with the man compel me to end this essay by partially deconstructing my own argument. Many contributors to this volume, and others as well, will quarrel with my conclusions and think that I have slighted or unfairly characterized his lasting achievement in Islamic religious studies. It seems clear to me now in retrospect that when I asked Fazlur Rahman to respond to the conference papers on "Islam and the History of Religion," it was assumed by me and by him that his role was that of a Muslim commentator. I had resorted to and thus reinforced the flawed relationship of Islamic studies to Religious Studies I now find so dismaying.

The problem, as I have labored to argue, is that Religious Studies has to be more than a combination of Buddhist studies, Judaic studies, Christian studies (itself complex and disparate), Islamic studies, and so on. To the extent that Religious Studies has nonetheless ended up being a concatenation of tradition studies, Fazlur Rahman's achievement has been enormous. His books are widely read in the Religious Studies curriculum, and will be for some time to come, and many of his students are now influential members of religion faculties in North America and in the Islamic world.

That being the case, perhaps religious studies as I have tried to define it is only an "imagined" discipline, or perhaps academic "discipline" is itself no longer viable in the postmodern age. I have just posed questions that those of us fortunate enough to be asked to write about Fazlur Rahman cannot answer in relation to his own work, but that nonetheless we must try to answer in relation to our own. I submit that it falls on our shoulders, as interpreters now of Fazlur Rahman's texts, to help those who come to his work to learn about Islam, also to learn how to interpret religion.

NOTES

1. Fazlur Rahman, "Approaches to Islam in Religious Studies: Review Essay," *Approaches to Islam in Religious Studies*, ed. Richard C. Martin (Tucson, AZ: University of Arizona Press, 1985), pp. 189–202.

2. In Robert K. Merton, *The Sociology of Science: Theoretical and Empirical Investigations*, ed. Norman W. Storer (Chicago and London: University of Chicago Press, 1973), pp. 99–136.

3. Fazlur Rahman, "Approaches to Islam in Religious Studies: Review Essay," *Approaches to Islam*, ed. Martin, p. 193.

4. It goes (almost) without saying that there are many important ways in which Fazlur Rahman and Rushdie are profoundly different intellectuals, especially when we move from axes of ethnicity and cultural displacement to the axis of religious intellectualism.

5. Akbar S. Ahmed, *Postmodernism and Islam: Predicament and Promise* (London and New York: Routledge, 1992).

6. Fazlur Rahman, *Prophecy in Islam: Philosophy and Orthodoxy* (London: George Allen & Unwin, 1958 [University of Chicago Press, 1979]).

7. "Biography of Dr. Fazlur Rahman."

8. Fazlur Rahman, *Islam and Modernity* (Chicago: University of Chicago Press, 1982), pp. 8–11.

9. Letter to the author dated January 12, 1994.

10. Ismail R. al-Faruqi (d. 1986) at Temple University.

11. Charles J. Adams, "The History of Religions and the Study of Islam," *The History of Religions: Essays on the Problem of Understanding*, ed. Joseph M. Kitagawa, with the collaboration of Mircea Eliade and Charles H. Long (Chicago and London: University of Chicago Press, 1967), p. 178.

12. It is true that some Religious Studies departments in the 1980s and 1990s have begun to include historians of religion, who specialize in Islam and in comparative studies of Islam, on their faculties. Significantly, this recent openness to Islam seems to have occurred in religion departments at public universities and smaller private colleges where Middle Eastern area studies are absent.

13. J.Z. Smith has stated the case with clarity in his chapter "On Comparison" in *Drudgery Divine: On the Comparison of Early Christianities and the Religions of Late Antiquity* (Chicago: University of Chicago Press, 1990), pp. 36–53.

14. Jacob Neusner, "Judaism within the Disciplines of Religious Studies: Perspectives on Graduate Education," *The Council on the Study of Religion Bulletin* 14/5 (1983):141. This passage was cited in my 1985 essay, "Islam and Religious Studies: An Introductory Essay," *Approaches to Islam in Religious Studies*, ed. Richard C. Martin (Tucson, AZ: University of Arizona Press, 1985), p. 17. I have borrowed freely from that essay in revising and constructing my argument here.

15. Mary Douglas, "The Effects of Modernization on Religious Change," *Daedalus* 111/1 (1982):1. That issue of the journal was dedicated to the

restoration of religion as a topic of study in the academy.

16. Leonard Binder, "Area Studies: A Critical Reassessment," *The Study of the Middle East: Research and Scholarship in the Humanities and the Social Sciences*, ed. Leonard Binder (New York: John Wiley and Sons, 1976), pp. 10–18.

BIBLIOGRAPHY OF FAZLUR RAHMAN

BOOKS

Avicenna's De Anima. New York: Oxford University Press, 1959.

Avicenna's Psychology: An English Translation of Kitāb al-Naāt, Book II, Chapter VI. New York: Oxford University Press, 1952. (Reprinted in Westport, CT: Hyperion Press, 1981).

Health and Medicine in the Islamic Tradition. New York: The Crossroad Publishing Company, 1989.

Intikhabāt-i makhtūbāt-i Shaykh Ahmad Sirhindi: Selected Letters of Sir Ahmad Sirhindi. Karachi: Iqbal Academy, 1968.

Islam. 2nd ed. Chicago: University of Chicago Press, 1979.

Islam and Modernity: Transformation of an Intellectual Tradition. Publications of the Center for Middle Eastern Studies, no. 15. Chicago: University of Chicago Press, 1982.

Islamic Methodology in History. Karachi: Iqbal Academy, 1965.

Major Themes of the Qur'ān. Chicago: Bibliotheca Islamica, 1980.

Philosophy of Mullā Sadrā Shīrāzī. Albany: State University of New York Press, 1976.

Prophecy in Islam: Philosophy and Orthodoxy. London: George Allen & Unwin, 1958; 2nd ed. Chicago: University of Chicago Press, 1979.

ARTICLES

"Approaches to Islam in Religious Studies: A Review." *Approaches to Islam in Religious Studies*. Ed. Richard C. Martin. Tucson: University of Arizona Press, 1985: 189-202.

"Avicenna and Orthodox Islam: An Interpretive Note on the Composition of his System." *Harry Austryn Wolfson, Jubilee Volume on the Occasion of his Seventy-Fifth Birthday*. Vol. II. Jerusalem: American Academy for Jewish Research, 1965: 667-76.

"Challenge of Modern Ideas and Social Values to Muslim Society." *International Islamic Colloquium, University of Punjab, 1957–1958, Papers*. Lahore: Punjab University Press, 1960.

"The Concept of *Hadd* in Islamic Law." *Islamic Studies*. 4, no. 3 (September 1965), 237–51.

"Concepts of Sunnah, Ijtihād and Ijmā in the Early Period." *Islamic Studies*. 1, no. 1 (March 1962), 5–21.

"Controversy Over the Muslim Family Laws Ordinance." *South Asian Politics and Religion*. Ed. Donald E. Smith. Princeton, NJ: Princeton University Press, 1966: 414-27.

"Currents of Religious Thought in Pakistan." *Islamic Studies*. 7, no. 1 (March 1968), 1–7.

"Divine Revelation and the Prophet." *Hamdard Islamicus*. 1, no. 2 (Fall 1978): 66-72.

"Dream, Imagination and *'Ālam al-Mithāl*." *Islamic Studies*. 4, no. 2 (June 1964), 167–80. (Reprinted in *The Dream and Human Societies*, Ed. C.E. von Grunebaum and R. Caillois. Berkeley: University of California Press, 1966.

"Economic Principles of Islam." *Islamic Studies*. 8, no. 1 (March 1969), 1–8.

"Elements of Belief in the Qur'ān." *Literature of Belief: Sacred Scripture and Religion*, Ed. Neal E. Lambert. Provo, UT: Brigham Young University 1981.

"Essence and Existence in Avicenna." *Medieval and Renaissance Studies*. 4 (1958), 1–16.

"Essence and Existence in Ibn Sīnā: The Myth and Reality." *Hamadard Islamicus*. 4, no. 1 (Spring 1981), 3–14.

"The Eternity of the World and the Heavenly Bodies." *Essays on Islamic Philosophy and Science*. Ed. George F. Hourani. Albany: State University of New York, 1975: 222-37.

"Evolution of Soviet Policy toward Muslims in Russia: 1917–1965." *Journal of the Institute for Muslim Minority Affairs*. 1/2 (1979–1980), 28–46.

"Fazlur Rahman." *The Courage of Convictions: Prominent Contemporaries Discus Their Beliefs and How They Put Them into Action*. Ed. Phillip L. Berman. Santa Barbara, CA: Dodd, Mead & Co., 1985: 153-9.

"Functional Interdependence of Law and Theology." *Theology and in Islam: Law Second Giorgio Levi Della Vida Conference, 1969*. Ed. G.E. von Grunebaum. Wiesbaden: Otto Harrassowitz, 1971: 89-97.

"The God-World Relationship in Mullā Sadrā." *Essays on Islamic Philosophy and Science*. Ed. George F. Hourani. Albany: State University of New York, 1975: 238-53.

"Human Rights in Islam." *Democracy and Human Rights in the Islamic Republic of Iran*. Chicago: Committee on Democracy and Human Rights, 1982.

"Ibn Sīnā." *A History of Muslim Philosophy*. Vol. I. Ed. M.M. Sharif. Wiesbaden: Otto Harrassowitz, 1966: 480-506.

"Ibn Sīnā's Theory of the God-World Relationship. *God and Creation: An Ecumenical Symposium*. Eds. David B. Burrell and Bernard McGinn. Notre Dame, IN: University of Notre Dame Press, 1990: 38-52.

"The Ideological Experience of Pakistan." *Islam and the Modern Age*. 2, no. 4 (November 1971), 1–20.

"The Impact of Modernity on Islam." *Islamic Studies*. 5, no. 2 (June 1966), 113–28. (Also in *Religious Plurality and World Community*. Ed. Edward J. Jurji. Leiden: E.J. Brill, 1969.)

"Implementation of the Islamic Concept of State in the Pakistani Milieu." *Islamic Studies*. 6, no. 3 (September 1967), 205–24. (Reprinted in abridged form as "Islamic Concept of State" in *Islam in Transition: Muslim Perspectives*. Eds. John J. Donahue and John L. Esposito. New York: Oxford University Press, 1982.)

"L'Intellectus Acquistus in Alfarābī." *Giornale Critico della Filosofia Italiana*. 3, 7 (1953), 351–57.

"Internal Religious Developments in the Present Century Islam." *Journal of World History*. 2 (1954–55), 862–79.

"Interpreting the Qur'ān." *Inquiry* 3, 5(May 1986): 45–9.

"Iqbal, the Visionary; Jinnah, the Technician; and Pakistan, the Reality." *Iqbal, Jinnah and Pakistan: The Vision and the Reality*, Ed. C.M. Naim. Syracuse, NY: Syracuse University, 1979.

"Iqbal's Idea of the Muslim." *Islamic Studies*. 2, no. 4 (December 1963), 439–45.

"Islam and Health: Some Theological, Historical, and Sociological Perspectives." *Hamdard Islamicus*. 5, no. 4 (Winter 1982), 75–88.

"Islam and Health/Medicine: A Historical Perspective." *Healing and Restoration: Health and Medicine in the World's Religious Traditions* Ed. Lawrence E. Sullivan. New York: MacMillan Publishing Company, 1989.

"Islam and Medicine—A General Overview." *Perspectives in Biology and Medicine*. 27, no. 4 (Summer 1984), 585–97.

"Islam and Political Action: Politics in the Service of Religion." *Cities of God: Faith, Politics and Pluralism in Judaism, Christianity and Islam*. Eds. Nigel Biggar, Jamie S. Scott and William Schweiker. New York: Greenwood Press, 1986.

"Islam and the Constitutional Problem of Pakistan." *Studia Islamica*. 32 (1970), 275–87.

"Islam and the New Constitution of Pakistan." *Journal of Asian and African Studies*. 8 (1973), 190–204. (Reprinted in *Contemporary Problems of Pakistan*. Ed. J. Henry Korson. Leiden: E.J. Brill, 1974.)

"Islam and the Problem of Economic Justice." *The Pakistan Economist*. 24 (August 1974), 14–39.

"Islam: Challenges and Opportunities." *Islam: Past Influence and Present Challenge, in Honor of W.M. Watt*. Eds. Alford T. Welch and Pierre Cachia. Edinburgh: Edinburgh University Press, 1979: 31-30.

"Islam: Legacy and Contemporary Challenge." *Islamic Studies*. 19, no. 4 (Winter 1980), 235–46. (Reprinted in *Islam in the Contemporary World*. Ed. Cyriac Pullapilly. Notre Dame, IN: Cross Roads Books, 1980.)

"Islam in Pakistan." *Journal of South Asian and Middle Eastern Studies*. 8, no. 4 (1985), 34–61.

"Islamic Philosophy." *The Encyclopedia of Philosophy*, ed. Paul Edwards. New York: MacMillan, 1967, 4: 219–24.

"Islamic Modernism: Its Scope, Method and Alternative." *International Journal of Middle Eastern Studies*. 1 (1970), 317–33.

"Islamic Studies and the Future of Islam." *Islamic Studies: A Tradition and its Problems, Seventh Giorgio Della Vida Conference, 1979*. Ed. Malcolm H. Kerr. Malibu, CA: Undena Publications, 1980: 125-33.

"Islamic Thought in the India-Pakistan Subcontinent and the Middle East." *Journal of Near Eastern Studies*. 32 (1973), 194–200.

"Islamization of Knowledge: A Response." *American Journal of Islamic Social Sciences*. 5, 1(1988), 3–11.

"Islam's Attitude Toward Judaism." *The Muslim World*. 72 (1982), 1–13.

"Law and Ethics in Islam." *Ethics in Islam: Ninth Giorgio Levi Della Vida Conference, 1983, in Honor of Fazlur Rahman*. Ed. R. Hovannisian. Malibu, CA: Undena Publications, 1985: 3-15..

"Law of Rebellion in Islam." *Islam in the Modern World, 1983 Paine Lectures in Religion*. 8th Series. Ed. Jill Raitt. Columbia: University of Missouri-Columbia, 1983.

"Letter to the Editor." *The Pakistan Times*. Lahore, December 25, 1967.

"The Message and the Messenger." *Islam: The Religious and Political Life of a World Community*. Ed. Marjorie Kelly. New York: Praeger Publications, 1984: 9-54.

"Mir Damad's Concept of Huduth Dahrl: A Contribution to the Study of the God-World Relationship Theories in Safavid Iran." *Journal of Near Eastern Studies*. 39 (1980), 139–50.

"Modern Muslim Thought." *Muslim World*. 45 (1955), 16–25.

"Modern Thought in Islam." *Colloquium on Islamic Culture in Its Relation to the Contemporary World, September 1953*. Princeton University Press, [n.d.].

"Muhammad Iqbal and Ataturk's Reform." *Journal of Near Eastern Studies*. 43 (1984), 157–62.

"Mullā Sadrā's Theory of Knowledge." *Philosophical Forum*. 4 (1972), 141–52.

"Muslim Attitudes toward Family Planning." Paper presented at Lahore Seminar in March, 1964.

"Muslim Modernism in the Indo-Pakistan Sub-Continent." *Bulletin of the School of Oriental and African Studies*. 21 (1958), 82–99.

"A Muslim Response to Christian Particularity and the Faith of Islam." *Christian Faith in a Religiously Plural World*. Eds. Donald G. Dawe and John B. Carman. Maryknoll, NY: Orbis Books, 1978.

"My Belief-in-Action." *The Courage of Conviction*. Ed. Phillip L. Berman. Santa Barbara, CA: Dodd, Mead & Company, 1985.

"Notification of the Government of Pakistan." *Pakistan Gazette*. July, 1961.

"The People of the Book and the Diversity of Religions." (Reprint of Appendix II of *Major Themes of the Qur'ān*). *Christianity Through Non-Christian Eyes*. Ed. Paul J. Griffiths. Maryknoll, NY: Orbis Books, 1990.

"Pre-foundations of the Muslim Community in Mecca." *Studia Islamica*. 43 (1976), 5–24.

"The Principle of *Shūrā* and the Role of the *Ummah* in Islam." *Journal of the University of Baluchistan*, 1982. (Reprinted in *American Journal of Islamic Studies*, 1 [1984], 1–9 and in *State Politics and Islam*, Ed. Mumtaz Ahmad, Indianapolis, IN: American Trust Publications, 1986: 1-13.)

"The Post-Formative Developments in Islam." *Islamic Studies*. 1, no. 4 (December 1962), 1–23 and 2, no. 3, (September 1963), 297–316.

"The Qur'ānic Concept of God, the Universe and Man." *Islamic Studies*. 6, no. 1 (March 1967), 1–19.

"The Qur'ānic Solution of Pakistan's Educational Problem." *Islamic Studies*. 6, no. 4 (December 1967), 315–26.

"A Recent Controversy over the Interpretation of *Shūrā* [in the Qur'ān]." *History of Religions*. 20, no. 4 (May 1981), pp. 291–301.

"The Religious Situation of Mecca from the Eve of Islam up to the Hijra." *Islamic Studies*. 16, no. 4 (Winter 1977), 289–301.

"Revival and Reform in Islam." *Cambridge History of Islam*. Eds. P.M. Holt. et al, Vol. II. Cambridge: Cambridge University Press, 1970: 635-56.

"Ribā and Interest." *Islamic Studies*. 3, no. 1 (March 1964), 1–43.

"Roots of Islamic Neo-Fundamentalism." *Change in the Muslim World*. Eds. Philip H. Stoddard, David C. Cuthell and Margaret W. Sullivan. Syracuse, NY: Syracuse University Press, 1981: 23-35.

"Social Change and the Early Sunnah." *Islamic Studies*. 2, no. 2 (June 1963), 159–20

"Some Islamic Issues in the Ayyūb Khān Era." *Essay on Islamic Civilization, Presented to Niyazi Berkes*. Ed. Donald P. Little. Leiden: E.J. Brill, 1976: 299-302.

"Some Key Ethical Concepts on the Qur'ān." *Journal of Religious Ethics*. 2 (1983), 170-185.

"Some Recent Books on the Qur'ān by Western Authors." *Journal of Religion*. 64, no. 1 (1984), 73–95.

"Some Reflections on the Reconstruction of Muslim Society in Pakistan." *Islamic Studies*. 6, no. 2 (June 1967), 103–120.

"Sources of Dynamism in Islam." *Al-Ijtihād*. 15, no. 1 (January 1978), 53–64.

"Sources and Meaning of Islamic Socialism." In *Religion* and *Political Modernization*, ed. D.E. Smith. New Haven & London: Yale University Press, 1974: 243–58.

"The Status of the Individual in Islam." *Islamic Studies*. 5, no. 4 (December 1966), 319–330.

"The Status of the Individual in Islam." *The Status of the Individual in East and West, Report of the Fourth East-West Philosopher's Conference*. Eds. Charles A. Moore and Aldyth V. Morris. Honolulu: University of Hawaii Press, 1968.

"The Status of Women in Islam: A Modernist Interpretation." *Separate Worlds: Studies of Purdah in South Asia*. Eds. Hanna Papanek and Gail Minault. Columbia: South Asia Books, 1982: 285-310.

"The Status of Women in the Qur'ān." *Women and Revolution in Iran*. Ed. Guity Nashat. Boulder, CO: Westview Press, 1983: 37-54.

"Sunnah and Hadīth." *Islamic Studies*. 1, no. 2 (June 1962), 1–36.

"A Survey of Modernization of Muslim Family Law." *International Journal of Middle Eastern Studies*. 2 (1980), 451–65.

"The Thinker of Crisis—Shah Wali-Ullah." *Pakistan Quarterly*. 6, no. 2 (1956), 44–8.

"Towards a Reformulation of the Theory of Islamic Law: Sheikh Yamani on Public Interest." *New York University Journal of International Law and Politics*. 12, no. 2 (Fall 1979), 219–24.

"Translating the Qur'ān." *Religion and Literature*. 20 (1988), 23–30.

UNPUBLISHED MANUSCRIPT

Revival and Reform in Islam: A Study of Islamic Fundamentalism (portions of this document are written and other portions remain on untranscribed tapes).

TRANSLATED WORKS

Indonesian

Tema Pokok al-Qur'ān [*Major Themes of the Qur'ān*], Ed. Ammar Haryono, Tran. Anas Mahyuddin. Bandung: Penerbit Pustaka, 1983.

Membuka Pintu Ijtihād [*Islamic Methodology in History*], Ed. Ammar Haryono, Tran. Anas Mahyuddin. Bandung: Penerbit Pustaka, 1984.

Islam dan Modernitas, Tentang Transformasi Intelektual [*Islam and Modernity: Transformation of an Intellectual Tradition*], Ed. Ammar Haryono, Tran. Ahsin Mohammad. Bandung: Penerbit Pustaka, 1985.

Islam [*Islam*], Ed. Ammar Haryono, Tran. Ahsin Mohammad. Bandung: Penerbit Pustaka, 195.

Serbo-Croatian

Duh Islama [*Islam*], Tran. Andrija Grosberger. Biblioteka Zenit Velike Avanture Coveka Series. Belgrade: Yugoslavia, 1983.

Turkish

Islâm [*Islam*], Trans. Mehmet Dağ and Mehmet Aydin. Hicrī 15, Asir Külliyāt, Series no. 2. Ankara: Selcuk Yayinlari, 1981.

Ana Konulariyla Kur'ān [*Major Themes of the Qur'ān*], Tran. Alparslan Açikgenç. Ankara: Fecr Yaninlari, 1987.

Islamiyet ve Iktisadi Adalet Meselesi [*Islamic Methodology in History*], Tran. Yusuf Ziya Kavakçi. Islāmi Ilimler Fakültesi Series, no. 4; Tercüme Serisi, no. 1. Ankara: Islâmi Ilimler Fakültesi, 1976.

ENCYCLOPEDIA ARTICLES

"ʿAkl," "Andjuman," "ʿArad," "Bahmanyār," "Bakā wa Fanā," "Barahima," "Basīt wa Murakkab," "Dhāt," and "Dhawk." *Encylopedia of Islam*, New Edition. Ed. H.A.R. Gibb, et al. Leiden: E.J. Brill, 1979.

"Islam," "Iqbal, Muhammad," and "Mullā Sadrā." *Encyclopedia of Religion*. Ed. Mircea Eliade. New York: MacMillan Publishing Company, 1987.

"Islamic Philosophy," *Encyclopedia of Philosophy*. Ed. Paul Edwards. New York: MacMillian Company and The Free Press, 1967.

"The Legacy of Muhammad," "Sources of Islamic Doctrine and Social Views," "Doctrines of the Qur'ān," "Fundamental Practices and Institutions of Islam," "Theology and Sectarianism," and "Religion and the Arts." *Encyclopedia Britannica*, 15th Edition. Ed. Philip W. Goetz, Chicago: Encyclopedia Britannica, Inc., 1974.

BOOK REVIEWS

Rahman, Fazlur. Review of *On Schacht's Origins of Muhammadan Jurisprudence*, by G.M. Azami, *Journal of Near Eastern Studies*, 47 (July 1988), 228–29.

ABOUT THE CONTRIBUTORS

Donald L. Berry graduated from the University of Chicago in 1993 with a Ph.D. in Islamic studies. His research specialization is in Islamic intellectual history.

Donna Lee Bowen is a professor of Political Science and Near Eastern Studies at Brigham Young University. Her research concerns the interface of politics, religion, and social issues in the Middle East and North Africa. She has been a consultant for the World Bank and USAID on issues concerning Islam and family planning. Her recent publications include "Abortion, Islam, and the 1994 Cairo Population Conference" (*International Journal of Middle East Studies*, 1997).

Daniel Brown graduated from the University of Chicago in 1993 with a Ph.D. in Islamic Studies. His research specialization is in Islamic intellectual history, and he is the author or *Rethinking Tradition in Modern Islamic Thought* (Cambridge University Press, 1996).

Frederick M. Denny teaches Islamic studies and the history of religions at the University of Colorado at Boulder. He is author of *An Introduction to Islam* (2nd edition, 1994) and *Islam and the Muslim Community* (revised edition, 1993). His most recent work is the co-authored *Jews, Christians, Muslims: An Introduction to Monotheism* (forthcoming, Prentice-Hall, 1997).

Marcia K. Hermansen is a professor of Religious Studies at San Diego State University, specializing in Islamic studies. Her research interests are classical Islamic thought, Islamic mysticism, Islamic cultural studies, Islam in South Asia,

Muslims in America, and Muslim women's studies. In 1996 she published *The Conclusive Argument from God: Shah Wali Allah of Delhi's Hujjat Allah al-Baligha* and she is currently writing a book on Islamic religious biography.

Valerie J. Hoffman is an associate professor in the Program for the Study of Religion at the University of Illinois at Urbana-Campaign. She is the author of *Sufism, Mystics, and Saints in Modern Egypt* (University of South Carolina Press, 1995), and has written a number of articles on Sufism, Islamic gender ideology, and contemporary Islamic movements.

Th. Emil Homerin is associate professor and chair of the Department of Religion and Classics at the University of Rochester, where he teaches Islam, mysticism and classical Arabic poetry. His publications include *From Arab Poet to Muslim Saint: Ibn al-Farid, His Verse and His Shrine* (University of South Carolina Press, 1994) and *Ibn al-Farid: Sufi Verse and Saintly Life* (forthcoming, Paulist).

Richard C. Martin is professor and chair of the Department of Religion, Emory University. He specializes in Islamic religious thought and comparative religions. His most recent book is *Defenders of Reason in Islam* (Oneworld, 1997).

Sheila McDonough is a professor in the Department of Religion at Concordia University, Montreal. Her recent publications include *Muslim Ethics and Modernity* (Wilfred Laurier, 1984) and *Gandhi's Responses to Islam* (Printword, 1994).

Michael A. Sells is Emily Judson Baugh and John Marshall Gest Professor of Comparative Religions at Haverford College. His writings include *The Bridge Betrayed: Religion and Genocide in Bosnia* (University of California Press, 1996); *Early Islamic Mysticism* (Classics of Western Spirituality, 1996); *Mystical Languages of Unsaying* (University of Chicago Press, 1994); *Desert Tracings: Six Classic Arabian Odes* (Wesleyan University Press, 1989); "Sound and Meaning in Surat al-Qari'a" (*Arabica*, 1993); and numerous articles on Quar'ānic language, Sufism, and Arabic poetry. He is founder and president of the Community of Bosnia Foundation, dedicated to supporting a multireligious Bosnia.

Tamara Sonn is professor of Religious Studies at the University of South Florida, specializing in Islamic studies. Her books include *Between Qur'ān and Crown: The Challenge of Political Legitimacy in the Arab World* (Westview, 1990), *Interpreting Islam: Bandali Jawzi's Islamic Intellectual History* (Oxford, 1996), *Islam and the Question of Minorities* (Scholars Press, 1996), and *Comparing Religions Through Law: Judaism and Islam* (with Jacob Neusner, forthcoming, Routledge, 1999), as well as numerous chapters and articles on Islamic intellectual history. She is also editor of "Islam and the World" for The University of South Florida.

Earle H. Waugh is professor of Religious Studies and chair of the Department of Modern Languages and Comparative Studies at the University of Alberta. He has written many articles about, and edited several texts on, Islam in North America, in addition to his work on the Middle East. He is currently writing a companion volume to his *The Munshidin of Egypt: Their World and Their Song* (University of South Carolina, 1989), entitled *Lyrics of the Soul: Texts From Egypt's Mystical Chanters.*

South Florida Studies in the History of Judaism

40001	Lectures on Judaism in the Academy and in the Humanities	Neusner
40002	Lectures on Judaism in the History of Religion	Neusner
40003	Self-Fulfilling Prophecy: Exile and Return in the History of Judaism	Neusner
40004	The Canonical History of Ideas: The Place of the So-called Tannaite Midrashim, Mekhilta Attributed to R. Ishmael, Sifra, Sifré to Numbers, and Sifré to Deuteronomy	Neusner
40005	Ancient Judaism: Debates and Disputes, Second Series	Neusner
40006	The Hasmoneans and Their Supporters: From Mattathias to the Death of John Hyrcanus I	Sievers
40007	Approaches to Ancient Judaism: New Series, Volume One	Neusner
40008	Judaism in the Matrix of Christianity	Neusner
40009	Tradition as Selectivity: Scripture, Mishnah, Tosefta, and Midrash in the Talmud of Babylonia	Neusner
40010	The Tosefta: Translated from the Hebrew: Sixth Division Tohorot	Neusner
40011	In the Margins of the Midrash: Sifre Ha'azinu Texts, Commentaries and Reflections	Basser
40012	Language as Taxonomy: The Rules for Using Hebrew and Aramaic in the Babylonia Talmud	Neusner
40013	The Rules of Composition of the Talmud of Babylonia: The Cogency of the Bavli's Composite	Neusner
40014	Understanding the Rabbinic Mind: Essays on the Hermeneutic of Max Kadushin	Ochs
40015	Essays in Jewish Historiography	Rapoport-Albert
40016	The Golden Calf and the Origins of the Jewish Controversy	Bori/Ward
40017	Approaches to Ancient Judaism: New Series, Volume Two	Neusner
40018	The Bavli That Might Have Been: The Tosefta's Theory of Mishnah Commentary Compared With the Bavli's	Neusner
40019	The Formation of Judaism: In Retrospect and Prospect	Neusner
40020	Judaism in Society: The Evidence of the Yerushalmi, Toward the Natural History of a Religion	Neusner
40021	The Enchantments of Judaism: Rites of Transformation from Birth Through Death	Neusner
40022	Åbo Addresses	Neusner
40023	The City of God in Judaism and Other Comparative and Methodological Studies	Neusner
40024	The Bavli's One Voice: Types and Forms of Analytical Discourse and their Fixed Order of Appearance	Neusner
40025	The Dura-Europos Synagogue: A Re-evaluation (1932-1992)	Gutmann
40026	Precedent and Judicial Discretion: The Case of Joseph ibn Lev	Morell
40027	Max Weinreich *Geschichte der jiddischen Sprachforschung*	Frakes
40028	Israel: Its Life and Culture, Volume I	Pedersen
40029	Israel: Its Life and Culture, Volume II	Pedersen
40030	The Bavli's One Statement: The Metapropositional Program of Babylonian Talmud Tractate Zebahim Chapters One and Five	Neusner

240031	The Oral Torah: The Sacred Books of Judaism: An Introduction: Second Printing	Neusne
240032	The Twentieth Century Construction of "Judaism:" Essays on the Religion of Torah in the History of Religion	Neusne
240033	How the Talmud Shaped Rabbinic Discourse	Neusne
240034	The Discourse of the Bavli: Language, Literature, and Symbolism: Five Recent Findings	Neusne
240035	The Law Behind the Laws: The Bavli's Essential Discourse	Neusne
240036	Sources and Traditions: Types of Compositions in the Talmud of Babylonia	Neusne
240037	How to Study the Bavli: The Languages, Literatures, and Lessons of the Talmud of Babylonia	Neusne
240038	The Bavli's Primary Discourse: Mishnah Commentary: Its Rhetorical Paradigms and their Theological Implications	Neusne
240039	Midrash Aleph Beth	Sawye
240040	Jewish Thought in the 20th Century: An Introduction in the Talmud of Babylonia Tractate Moed Qatan	Schwei
240041	Diaspora Jews and Judaism: Essays in Honor of, and in Dialogue with, A. Thomas Kraabel	Overman/MacLenna
240042	The Bavli: An Introduction	Neusne
240043	The Bavli's Massive Miscellanies: The Problem of Agglutinative Discourse in the Talmud of Babylonia	Neusne
240044	The Foundations of the Theology of Judaism: An Anthology Part II: Torah	Neusne
240045	Form-Analytical Comparison in Rabbinic Judaism: Structure and Form in *The Fathers* and *The Fathers According to Rabbi Nathan*	Neusne
240046	Essays on Hebrew	Weinber
240047	The Tosefta: An Introduction	Neusne
240048	The Foundations of the Theology of Judaism: An Anthology Part III: Israel	Neusne
240049	The Study of Ancient Judaism, Volume I: Mishnah, Midrash, Siddur	Neusne
240050	The Study of Ancient Judaism, Volume II: The Palestinian and Babylonian Talmuds	Neusne
240051	Take Judaism, for Example: Studies toward the Comparison of Religions	Neusne
240052	From Eden to Golgotha: Essays in Biblical Theology	Moberl
240053	The Principal Parts of the Bavli's Discourse: A Preliminary Taxonomy: Mishnah Commentary, Sources, Traditions and Agglutinative Miscellanies	Neusne
240054	Barabbas and Esther and Other Studies in the Judaic Illumination of Earliest Christianity	Au
240055	Targum Studies, Volume I: Textual and Contextual Studies in the Pentateuchal Targums	Fleshe
240056	Approaches to Ancient Judaism: New Series, Volume Three, Historical and Literary Studies	Neusne
240057	The Motherhood of God and Other Studies	Grube
240058	The Analytic Movement: Hayyim Soloveitchik and his Circle	Solomo
240059	Recovering the Role of Women: Power and Authority in Rabbinic Jewish Society	Haa

40060	The Relation between Herodotus' *History* and Primary History	Mandell/Freedman
40061	The First Seven Days: A Philosophical Commentary on the Creation of Genesis	Samuelson
40062	The Bavli's Intellectual Character: The Generative Problematic: In Bavli Baba Qamma Chapter One And Bavli Shabbat Chapter One	Neusner
40063	The Incarnation of God: The Character of Divinity in Formative Judaism: Second Printing	Neusner
40064	Moses Kimhi: Commentary on the Book of Job	Basser/Walfish
40066	Death and Birth of Judaism: Second Printing	Neusner
40067	Decoding the Talmud's Exegetical Program	Neusner
40068	Sources of the Transformation of Judaism	Neusner
40069	The Torah in the Talmud: A Taxonomy of the Uses of Scripture in the Talmud, Volume I	Neusner
40070	The Torah in the Talmud: A Taxonomy of the Uses of Scripture in the Talmud, Volume II	Neusner
40071	The Bavli's Unique Voice: A Systematic Comparison of the Talmud of Babylonia and the Talmud of the Land of Israel, Volume One	Neusner
40072	The Bavli's Unique Voice: A Systematic Comparison of the Talmud of Babylonia and the Talmud of the Land of Israel, Volume Two	Neusner
40073	The Bavli's Unique Voice: A Systematic Comparison of the Talmud of Babylonia and the Talmud of the Land of Israel, Volume Three	Neusner
40074	Bits of Honey: Essays for Samson H. Levey	Chyet/Ellenson
40075	The Mystical Study of Ruth: *Midrash HaNe'elam* of the Zohar to the Book of Ruth	Englander
40076	The Bavli's Unique Voice: A Systematic Comparison of the Talmud of Babylonia and the Talmud of the Land of Israel, Volume Four	Neusner
40077	The Bavli's Unique Voice: A Systematic Comparison of the Talmud of Babylonia and the Talmud of the Land of Israel, Volume Five	Neusner
40078	The Bavli's Unique Voice: A Systematic Comparison of the Talmud of Babylonia and the Talmud of the Land of Israel, Volume Six	Neusner
40079	The Bavli's Unique Voice: A Systematic Comparison of the Talmud of Babylonia and the Talmud of the Land of Israel, Volume Seven	Neusner
240080	Are There Really Tannaitic Parallels to the Gospels?	Neusner
240081	Approaches to Ancient Judaism: New Series, Volume Four, Religious and Theological Studies	Neusner
240082	Approaches to Ancient Judaism: New Series, Volume Five, Historical, Literary, and Religious Studies	Basser/Fishbane
240083	Ancient Judaism: Debates and Disputes, Third Series	Neusner
240084	Judaic Law from Jesus to the Mishnah	Neusner
240085	Writing with Scripture: Second Printing	Neusner/Green
240086	Foundations of Judaism: Second Printing	Neusner

240087	Judaism and Zoroastrianism at the Dusk of Late Antiquity	Neusn
240088	Judaism States Its Theology	Neusn
240089	The Judaism behind the Texts I.A	Neusn
240090	The Judaism behind the Texts I.B	Neusn
240091	Stranger at Home	Neusn
240092	Pseudo-Rabad: Commentary to Sifre Deuteronomy	Basse
240093	FromText to Historical Context in Rabbinic Judaism	Neusne
240094	Formative Judaism	Neusne
240095	Purity in Rabbinic Judaism	Neusne
240096	Was Jesus of Nazareth the Messiah?	McMicha
240097	The Judaism behind the Texts I.C	Neusne
240098	The Judaism behind the Texts II	Neusne
240099	The Judaism behind the Texts III	Neusne
240100	The Judaism behind the Texts IV	Neusne
240101	The Judaism behind the Texts V	Neusne
240102	The Judaism the Rabbis Take for Granted	Neusne
240103	From Text to Historical Context in Rabbinic Judaism V. II	Neusne
240104	From Text to Historical Context in Rabbinic Judaism V. III	Neusne
240105	Samuel, Saul, and Jesus: Three Early Palestinian Jewish Christian Gospel Haggadoth	Au
240106	What is Midrash? And a Midrash Reader	Neusne
240107	Rabbinic Judaism: Disputes and Debates	Neusne
240108	Why There Never Was a "Talmud of Caesarea"	Neusne
240109	Judaism after the Death of "The Death of God"	Neusne
240110	Approaches to Ancient Judaism	Neusne
240112	The Judaic Law of Baptism	Neusne
240113	The Documentary Foundation of Rabbinic Culture	Neusne
240114	Understanding Seeking Faith, Volume Four	Neusne
240115	Paul and Judaism: An Anthropological Approach	Laat
240116	Approaches to Ancient Judaism, New Series, Volume Eight	Neusne
240119	Theme and Context in Biblical Lists	Scolni
240120	Where the Talmud Comes From	Neusne
240121	The Initial Phases of the Talmud, Volume Three: Social Ethics	Neusne
240122	Are the Talmuds Interchangeable? Christine Hayes's Blunder	Neusne
240123	The Initial Phases of the Talmud, Volume One: Exegesis of Scripture	Neusne
240124	The Initial Phases of the Talmud, Volume Two: Exemplary Virtue	Neusne
240125	The Initial Phases of the Talmud, Volume Four: Theology	Neusne
240126	From Agnon to Oz	Barga
240127	Talmudic Dialectics, Volume I: Tractate Berakhot and the Divisions of Appointed Times and Women	Neusne
240128	Talmudic Dialectics, Volume II: The Divisions of Damages and Holy Things and Tractate Niddah	Neusne
240129	The Talmud: Introduction and Reader	Neusne
240130	*Gesher Vakesher:* Bridges and Bonds The Life of Leon Kronish	Greer
240131	Beyond Catastrophe	Neusne

40132 Ancient Judaism, Fourth Series — Neusner
40133 Formative Judaism, New Series: Current Issues and Arguments Volume One — Neusner
40134 Sects and Scrolls — Davies
40135 Religion and Law — Neusner
40136 Approaches to Ancient Judaism, New Series, Volume Nine — Neusner
40137 Uppsala Addresses — Neusner
40138 Jews and Christians in the Life and Thought of Hugh of St. Victor — Moore
40140 Jews, Pagans, and Christians in the Golan Heights — Gregg/Urman
40141 Rosenzweig on Profane/Secular History — Vogel
40142 Approaches to Ancient Judaism, New Series, Volume Ten — Neusner
40143 Archaeology and the Galilee — Edwards/McCullough
40144 Rationality and Structure — Neusner
40145 Formative Judaism, New Series: Current Issues and Arguments Volume Two — Neusner
40146 Ancient Judaism, Religious and Theological Perspectives First Series — Neusner
40147 The Good Creator — Gelander
40148 The Mind of Classical Judaism, Volume IV, The Philosophy and Political Economy of Formative Judaism: The Mishnah's System of the Social Order — Neusner
40149 The Mind of Classical Judaism, Volume I, Modes of Thought:: Making Connections and Drawing Conclusions — Neusner
40150 The Mind of Classical Judaism, Volume II, From Philosophy to Religion — Neusner
41051 The Mind of Classical Judaism, Volume III, What is "Israel"? Social Thought in the Formative Age — Neusner
40152 The Tosefta, Translated from the Hebrew: Fifth Division, Qodoshim, The Order of Holy Things — Neusner
40153 The Theology of Rabbinic Judaism: A Prolegomenon — Neusner
40154 Approaches to Ancient Judaism, New Series, Volume Eleven — Neusner
40155 Pesiqtå Rabbati: A Synoptic Edition of Pesiqta Rabbati Based upon all Extant Manuscripts and the Editio Princeps, V. I — Ulmer
40156 The Place of the Tosefta in the Halakhah of Formative Judaism: What Alberdina Houtman Didn't Notice — Neusner
40157 "Caught in the Act," Walking on the Sea, and The Release of Barabbas Revisited — Aus
40158 Approaches to Ancient Judaism, New Series, Volume Twelve — Neusner
40159 The Halakhah of the Oral Torah, A Religious Commentary, Introduction and Volume I, Part One, Between Israel and God — Neusner
40160 Claudian Policymaking and the Early Imperial Repression of Judaism at Rome — Slingerland
40161 Rashi's Commentary on Psalms 1–89 with English Translation, Introducion and Notes — Gruber
40162 Peace, In Deed — Garber/Libowitz
40163 Mediators of the Divine — Berchman
40164 Approaches to Ancient Judaism, New Series, Volume Thirteen — Neusner
40165 Targum Studies, Volume Two: Targum and Peshitta — Flesher
40166 The Text and I: Writings of Samson H. Levey — Chyet

240167	The Documentary Form-History of Rabbinic Literature, I. The Documentary Forms of Mishnah	Neusne
240168	Louis Finkelstein and the Conservative Movement	Greenbaur
240169	Invitation to the Talmud: A Teaching Book	Neusne
240170	Invitation to Midrash: The Workings of Rabbinic Bible Interpretation, A Teaching Book	Neusne
240171	The Documentary Form-History of Rabbinic Literature, II. The Aggadic Sector:Tractate Abot, Abot deRabbi Natan, Sifra, Sifré to Numbers and Sifré to Deuteronomy	Neusne
240172	The Documentary Form-History of Rabbinic Literature, III. The Aggadic Sector: Mekhilta Attributed to R. Ishmael and Genesis Rabbah	Neusne
240173	The Documentary Form-History of Rabbinic Literature, IV. The Aggadic Sector: Leviticus Rabbah and Pesiqta deRab Kahana	Neusne
240174	The Documentary Form-History of Rabbinic Literature, V. The Aggadic Sector: Song of Songs Rabbah, Ruth Rabbah, Lamentations Rabbati, and Esther Rabbah I	Neusne
240175	The Documentary Form-History of Rabbinic Literature, VI. The Halakhic Sector: The Talmud of the Land of Israel A. Tractates Berakhot and Shabbat through Taanit	Neusne
240176	The Documentary Form-History of Rabbinic Literature, VI. The Halakhic Sector: The Talmud of the Land of Israel B. Tractates Megillah through Qiddushin	Neusne
240177	The Documentary Form-History of Rabbinic Literature, VI. The Halakhic Sector: The Talmud of the Land of Israel C. Tractates Sotah through Horayot and Niddah	Neusne
240178	The Documentary Form-History of Rabbinic Literature, VII. The Halakhic Sector: The Talmud of the Land of Israel A. Tractates Berakhot and Shabbat through Pesahim	Neusne
240179	The Documentary Form-History of Rabbinic Literature, VII. The Halakhic Sector: The Talmud of Babylonia B. Tractates Yoma through Ketubot	Neusne
240180	The Documentary Form-History of Rabbinic Literature, VII. The Halakhic Sector: The Talmud of Babylonia C. Tractates Nedarim through Baba Mesia	Neusne
240181	The Documentary Form-History of Rabbinic Literature, VII. The Halakhic Sector: The Talmud of Babylonia D. Tractates Baba Batra through Horayot	Neusne
240182	The Documentary Form-History of Rabbinic Literature, VII. The Halakhic Sector: The Talmud of Babylonia E. Tractates Zebahim through Bekhorot	Neusne
240183	The Documentary Form-History of Rabbinic Literature, VII. The Halakhic Sector: The Talmud of Babylonia F. Tractates Arakhin through Niddah and Conclusions	Neusne
240184	Messages to Moscow: And Other Current Lectures on Learning and Community in Judaism	Neusne
240185	The Economics of the Mishnah	Neusne
240186	Approaches to Ancient Judaism, New Series, Volume Fourteen	Neusne
240187	Jewish Law from Moses to the Mishnah	Neusne
240188	The Language and the Law of God	Cala

40189	Pseudo-Rabad: Commentary to Sifre Numbers	Basser
40190	How Adin Steinsalz Misrepresents the Talmud	Neusner
40191	How the Rabbis Liberated Women	Neusner
40192	From Scripture to 70	Neusner
40193	The Levites: Their Emergence as a Second-Class Priesthood	Nurmela
40194	Sifra	Ginsberg
40195	Approaches to Ancient Judaism, New Series, Volume Fifteen	Neusner
40196	What, Exactly, Did the Rabbinic Sages Mean by the "Oral Torah"?	Neusner

South Florida Academic Commentary Series

43001	The Talmud of Babylonia, An Academic Commentary, Volume XI, Bavli Tractate Moed Qatan	Neusner
43002	The Talmud of Babylonia, An Academic Commentary, Volume XXXIV, Bavli Tractate Keritot	Neusner
43003	The Talmud of Babylonia, An Academic Commentary, Volume XVII, Bavli Tractate Sotah	Neusner
43004	The Talmud of Babylonia, An Academic Commentary, Volume XXIV, Bavli Tractate Makkot	Neusner
43005	The Talmud of Babylonia, An Academic Commentary, Volume XXXII, Bavli Tractate Arakhin	Neusner
43006	The Talmud of Babylonia, An Academic Commentary, Volume VI, Bavli Tractate Sukkah	Neusner
43007	The Talmud of Babylonia, An Academic Commentary, Volume XII, Bavli Tractate Hagigah	Neusner
43008	The Talmud of Babylonia, An Academic Commentary, Volume XXVI, Bavli Tractate Horayot	Neusner
43009	The Talmud of Babylonia, An Academic Commentary, Volume XXVII, Bavli Tractate Shebuot	Neusner
43010	The Talmud of Babylonia, An Academic Commentary, Volume XXXIII, Bavli Tractate Temurah	Neusner
43011	The Talmud of Babylonia, An Academic Commentary, Volume XXXV, Bavli Tractates Meilah and Tamid	Neusner
43012	The Talmud of Babylonia, An Academic Commentary, Volume VIII, Bavli Tractate Rosh Hashanah	Neusner
43013	The Talmud of Babylonia, An Academic Commentary, Volume V, Bavli Tractate Yoma	Neusner
43014	The Talmud of Babylonia, An Academic Commentary, Volume XXXVI, Bavli Tractate Niddah	Neusner
43015	The Talmud of Babylonia, An Academic Commentary, Volume XX, Bavli Tractate Baba Qamma	Neusner
43016	The Talmud of Babylonia, An Academic Commentary, Volume XXXI, Bavli Tractate Bekhorot	Neusner
43017	The Talmud of Babylonia, An Academic Commentary, Volume XXX, Bavli Tractate Hullin	Neusner
43018	The Talmud of Babylonia, An Academic Commentary, Volume VII, Bavli Tractate Besah	Neusner

243019	The Talmud of Babylonia, An Academic Commentary, Volume X, Bavli Tractate Megillah	Neusn
243020	The Talmud of Babylonia, An Academic Commentary, Volume XXVIII, Bavli Tractate Zebahim A. Chapters I through VII	Neusn
243021	The Talmud of Babylonia, An Academic Commentary, Volume XXI, Bavli Tractate Baba Mesia, A. Chapters I through VI	Neusn
243022	The Talmud of Babylonia, An Academic Commentary, Volume XXII, Bavli Tractate Baba Batra, A. Chapters I through VI	Neusn
243023	The Talmud of Babylonia, An Academic Commentary, Volume XXIX, Bavli Tractate Menahot, A. Chapters I through VI	Neusn
243024	The Talmud of Babylonia, An Academic Commentary, Volume I, Bavli Tractate Berakhot	Neusn
243025	The Talmud of Babylonia, An Academic Commentary, Volume XXV, Bavli Tractate Abodah Zarah	Neusn
243026	The Talmud of Babylonia, An Academic Commentary, Volume XXIII, Bavli Tractate Sanhedrin, A. Chapters I through VII	Neusn
243027	The Talmud of Babylonia, A Complete Outline, Part IV, The Division of Holy Things; A: From Tractate Zabahim through Tractate Hullin	Neusn
243028	The Talmud of Babylonia, An Academic Commentary, Volume XIV, Bavli Tractate Ketubot, A. Chapters I through VI	Neusn
243029	The Talmud of Babylonia, An Academic Commentary, Volume IV, Bavli Tractate Pesahim, A. Chapters I through VII	Neusn
243030	The Talmud of Babylonia, An Academic Commentary, Volume III, Bavli Tractate Erubin, A. ChaptersI through V	Neusn
243031	The Talmud of Babylonia, A Complete Outline, Part III, The Division of Damages; A: From Tractate Baba Qamma through Tractate Baba Batra	Neusn
243032	The Talmud of Babylonia, An Academic Commentary, Volume II, Bavli Tractate Shabbat, Volume A, Chapters One through Twelve	Neusn
243033	The Talmud of Babylonia, An Academic Commentary, Volume II, Bavli Tractate Shabbat, Volume B, Chapters Thirteen through Twenty-four	Neusn
243034	The Talmud of Babylonia, An Academic Commentary, Volume XV, Bavli Tractate Nedarim	Neusn
243035	The Talmud of Babylonia, An Academic Commentary, Volume XVIII, Bavli Tractate Gittin	Neusn
243036	The Talmud of Babylonia, An Academic Commentary, Volume XIX, Bavli Tractate Qiddushin	Neusn
243037	The Talmud of Babylonia, A Complete Outline, Part IV, The Division of Holy Things; B: From Tractate Berakot through Tractate Niddah	Neusn

43038	The Talmud of Babylonia, A Complete Outline, Part III, The Division of Damages; B: From Tractate Sanhedrin through Tractate Shebuot	Neusner
43039	The Talmud of Babylonia, A Complete Outline, Part I, Tractate Berakhot and the Division of Appointed Times A: From Tractate Berakhot through Tractate Pesahim	Neusner
43040	The Talmud of Babylonia, A Complete Outline, Part I, Tractate Berakhot and the Division of Appointed Times B: From Tractate Yoma through Tractate Hagigah	Neusner
43041	The Talmud of Babylonia, A Complete Outline, Part II, The Division of Women; A: From Tractate Yebamot through Tractate Ketubot	Neusner
43042	The Talmud of Babylonia, A Complete Outline, Part II, The Division of Women; B: From Tractate Nedarim through Tractate Qiddushin	Neusner
43043	The Talmud of Babylonia, An Academic Commentary, Volume XIII, Bavli Tractate Yebamot, A. Chapters One through Eight	Neusner
43044	The Talmud of Babylonia, An Academic Commentary, XIII, Bavli Tractate Yebamot, B. Chapters Nine through Seventeen	Neusner
43045	The Talmud of the Land of Israel, A Complete Outline of the Second, Third and Fourth Divisions, Part II, The Division of Women, A. Yebamot to Nedarim	Neusner
43046	The Talmud of the Land of Israel, A Complete Outline of the Second, Third and Fourth Divisions, Part II, The Division of Women, B. Nazir to Sotah	Neusner
43047	The Talmud of the Land of Israel, A Complete Outline of the Second, Third and Fourth Divisions, Part I, The Division of Appointed Times, C. Pesahim and Sukkah	Neusner
43048	The Talmud of the Land of Israel, A Complete Outline of the Second, Third and Fourth Divisions, Part I, The Division of Appointed Times, A. Berakhot, Shabbat	Neusner
43049	The Talmud of the Land of Israel, A Complete Outline of the Second, Third and Fourth Divisions, Part I, The Division of Appointed Times, B. Erubin, Yoma and Besah	Neusner
43050	The Talmud of the Land of Israel, A Complete Outline of the Second, Third and Fourth Divisions, Part I, The Division of Appointed Times, D. Taanit, Megillah, Rosh Hashannah, Hagigah and Moed Qatan	Neusner
43051	The Talmud of the Land of Israel, A Complete Outline of the Second, Third and Fourth Divisions, Part III, The Division of Damages, A. Baba Qamma, Baba Mesia, Baba Batra, Horayot and Niddah	Neusner
43052	The Talmud of the Land of Israel, A Complete Outline of the Second, Third and Fourth Divisions, Part III, The Division of Damages, B. Sanhedrin, Makkot, Shebuot and Abldah Zarah	Neusner
43053	The Two Talmuds Compared, II. The Division of Women in the Talmud of the Land of Israel and the Talmud of Babylonia, Volume A, Tractates Yebamot and Ketubot	Neusner

243054 The Two Talmuds Compared, II. The Division of Women in the Talmud of the Land of Israel and the Talmud of Babylonia, Volume B, Tractates Nedarim, Nazir and Sotah — Neusn

243055 The Two Talmuds Compared, II. The Division of Women in the Talmud of the Land of Israel and the Talmud of Babylonia, Volume C, Tractates Qiddushin and Gittin — Neusn

243056 The Two Talmuds Compared, III. The Division of Damages in the Talmud of the Land of Israel and the Talmud of Babylonia, Volume A, Tractates Baba Qamma and Baba Mesia — Neusn

243057 The Two Talmuds Compared, III. The Division of Damages in the Talmud of the Land of Israel and the Talmud of Babylonia, Volume B, Tractates Baba Batra and Niddah — Neusn

243058 The Two Talmuds Compared, III. The Division of Damages in the Talmud of the Land of Israel and the Talmud of Babylonia, Volume C, Tractates Sanhedrin and Makkot — Neusn

243059 The Two Talmuds Compared, I. Tractate Berakhot and the Division of Appointed Times in the Talmud of the Land of Israel and the Talmud of Babylonia, Volume B, Tractate Shabbat — Neusn

243060 The Two Talmuds Compared, I. Tractate Berakhot and the Division of Appointed Times in the Talmud of the Land of Israel and the Talmud of Babylonia, Volume A, Tractate Berakhot — Neusn

243061 The Two Talmuds Compared, III. The Division of Damages in the Talmud of the Land of Israel and the Talmud of Babylonia, Volume D, Tractates Shebuot, Abodah Zarah and Horayot — Neusn

243062 The Two Talmuds Compared, I. Tractate Berakhot and the Division of Appointed Times in the Talmud of the Land of Israel and the Talmud of Babylonia, Volume C, Tractate Erubin — Neusn

243063 The Two Talmuds Compared, I. Tractate Berakhot and the Division of Appointed Times in the Talmud of the Land of Israel and the Talmud of Babylonia, Volume D, Tractates Yoma and Sukkah — Neusn

243064 The Two Talmuds Compared, I. Tractate Berakhot and the Division of Appointed Times in the Talmud of the Land of Israel and the Talmud of Babylonia, Volume E, Tractate Pesahim — Neusn

243065 The Two Talmuds Compared, I. Tractate Berakhot and the Division of Appointed Times in the Talmud of the Land of Israel and the Talmud of Babylonia, Volume F, Tractates Besah, Taanit and Megillah — Neusn

243066 The Two Talmuds Compared, I. Tractate Berakhot and the Division of Appointed Times in the Talmud of the Land of Israel and the Talmud of Babylonia, Volume G, Tractates Rosh Hashanah and Moed Qatan — Neusn

243067 The Talmud of Babylonia, An Academic Commentary, Volume XXII, Bavli Tractate Baba Batra, B. Chapters VII through XI — Neusn

243068 The Talmud of Babylonia, An Academic Commentary, Volume XXIII, Bavli Tractate Sanhedrin, B. Chapters VIII through XII — Neusn

243069 The Talmud of Babylonia, An Academic Commentary, Volume XIV, Bavli Tractate Ketubot, B. ChaptersVII through XIV — Neusn

143070 The Talmud of Babylonia, An Academic Commentary, Volume IV, Bavli Tractate Pesahim, B. Chapters VIII through XI — Neusner
143071 The Talmud of Babylonia, An Academic Commentary, Volume XXIX, Bavli Tractate Menahot, B. Chapters VII through XIV — Neusner
143072 The Talmud of Babylonia, An Academic Commentary, Volume XXVIII, Bavli Tractate Zebahim B. Chapters VIII through XV — Neusner
143073 The Talmud of Babylonia, An Academic Commentary, Volume XXI, Bavli Tractate Baba Mesia, B. Chapters VIII through XI — Neusner
143074 The Talmud of Babylonia, An Academic Commentary, Volume III, Bavli Tractate Erubin, A. ChaptersVI through XI — Neusner
143075 The Components of the Rabbinic Documents: From the Whole to the Parts, I. Sifra, Part One — Neusner
143076 The Components of the Rabbinic Documents: From the Whole to the Parts, I. Sifra, Part Two — Neusner
143077 The Components of the Rabbinic Documents: From the Whole to the Parts, I. Sifra, Part Three — Neusner
143078 The Components of the Rabbinic Documents: From the Whole to the Parts, I. Sifra, Part Four — Neusner
143079 The Components of the Rabbinic Documents: From the Whole to the Parts, II. Esther Rabbah I — Neusner
143080 The Components of the Rabbinic Documents: From the Whole to the Parts, III. Ruth Rabbah — Neusner
143081 The Components of the Rabbinic Documents: From the Whole to the Parts, IV. Lamemtations Rabbah — Neusner
143082 The Components of the Rabbinic Documents: From the Whole to the Parts, V. Song of Songs Rabbah, Part One — Neusner
143083 The Components of the Rabbinic Documents: From the Whole to the Parts, V. Song of Songs Rabbah, Part Two — Neusner
143084 The Components of the Rabbinic Documents: From the Whole to the Parts, VI. The Fathers According to Rabbi Nathan — Neusner
143085 The Components of the Rabbinic Documents: From the Whole to the Parts, VII. Sifré to Deuteronomy, Part One — Neusner
143086 The Components of the Rabbinic Documents: From the Whole to the Parts, VII. Sifré to Deuteronomy, Part Two — Neusner
143087 The Components of the Rabbinic Documents: From the Whole to the Parts, VII. Sifré to Deuteronomy, Part Three — Neusner
143088 The Components of the Rabbinic Documents: From the Whole to the Parts, VIII. Mekhilta Attributed to Rabbi Ishmael, Part One — Neusner
143089 The Components of the Rabbinic Documents: From the Whole to the Parts, VIII. Mekhilta Attributed to Rabbi Ishmael, Part Two — Neusner
143090 The Components of the Rabbinic Documents: From the Whole to the Parts, VIII. Mekhilta Attributed to Rabbi Ishmael, Part Three — Neusner
143092 The Components of the Rabbinic Documents: From the Whole to the Parts, IX. Genesis Rabbah, Part One, Introduction and Chapters One through Twenty-two — Neusner

243093	The Components of the Rabbinic Documents: From the Whole to the Parts, IX. Genesis Rabbah, Part Two, Chapters Twenty-three through Fifty	Neusn
243094	The Components of the Rabbinic Documents: From the Whole to the Parts, IX. Genesis Rabbah, Part Three, Chapters Fifty-one through Seventy-five	Neusn
243095	The Components of the Rabbinic Documents: From the Whole to the Parts, X. Leviticus Rabbah, Part One , Introduction and Parashiyyot One through Seventeen	Neusn
243096	The Components of the Rabbinic Documents: From the Whole to the Parts, X. Leviticus Rabbah, Part Two, Parashiyyot Eighteen through Thirty-seven	Neusn
243097	The Components of the Rabbinic Documents: From the Whole to the Parts, X. Leviticus Rabbah, Part Three, Topical and Methodical Outline	Neusn
243098	The Components of the Rabbinic Documents: From the Whole to the Parts, XI. Pesiqta deRab Kahana, Part One, Introduction and Pisqaot One through Eleven	Neusn
243099	The Components of the Rabbinic Documents: From the Whole to the Parts, XI. Pesiqta deRab Kahana, Part Two, Pisqaot Twelve through Twenty-eight	Neusn
243100	The Components of the Rabbinic Documents: From the Whole to the Parts, XI. Pesiqta deRab Kahana, Part Three, A Topical and Methodical Outline	Neusn
243101	The Components of the Rabbinic Documents: From the Whole to the Parts, IX. Genesis Rabbah, Part Four, Chapters Seventy-six through One Hundred	Neusn
243102	The Components of the Rabbinic Documents: From the Whole to the Parts, IX. Genesis Rabbah, Part Five, A Methodical and Topical Outline; Bereshit through Vaere, Chapters One through Fifty-seven	Neusn
243103	The Components of the Rabbinic Documents: From the Whole to the Parts, IX. Genesis Rabbah, Part Six, A Methodical and Topical Outline; Hayye Sarah through Miqqes, Chapters Fifty-eight through One Hundred	Neusn
243104	The Components of the Rabbinic Documents: From the Whole to the Parts, XII., Sifré to Numbers, Part One, Introduction and Pisqaot One through Seventy-one	Neusn
243105	The Components of the Rabbinic Documents: From the Whole to the Parts, XII., Sifré to Numbers, Part Two, Pisqaot Seventy-two through One Hundred Twenty-two	Neusn
243106	The Components of the Rabbinic Documents: From the Whole to the Parts, XII., Sifré to Numbers, Part Three, Pisqaot One Hundred Twenty-three through One Hundred Sixty-one	Neusn
243107	The Components of the Rabbinic Documents: From the Whole to the Parts, XII., Sifré to Numbers, Part Four, A Topical and Methodical Outline	Neusn
243108	The Talmud of the Land of Israel: An Academic Commentary of the Second, Third, and Fourth Divisions, I. Yerushalmi Tractate Berakhot (Based on the Translation by Tzvee Zahavy)	Neusn

43109	The Talmud of the Land of Israel: An Academic Commentary of the Second, Third, and Fourth Divisions, II. Yerushalmi Tractate Shabbat. A. Chapters One through Ten	Neusner
43110	The Talmud of the Land of Israel: An Academic Commentary of the Second, Third, and Fourth Divisions, II. Yerushalmi Tractate Shabbat. B. Chapters Eleven through Twenty-Four and The Structure of Yerushalmi Shabbat	Neusner
43111	The Talmud of the Land of Israel: An Academic Commentary of the Second, Third, and Fourth Divisions, ÎII. Yerushalmi Tractate Erubin	Neusner
43112	The Talmud of the Land of Israel: An Academic Commentary of the Second, Third, and Fourth Divisions, IV. Yerushalmi Tractate Yoma	Neusner
43113	The Talmud of the Land of Israel: An Academic Commentary of the Second, Third, and Fourth Divisions, V. Yerushalmi Tractate Pesahim A. Chapters One through Six, Based on the English Translation of Baruch M. Bokser with Lawrence Schiffman	Neusner
43114	The Talmud of the Land of Israel: An Academic Commentary of the Second, Third, and Fourth Divisions, V. Yerushalmi Tractate Pesahim B. Chapters Seven through Ten and The Structure of Yerushalmi Pesahim, Based on the English Translation of Baruch M. Bokser with Lawrence Schiffman	Neusner
43115	The Talmud of the Land of Israel: An Academic Commentary of the Second, Third, and Fourth Divisions, VI. Yerushalmi Tractate Sukkah	Neusner
43116	The Talmud of the Land of Israel: An Academic Commentary of the Second, Third, and Fourth Divisions, VII. Yerushalmi Tractate Besah	Neusner
43117	The Talmud of the Land of Israel: An Academic Commentary of the Second, Third, and Fourth Divisions, VIII. Yerushalmi Tractate Taanit	Neusner
43118	The Talmud of the Land of Israel: An Academic Commentary of the Second, Third, and Fourth Divisions, IX. Yerushalmi Tractate Megillah	Neusner
43119	The Talmud of the Land of Israel: An Academic Commentary of the Second, Third, and Fourth Divisions, X. Yerushalmi Tractate Rosh Hashanah	Neusner
43120	The Talmud of the Land of Israel: An Academic Commentary of the Second, Third, and Fourth Divisions, XI. Yerushalmi Tractate Hagigah	Neusner
43121	The Talmud of the Land of Israel: An Academic Commentary of the Second, Third, and Fourth Divisions, XII. Yerushalmi Tractate Moed Qatan	Neusner
43122	The Talmud of the Land of Israel: An Academic Commentary of the Second, Third, and Fourth Divisions, XIII. Yerushalmi Tractate Yebamot, A. Chapters One through Ten	Neusner
43123	The Talmud of the Land of Israel: An Academic Commentary of the Second, Third, and Fourth Divisions, XIII. Yerushalmi Tractate Yebamot, B. Chapters Eleven through Seventeen	Neusner

243124	The Talmud of the Land of Israel: An Academic Commentary of the Second, Third, and Fourth Divisions, XIV. Yerushalmi Tractate Ketubot	Neusn
243125	The Talmud of the Land of Israel: An Academic Commentary of the Second, Third, and Fourth Divisions, XV. Yerushalmi Tractate Nedarim	Neusn
243126	The Talmud of the Land of Israel: An Academic Commentary of the Second, Third, and Fourth Divisions, XVI. Yerushalmi Tractate Nazir	Neusn
243127	The Talmud of the Land of Israel: An Academic Commentary of the Second, Third, and Fourth Divisions, XVII. Yerushalmi Tractate Gittin	Neusn
243128	The Talmud of the Land of Israel: An Academic Commentary of the Second, Third, and Fourth Divisions, XVIII. Yerushalmi Tractate Qiddushin	Neusn
243129	The Talmud of the Land of Israel: An Academic Commentary of the Second, Third, and Fourth Divisions, XIX. Yerushalmi Tractate Sotah	Neusn
243130	The Talmud of the Land of Israel: An Academic Commentary of the Second, Third, and Fourth Divisions, XX. Yerushalmi Tractate Baba Qamma	Neusn

South Florida-Rochester-Saint Louis Studies on Religion and the Social Order

245001	Faith and Context, Volume 1	Or
245002	Faith and Context, Volume 2	Or
245003	Judaism and Civil Religion	Breslau
245004	The Sociology of Andrew M. Greeley	Greel
245005	Faith and Context, Volume 3	Or
245006	The Christ of Michelangelo	Dixo
245007	From Hermeneutics to Ethical Consensus Among Cultures	Bo
245008	Mordecai Kaplan's Thought in a Postmodern Age	Breslau
245009	No Longer Aliens, No Longer Strangers	Eckar
245010	Between Tradition and Culture	Ellensc
245011	Religion and the Social Order	Neusn
245012	Christianity and the Stranger	Nicho
245013	The Polish Challenge	Czosnyk
245014	Islam and the Question of Minorities	Son
245015	Religion and the Political Order	Neusne
245016	The Ecology of Religion	Neusne
245017	The Shaping of an American Islamic Discourse	Waugh/Denn
245018	The Muslim Brotherhood and the Kings of Jordan, 1945–1993	Boulb
245019	Muslims on the Americanization Path	Esposito/Hadda
245020	Protean Prejudice: Anti-semitism in England's Age of Reason	Glassma
245021	The Study of Religion: In Retrospect and Prospect	Gree
245024	Jacques Ellul on Religion, Technology and Politics: Conversations with Patrick Troude-Chastenet	Franc

South Florida International Studies in Formative Christianity and Judaism

2501	The Earliest Christian Mission to 'All Nations'	La Grand
2502	Judaic Approaches to the Gospels	Chilton
2503	The "Essence of Christianity"	Forni Rosa
2504	The Wicked Tenants and Gethsemane	Aus
2505	A Star Is Rising	Laato
2506	Romans 9–11: A Reader-Response Analysis	Lodge
2507	The Good News of Peter's Denial	Borrell